Ann(ie) Blum in Our Lives

Edited by

Peter J. Taylor

The Pumping Station
Arlington, MA

© 2016 Peter J. Taylor

Published by The Pumping Station
61 Cleveland Street #2, Arlington, MA 02474-6935, USA
thepumpingstation.org

No part of this publication may be reproduced, stored in a retrieval system, or transmitted in any form or by any means electronic, mechanical, photocopying, recording or otherwise without the prior permission of the publisher.

Online purchasers of this book who have not paid sales tax in their own jurisdiction (http://bit.ly/SalesTaxRates) should, out of fairness to brick-and-mortar bookstores, file use tax returns to report the purchase.

Proceeds from this publication are directed to "The Ann S. Blum Memorial Scholarship in Latin American Studies" at the University of Massachusetts Boston. Gifts can also be made at http://www.umb.edu/giving

Cover, interior design, and photo preparation by Ciampa Creative. Transcription of recordings by Laura White. Editorial advice from Terry Hill.

Library of Congress Cataloging-in-Publication Data

Ann(ie) Blum in Our Lives / Peter J. Taylor
p. cm.

Library of Congress Control Number: 2016951088

ISBN 978-0-9849216-8-3   (pbk)

October 2016, second printing
Printed by Lightning Source in **Arno Pro**, Adobe Garamond Pro, and **SCALA SANS**
Available in digital form as a pdf from the Publisher, http://bit.ly/ABIOL2016

Ann (center) with sister Pamela and brother Tom, c. 2002. The joke has been forgotten; the laugh remains with us.

This book is dedicated to all the caregivers and healthcare practitioners who looked after Ann caringly and carefully from July 2014 to November 2015,

and to the memory of Ann's parents,
Pamela Z. Blum (1923-2015)
and John M. Blum (1921-2011)

Ann(ie) Blum in Our Lives

What does it mean to have had Ann—Annie to some—Blum in our lives? The letters and stories from family and friends assembled here, together with photos and words of Ann's own, evoke her presence. They allow us to think about what we want to carry forward, into the lives we still have.

----
17 FEBRUARY 2015
When Ann finished chemo a month ago, the challenge shifted from the weekly routine of treatment and its after-effects to living well in the indefinite period of remission—hanging out with local friends, weekend trips to see not-so-distant friends, bed-time reading aloud from favorite books (indeed getting the bookcases built so we could bring up books from basement storage). For friends and family afar, as well as for other friends between visits, I have been thinking about some other way—not busy or tiring—of affirming connectedness.

A short sentence in a weekend email that I read out to Ann pointed the way—"Ann, I think of you every day when I put some clementines or oranges in one of the Mexican bowls." Following that lead, it'd be great if you could send me sentences or vignettes about ways that having Ann in your life has affected you. (No minimum word length or expectations of profundity. Nor a limit to how frequently you can send something-- as they say, "vote early and often.")

These contributions will be all the more valued right now because fewer visits will be possible. The news this weekend is that remission has, unfortunately, been short-lived—a new round of medical steps (not yet clear) lie ahead so contributions to buoy our spirits will be warmly appreciated. Of course, you may prefer to communicate with Ann in other modes than I have suggested—please don't feel inhibited by my request.

----
29 NOVEMBER 2015

I started a blog in February 2015 using it as a private repository of communications that captured some aspects of having had Ann(ie) Blum in the person's life. With her death on 28 November 2015, public contributions are welcome… I hope that the vignettes and other posts will help us see new ways to keep on keeping Ann(ie) Blum in our lives.

----
23 SEPTEMBER 2016

The order of the items is mostly according to the earliest of the periods of Ann's life the item recalls. Not always—the collections of stories and remembrances at a December 2015 party and two memorials in April 2016 are included at the dates of those events. The result is less a chronological unfolding as it is a series of flashbacks and rolls forward. Apologies for overlooking some 2015 letters and for mistakes in dates or other details—if you inform me of them, these can be readily corrected in new printings. Full names and the contributor's relationship to Ann are given at the very end. In assembling these electronically sent or recorded items, I do not mean to diminish the value of the phone calls, visits, handwritten letters, conversations, and distractions during these last two years.

Much thanks to all.
With love.

PETER

1950s

Caught by Pamela using her Brownie Hawkeye Camera

John, Tommie, Annie, Pam Blum, New Haven, 1959

Drawn from the basement archives

Annie Blum (third from right in front row), 4th Grade, 1959

1960s

Never far from each other's thoughts

I met Ann in 1962-3 when her family had a sabbatical in Cambridge, England. We were in the same class at school and became best friends straight away. Our homes were near each other, so we often walked between home and school together.

We were lucky to be able to keep seeing each other, as I visited my father in Washington DC most summers, and my English family had a sabbatical term at Harvard in 1965. I remember staying with the Blums in New Haven and cycling with Ann in the nearby woods.

After that we met less, and wrote occasionally, but were never far from each other's thoughts. In 1976 Ann wrote to me "A year ago when you wrote the news of your marriage, I was so negative and cynical about the possibilities between men and women that I hardly knew how to respond." But ten years later, she wrote "Peter moved in here at Foster Street at the end of last March and before long neither of us could imagine how we had lived apart." By that time I was writing about the joys of motherhood, which was much harder for Ann to reach than for me. But our sons are only a year apart; I met Ann with year-old Vann in Ithaca, and as teenagers the two boys got on well. We talked about the trials and rewards of balancing families with demanding work; nobody has understood me better than Ann did.

When my mother died in 1982, Ann wrote to me "It's wrenching to even imagine the loss. But I am slowly learning something that you probably already know, and that is – that we don't have to stop loving the person who has died." That thought is now my comfort. Our friendship has mostly been at a distance, and it will go on that way, as strong as ever.

CLAIRE
29 NOVEMBER 2015

High school Commencement speech, June 1968

Since you were the one who succeeded in accomplishing my selection as the Commencement speaker

– an honor which I shall long cherish – I want you to have a copy of my thoughts.

Sincerely,

LOU
7 JUNE 1968

Ann, High School yearbook, 1968

Commencement Address - Day Prospect Hill School, New Haven
June 5, 1968

We meet on a day when terror and beauty converge. Terror because of the madness which strikes down our gallant young men -- John Kennedy; Martin Luther King; and now, hovering between life and death, Robert Kennedy. A madness which has its analogue in the killing of thousands of ordinary men -- yellow and black and white -- in the forests and villages and city-streets of Vietnam. A madness which reminds us that killing is only the outer and monstrous face of humdrum inner corruptions -- that even in our own beloved land it remains the case, as Thoreau told us over a century ago, that "Most men live lives of quiet desperation." Desperation not alone in Watts, or down over the hill in Newhallville -- desperation not alone for those whose lives are circumscribed by rats, or by hostile or condescending or apathetic whites, or by the dole; but desperation also in the midst of affluence -- a corrosive doubt about whether we mean any substantial measure of our highest rhetoric, or whether our farthest horizon remains that painted luminously before us by the presidential candidate who won forty years ago: "a chicken in every pot, and two cars in every garage."

And, at the same time, the beauty -- the beauty of this place; the beauty of this warm and loving event -- a day properly set apart to mark your high accomplishments, and to record our high confidence in your future, and hence in ours; and the beauty in each of you.

Does the sunshine on this lovely June day play tricks with us? Does it pretend a brightness of fortune which is all illusion? Are we to say that values are false, hope is folly, action is futile and self-deceiving, and the curve from this day onward an ever-downward one? Are we condemned, as we look ahead together from Prospect Hill, by MacLeish's dread words? --

> And here face down beneath the sun
> And here upon earth's noonward height
> I feel the always coming on
> The always rising of the night.

I think not. I insist not.

Martin King was not yet forty when he fell. Though he did not seek death, he was ready for it, knowing that others -- people like Ralph Abernathy and Bill Coffin and hundreds of thousands of others, perhaps including some of you -- would come forward to take his place. This is what he said the day before he died:

> Like anybody, I would like to live a long life. Longevity has its place. But I'm not concerned about that now. I just want to do God's will. . . . I've looked over and I've seen the promised land. I may not get there with you, but I want you to know tonight that we as a people will get to the promised land.

Which way to the promised land?

> Our answer [wrote Robert Kennedy last fall] is the world's hope; it is to rely on youth -- not a time of life but a state of mind, a temper of the will, a quality of the imagination, a predominance of courage over timidity, of the appetite for adventure over the love of ease. The cruelties and obstacles of this swiftly changing planet will not yield to obsolete dogmas and outworn slogans. It cannot be moved by those who cling to a present that is already dying, who prefer the illusion of security to the excitement and danger that come with even the most peaceful progress. It is a revolutionary world we live in; and this generation, at home and around the world, has had thrust upon it a greater burden of responsibility than any generation that has ever lived.

The title of the Senator's book is "To Seek A Newer World." You doubtless remember Tennyson's phrases--

>Come, my friends
>'Tis not too late to seek a newer world.
>Push off, and sitting well in order smite
>The sounding furrows; for my purpose holds
>To sail beyond the sunset, and the baths
>Of all the western stars, until I die.

But it was not the young Ulysses who was talking. It was the aging captain unwilling

>. . . to pause, to make an end,
>To rust unburnish'd, not to shine in use!
>As tho' to breathe were life. Life piled on life
>Were all too little, and of one to me
>Little remains: but every hour is saved
>From that eternal silence, something more,
>A bringer of new things. . . .

Ulysses' son, his "well-loved" Telemachus, was cast in a different mold. "Most blameless . . ., centered in the sphere/Of common duties," Telemachus was deeply mired in the dying present of Ithaca. "He works his work" -- said Ulysses -- "I mine." And so Ulysses turned for the companionship, in his last adventure, to his mariners--

>Souls that have toil'd, and wrought, and
>   thought with me--
>That ever with a frolic welcome took
>The thunder and the sunshine, and opposed
>Free hearts, free foreheads--you and I are old;
>Old age hath yet his honour and his toil;
>Death closes all: but something ere the end,
>Some work of noble note, may yet be done,
>Not unbecoming men that strove with Gods.
>   * * * * *
>Tho' much is taken, much abides; and tho'
>We are not now that strength which in old days
>Moved earth and heaven; that which we are, we are;
>One equal temper of heroic hearts,
>Made weak by time and fate, but strong in will
>To strive, to seek, to find, and not to yield.

Youth, the Senator told us, is "not a time of life but a state of mind, a temper of the will. . . ." Some among us gain youth when they are young, only to lose it. Some, like Telemachus, are never really young at all. The great feat -- perhaps the only one in life that matters -- is, at whatever age you achieve youth, to hold it fast. These are the blessed among us.

One such was my dear friend and colleague Jack Tate -- the late husband of your beloved teacher: Dean Tate died, just over two months ago, in his mid-sixties, the youngest of men. Two others I think of are sisters -- my wife's great aunt Lucile, now eighty-five, and my wife's grandmother, Nanny, who turned ninety-eight just a few days ago. (Nanny graduated from college in Barnard's first class, just seventy-five commencements ago.) Two years ago, when Nanny was only ninety-six, she spoke at a dinner honoring her and her baby sister. She started her speech this way:

> I think it would be appropriate for me
> to begin by reciting the part assigned to
> me in our class play when I was in first grade,
> ninety-years ago:
>
> It must seem odd for one my age
> To speak in public on a stage.

But of course it is not odd at all. Her eyes, though almost sightless now, look only forward.

Even the most far-sighted among us can only see a little way:

> Our future [wrote Senator Kennedy] may
> lie beyond our vision, but it is not completely
> beyond our control. It is the shaping impulse
> of America that neither fate nor nature nor the
> irresistible tides of history, but the work of
> our own hands, matched to reason and principle . . .

> will determine destiny. There is pride in
> that, even arrogance, but there is also
> experience and truth. In any event, it is
> the only way we can live.

*   *   *   *

We are assembled on Prospect Hill, on this golden afternoon, to look to your future, and thus to our own, and our country's. My mind runs back twenty-five years, to May of 1943, to my last college class. The golden sun streamed in the second-floor windows of Harvard Hall on some ninety young men who were going off to war.

The course was Shakespeare. The teacher was F. O. Matthiessen -- "Matty" as he was known to his contemporaries. Matty was talking about the last of the plays, "The Tempest." He came to the Epilogue, where Prospero promises "calm seas, auspicious gales. . . ." And then, at five minutes of one, Matty closed his book.

I cannot promise you "calm seas, auspicious gales." But I can prophesy that you will meet with courage the heavy seas and strong gales which will come. Also, I can tell you what Matty told us in the waning minutes of that last class, after he closed his book:

> You will be leaving this place and
> going to all parts of the world. Wherever
> you are, there will, I hope, be occasional
> quiet moments when you will be thinking about
> Shakespeare and what we have read and talked
> of here together. And I will be thinking
> about all of you.

A woman of conviction and strong boundaries

Ann was a woman of conviction and strong boundaries. Academics' daughter, we met at college, in 1969.

She left to work for several years before finishing her degree. Ann wrote the book on American illustration and science. She learned Spanish later in life and became a professor of Latin American Studies. With Peter, Ann raised Vann in an open adoption. To accomplish all this, often she needed to focus without us. When she let us in, her laugh and engagement sparked us onward.

Missing Ann

Ann had her own spare style.
In her home, she kept a few beautiful things:
    a wooden bowl.
    a modern chair.
She dressed with a clean simple line-
    often in black.
She chose the right accent:
    thin gold hoop earrings.
She was a good editor:
    she knew what to edit out
    and what to leave in.
Her thinking was that way:
    clear and incisive.

Her last edit
was not about us.

It was about her.
We try to understand.

This is about us
being without her.
We try to understand.

Spare
        into thin air
                sparrow's arrow
                      to the heart
                              aches the breath
                                      away.

Love, stV

STEVE
3 DECEMBER 2015

1970s

The years of our adolescent turmoil over

One Summer's Day in the early 1970s.

So I clicked two pictures of Ann as she lay on the grass sunning herself, blooming, radiant, serene.

The years of our adolescent turmoil over, I simply loved my sister.

With love and admiration,

PAMELA
20 FEBRUARY 2015

A moment in the 1970's

Had Mother given her the red knit dress she wore? We passed her on Broadway while we drove towards Harvard Square. "She walks like a queen," Mother said.

And she did—slim, introspective, her hair pulled back with escaped red "flames," elegant strides, a sense of self, a sense of purpose.

Remembered with love and admiration,

PAMELA
18 FEBRUARY 2015

Annie at the MCZ

I met Annie when she came to replace me as the Archives Assistant at the MCZ library – this would have been somewhere around 1975. I think it was the only time in my life that I became friends with the person who replaced me at work!

We worked together briefly during the transition, and I enjoyed her enthusiasm for life, including the fairly humdrum work we were doing. For several years afterwards, until I moved out of state, we got together to enjoy a meal, a swim, or a walk in the woods of Lincoln where I was living. A few years ago we re-connected over a cup of coffee and laughed about those old times. Of course, there was the same spark in her eye and smile on her face. I regret that we didn't keep in better touch over these many years, but I will always have fond memories.

DAVID LAKARI
22 DECEMBER 2015

The way she looked at me as I explained my arcane problem

I first met Ann briefly at Harvard in the early 70s. She was working at the Museum of Comparative Zoology library. I was a new employee at the Peabody Museum looking for a way to identify some animal part or other on an artifact in the museum's collections.

It was only a few minutes but I remember the way she looked at me as I explained my arcane problem. She made me think I was the smartest and most fascinating guy at Harvard. As soon as I left her presence the world turned normal again and while I saw myself as something much less than a Harvard luminary I left feeling good about myself.

Almost 30 years later I saw Ann again as we walked the halls of the McCormack Building at our new jobs at UMass Boston. Amazingly we'd both remembered that short encounter in the 70s. So over the next 15 years now and then we'd pass one another with just a smile and a nod and sometimes stop for a short chat. She always left me feeling good about myself.

Thank you Ann.

DENNIS PIECHOTA
4 DECEMBER 2015

Now I have love and music back in my life

There are moments in a person's life that stand out as good (or not so good) memories, but those things that stay with you and send a bit of a twinge of recognition when they come to mind. And Annie and Peter, so many moments they we shared that have stayed with me for all of these years, and bring a smile and a tear whenever I see them in my mind's eye.

The first time you and I went out together by ourselves, leaving the boys at the Harvard Bookstore, is one of those times. Until that night, we were the "old ladies" (to use a motorcycle gang reference) of our bookstore bozos. But I think we knew that the two of us had friend material. So we met at your apartment, had a little bit of an intoxicant, went to dinner (probably Greek!) and had one of the nicest, warmest and loveliest nights of my life. I thought you had this aura about you that you have to this very day.

Then there was "aBrook aStreet" midnight dinners, waiting for Abdul to come and clear the dishes (by the way, he never came). Drinking café au lait out of bowls. Saturday trips to the North End and Haymarket for our stash of coffee, wine, cheese and pasta. Coming home, opening one of those bottles of wine, getting one of the three copies of the New Yorker that were delivered, and then retreating for the afternoon nap, until it was time to start the escapades all over again.

Did you know that after Christmas at your parent's house I wished I were an Episcopalian? That was the most beautiful Christmas I'd ever seen. You gave me silk eggplants and peppers that I have to this day.

So many, so many, so many little clips in my head and heart. Victor, Alan, Emily, Jon

Jill, the Bromell bunch, Tom, Christopher, and then wonderful Peter. We all dispersed to all ends of the earth, Vermont, California, New Jersey, but came together for lovely visits to Vermont, coffee in our jammies, then children, Bar Mitzvahs, and reconnections not so many years ago. I wish the reconnection had been many many years ago, but life became complicated. You know. But now I have love and music back in my life, and I feel that contentment I was always looking for.

But we'll laugh about all of it the next time we see you. I love you and you're with me every day.

All my love,

MERI
12 AUGUST 2016

Not long after, of course, I meet Annie, who is pals with all these wonderful Cantabrigians I'm meeting

It is 1976. I am an English graduate student at UNH when I meet Alan, one of a wonderful group of ragtag, nascent poets and writers, known lovingly as the "Harvard Bookstore Bozos."

A/k/a, the "Grolier Rhymes." Tom, Victor, Roger, Meri Sue. Not long after, of course, I meet Annie, who is pals with all these wonderful Cantabrigians I'm meeting. Everyone's in love with her, sweetly and chastely. She works at the Agassiz Museum, studying, cataloguing and archiving, in some mysterious way, arcana involving all things animal and vegetable. She's smart and wonderfully scholarly. And ethereally beautiful. And funny. And open-hearted. As I get integrated into this group of new friends, I am so happy to get to know Annie better.
Those carefree Cambridge years. It is such fun hanging out with Annie.

By 1982, I'm finally done with law school (what was I thinking?), and we relocate to northern Vermont. Other pals are finding careers and moving from Cambridge as well. But amidst all the moves, we find ways and places to gather. Just after we arrive in our new Calais home, we need our pals to inaugurate our new lives—and launch the Reggae Tweetie Bird!

Turns out, Annie has her own wonderful connections to Vermont. Here, as in so many places in the world, she's at home, having lived through many seasons at her family's summerhouse in the mountains east of Rutland. And, she's spent hours at the Rutland Fair! So, she's our tour guide on our many fair-going expeditions.

Skip to around 1984, '85. We've left bucolic Calais and moved to Middlebury, where we find a sweet spot on Lake Dunmore. Again, how can it be home unless our friends can find it, and bless it with their presence? They do. By this time, Meri Sue has beaten us all to the parenting punch, and become the proud mother of Ben. So he joins the gang.

Life goes on. We are all finding our careers, and life partners. Annie calls to tell us she has someone she wants us to meet! His name is Peter, and he's tall, handsome, and an Aussie! We are, of course, charmed.

And somehow, how does it happen? Decades pass. Turn around and Annie's back from California, having earned her PhD. While we're all still relatively mobile, we gather, again and again, as often as possible. We just don't pause to take as many photos as (in retrospect) we wish we had.

Turn around again, and Annie has published her first book – on those beautiful scientific illustrations she discovered and shared with us all at the Agassiz! Soon, Annie and Peter are both academics—Annie in Latin American & Iberian Studies; Peter in Critical & Creative Thinking! Her first book is certainly not her last. Indeed, she becomes a pioneer, leaving her mark in a whole new world of scholarship:

> "Blum's work is a major contribution to the nascent field of childhood history in Latin America. She draws from the historiography of gender and welfare to reflect how class, race, and gender interplayed in defining family relations and nation-state formation in modern Mexico."—Sandra Aguilar, *H-Net*

> "Ann Blum makes an important contribution to the history of childhood, family, and labor and helps tie together labor, cultural, and political histories."—Susie S. Porter, *Americas*

> "Blum uses an impressive array of sources—legal codes, decrees, censuses, court cases, articles, and welfare records. Her work sits at the intersection of multiple historiographies, not just family history, but also the history of women, gender, legal, labor, medical, and childhood as well."—Nicole Sanders, *Mexican Studies*

My, my. The acorn doesn't fall far from the tree.

And then, once we all have kids, the years start passing even faster. Annie and Peter are blessed with Vann; we with Nate and Adam. Suddenly, our kids are out of high school, trying on careers of their own! Visits are harder, but not impossible, to schedule. But alas, where are all the photos?

Annie, we smile when we think of these moments with you and Peter.

We are sending you so much love. When you're up for it, we so want to come visit, even briefly (we have already arranged our housing!). We are excellent dishwasher-emptiers, and bed makers, and vacuumers (Alan, especially). We love to run errands. Bake bread. Make tea. Read out loud. Act as secretary. Laugh. Dust. Sit quietly. Just send word.

You are both in our hearts.

EMILY
21 FEBRUARY 2015

The gang in Vermont at different times

Ann- Greetings from Columbia, CT. We know you are going through a tough siege and are thinking of you often.

I have enclosed some pictures of the gang in Vermont at different times. How proud you must be to have been a part of the launching of that notable inflatable christened by Alan as the "Reggae Tweety Bird" (I can't remember how he came up with that name).

We love you---
JON AND JILL ZORN
19 FEBRUARY 2015

Jill, Annie, Meri Sue; Jon, Emily, Alan
Vermont 1982

Poise and elegance since 1976

In 1976 you, Polly, and I had lunch to talk about Polly's book on the history of the MCZ and there it began, in a restaurant in Harvard Square. And I remember being struck by your poise and elegance, such a contrast from my feelings of awkward insecurity, of not having a clue.

You had radiance, and my memories are always of radiance. You would stroll into the MCZ in the mornings, wearing a black loose-fitting dress with wide shoulder straps which looked so good on you, bottom of dress swaying, and sandals clicking on the hard floor, and it would be a lift just to see you walking over to the little archive cage at the back of the room and settle in each morning. I still see you there. And dinners out in Central Square, usually Italian or Middle Eastern; pumpkin kibby was a favorite. And dinners at your apartment, avocado and buttermilk soup in those oblong bowls, with fresh bread and butter. I still make that recipe every summer when it's too hot to cook in Baltimore. Or bluefish poached in a little wine, simple but somehow grand.

And me bringing over some pears from the market, but still green and hard, and you commenting "Oh, they aren't ripe yet!" and this cluing me in to the fact that green pears are supposed to ripen before you eat them, and that green and hard is not their normal state! Such was my impoverished upbringing: when I was a child we rarely ate ripe pears, for my father would always put the green pears in the fridge and we'd eat the cold, hard green pears out of the fridge, and that's what we thought they were supposed to be like. Sometimes my mother would buy already ripe pears, which were soft and yellow, and I always believed there were two kinds of pears, green and hard ones and soft and yellow ones. And I laughed so much at the revelation that the green ones weren't supposed to be eaten that way. To think that had you not mentioned this, I would probably still be eating them like that.

And over dinner we'd talk and tell stories and laugh—always something to laugh over. You were so good at seeing what was funny in odd quirky aspects of human behavior. Three summers at the MCZ, those blazing hot, steamy Boston summers, but full of charm. And one year, at a reception at the MCZ, I seem to recall that Peter was there also, but it would be a while yet before I would make his acquaintance. As for Polly, no book in sight; that would take many more years.

I moved to Baltimore in 1981 and had to host the Joint Atlantic Seminar about two years later and you came down to help me out. In those days we had no budget, for my department was useless in providing help, but you came down a day early and we shopped and put together a lovely reception for Friday evening, complete with giant polished mushrooms piled in a colander for a table decoration, their gleaming whiteness contrasting with the red strawberries we had bought. And you explained that when you wiped mushrooms with a damp towel to clean them, you imagined yourself wiping a baby. From that day on, I have always associated mushrooms with cleaning babies. And Owen Hannaway exclaimed at the mushrooms and asked you where we had found them, and you said with a twinkle, we just found them!

You were already working on what would become the mammoth project leading to *Picturing Nature*, which had started quietly with a short article in the Harvard alumni magazine. It got quite a bit of attention. And you spoke on the subject in Baltimore, and over the years it grew into the magnificent study, which no one has surpassed, despite all the interest in visual images. Your great discovery of Sonrel, and those astonishing jellyfish lithographs! Turtles all facing left, and their eggs floating on the pages. I will always treasure your book. Every page brings me to your voice, your ideas and observations, your artistic sensitivity, your attention not just to the images but also to how they were made and what it took to produce these great works of natural history. And I was so excited at what you did with Abbott Thayer! What an astute analysis and so right, and something I could not have thought of. So full of creative insight.

By then Peter was on the scene and soon Vann too, about four years after Dave joined us in 1987. You came down to visit when Dave was about 6 weeks or 8 weeks old, when we were in our little row house in the city, near to the campus. Your visit then was a wonderful treat. And it was warm enough that we packed a picnic to go to Fort McHenry in the early morning, but when we got there, I discovered that I had forgotten to put the food in the car, so we starved.

And Ithaca—the little blue house slowly coming together, the garden blooming out back with a profusion of wildflowers randomly sown but producing such a lovely total effect, as though each one had been carefully and deliberately positioned to produce an artistic creation. I remember especially the coneflowers. And Vann, quite young then, but growing up quickly into a young man so fine, kind-hearted, and generous (not to mention handsome). Walking down the beach with Vann at Cape May, looking for interesting rocks (he had an acute eye for unusual rocks), we encountered a group of boys who were wreaking havoc on the shoreline, pulling things out of the water and in general behaving destructively; and Vann, though much younger, admonished them for their thoughtlessness and lack of respect for nature. And how astonished they were to find another kid telling them off! So wise and so bold; may he be like that throughout his life.

And new scholarly directions—from Berkeley to Ithaca and back to Boston. What a delight to get a copy of your book while having dinner while attending yet another Joint Atlantic Seminar, this time at Harvard!

So many memories; many, many more flood into one's mind; none ever to be forgotten, and always full of radiance. Many years ago we were talking about seasons and you mentioned that your mother did not like autumn as much as the other seasons because it was the time of nature shutting down. But for me it is not the fall but mid-August, when we received your note, which will forever be the saddest time of year.

Forty years of friendship is a long time, but not nearly long enough. I'm not ready to say good-bye; for now, I can only say thank you. Thank you for being such a wonderful friend. Thank you for helping me be a better person. You will be in our thoughts and dreams always.

Much love,

SHARON KINGSLAND
14 AUGUST 2015

This issue
HARVARD MAGAZINE
May/June 1977.

The cover of this issue first took shape in the mind of **Sarah Landry**, illustrator *par excellence* and co-author of "In loving detail" (page 38). She got **Steve Grohe** to render her idea in photographic form, and the result, she says, is exactly what she had visualized.

As a contributing editor of this magazine, Sally Landry thinks up cover and story ideas, creates resourceful illustrations—for instance, the one on page 54—and designs some of our page layouts. Her drawings and paintings also appear in Scientific American and International Wildlife, as well as in books and monographs. At Harvard she draws for scientists at the Museum of Comparative Zoology and the Gray Herbarium. She illustrated Professor E. O. Wilson's celebrated *Sociobiology*, and is now illustrating a book on coastal marine resources. She sails, backpacks, and collects old scientific drawings.

Her collaborator, **Ann Blum**, is archives assistant at the Museum of Comparative Zoology. After studying earth and life sciences at Smith College, she left to work at the School of American Research in Santa Fe, cataloguing photographs of archaeological digs. She and Sally Landry discovered their shared enthusiasm for scientific illustration a year ago, when both were involved in an MCZ exhibit on nineteenth-century illustrators. She is currently a research assistant for a history of the

above: Authors Landry and Blum,

MCZ funded by a National Science Foundation grant. Her interests include dance and drawing.

Eleven years of letters from Ann to Sharon

3 October. 1977

Dear Sharon,

Almost predictably, a problem has come up about a missing key to Archives. I said that I'd write to you although I doubt that you have it: a little brass key with KVF engraved on one side.

Rain, rain, rain in Cambridge, good weather for working but where is our Indian Summer? Harvard in full swing, and this year even the graduate students look too young to me. I am taking two wonderful courses: one, a seminar-workshop in the history of prints and printing: the other, an evening seminar through the Friends of the Fogg Museum, on connoisseurship of Old Master Drawings. Either way I have been spending a lot of time with Rembrandt lately, and feel properly uplifted.

The editor from Pantheon Books comes to the Museum of Friday afternoon, and I am preparing an outline and assembling books to show him; and suffering from butterflies.

How are you? I miss you. Have you managed to establish a Toronto Philosophical Society?

love,

Ann

MUSEUM OF COMPARATIVE ZOOLOGY
The Agassiz Museum

HARVARD UNIVERSITY · CAMBRIDGE, MASSACHUSETTS 02138 · TEL. 617-495-2475

The Library   Oct. 19

Dear Sharon —

Thank you for writing about the key. The Library is in a barely suppressed uproar over a large number of recently discovered thefts of plates from valuable books, so all matters re: keys are very sensitive.

Pantheon has come and gone. He certainly was the editor for me for my first experience. Young, friendly + relaxed but business-like, plenty of counter-culture to make me feel comfortable, he was encouraging but very straightforward: "Don't get your hopes up". We talked as much about Pantheon and what kinds of books they publish (few picture books. They always lose money) as we did about my topic. We had a good time looking at pictures in the Archives. He is a bird watcher — Natural History lives!

When I told him about the other publishing company he said frankly publishing is a business against authors and I should try for whatever I can get. We also had a nice, long conversation about working – personal attitudes, etc. In the end, for such a big-deal, it was all very pleasant + comfortable and interesting.

Your philosophy reading sounds wonderful. Do you really wish you could be a philosopher? I met a guy at a party recently who was horribly over-educated, but with whom I enjoyed talking about, of all things, Ezra Pound and Agassiz. Between puffs on his foul-smelling pipe he was dropping mots philosophiques right and left and I could barely keep up, but by frantically remembering as much of what you have ever told me about philosophy, as I could, I managed, in a stoned-out way, to keep face.

Last week I signed on to R. Cook's payroll. I'm looking forward to the work, too.
Best wishes for the success of your Phil. Soc. and carrying on with everything. love,
Ann

31 Jan 78

Dear Sharon—

You letter arrived at a moment when I was feeling comparatively cheery, so I agree that you are quite right. Things do get better. But I am still at the mercy of a revolving disc of circular emotions that carries me by its own laws of physics from relatively free, alive aware and cheerful down down down to rage, blame and total non-acceptance of the situation with ▇▇. At the top of the cycle I know with all of my being, that in separation we can individually achieve wholeness and that, probably _only_ by separating. And I embrace the challenge and get excited imagining who I might really be if I express myself totally. And then at the bottom I storm and rage against being rejected and not being loved the way I want to be, and I refuse to listen to reason and work myself into a collossal state. In between lie all degrees and proportions of compromise — compromise of my true feelings ▇▇▇▇▇▇▇▇ ▇▇▇▇▇▇▇▇. Round + round I go, pretty regularly at my best around Wednesday and at my worst by Friday night or Saturday. I would probably turn to drink if I weren't so broke and afraid of getting fat on liquor calories. My main drug has been reading. But it was ½-comic how the chapters about Anna Karenin's despair + suicide threw me into a total relapse.

21 February 1978

Dear Sharon —

Time passes and things __do improve__! Nothing is different about my situation except the way I feel about it, and I feel so much better. The pain evaporates, and more and more I simply feel good, lighter, relaxed, humorous — still reflective, but steady. Thank you for your letter.

Pantheon has made me an offer and it's __good__. And "my" editor, Tom Engelhardt, is neat. He's as delighted and enthusiastic as I am (Except, of course, it's only __part__ of his life, whereas The __Book__ is __all__ of mine!)

I dealt with post-blizzard restlessness by taking a work visit to New Haven. 2 days of archival survey work in the Hutchinson papers for Bob Cook and much-needed $. Delightful visits to the Yale __Animals in Art__ exhibitions at Sterling, Beinecke, Peabody — a good, gentle, fun, ease-into the natural-history illustration frame of mind. Food, rest + nurture with my parents — including a deluxe noon out for oysters + white wine — truly more festive than Christmas, because more spontaneous.

I made my report to Bob Cook today + he mentioned that you may be passing through New England after your exam. I'm delighted, + eager to see you. Or what's left of you after your ordeal. Courage! camarade! Oh, Sharon, how you must feel these days....
I won't bother to say anything about how your friends believe in you — that's useless, it doesn't allay the anxiety one wit. I just simply look forward to the day your exams are over and you can have a more balanced view of your true qualities, the ones we, I, love you for.

      Best, best of everything, don't bother
      to write unless you're moved to, but I'm
      fine — love,
           Ann.

6 March 78

Dear Sharon —

You're so far ahead of me with your correspondence that I'm going to take the lazy way out + enclose two unfinished, unsent letters — as landmarks.

It's wonderful the way you perscribed the perfect affair for yourself — and then took it. You must have had the man in mind when you wrote 2nd-to-last. Oh, Love + Work — and what else is there?

▮ is constantly on my mind, but just there, with no weight, pain or difficulty. And I think about the Book constantly, from the basic tasks of discipline + concentration, to all the crazy 19th-century things I want to weave into it. And so I sort of float along in this medium, and all the good things that come in bond or cohere to one or the other of the two principal elements.

And many good things come in, not only by chance, but to some extent I feel in control of providing them for myself. I go as often as I can to a lecture course on Italian painting, to the sauna at M.I.T. (bliss), to art and music around town. I'm on a binge of luxurious, romantic food + eating, inspired by reading Colette + M.F.K. Fisher during the blizzard-week — oysters + white wine, etc.

Sometimes I think I must be dangerously deluded — that I can't be really feeling this good so quickly. But I pay attention to my dreams, which are powerfully positive these days. And also, people come up to me on the street, strangers and friends, and say — you look beautiful, or radiant, or very happy. (Which just, of course, makes me feel more so.)

I'm really counting on seeing you soon.
Love and <u>encouragement</u>. Ann

MUSEUM OF COMPARATIVE ZOOLOGY
The Agassiz Museum

HARVARD UNIVERSITY · CAMBRIDGE, MASSACHUSETTS 02138 · TEL. 617 495-2466

21 August 78

Dear Sharon— Washington was wonderful. The S.I. Archives have more than I could cope with in 3 days. I concentrated on the Baird papers, incoming letters from artists, lithographers— people whose "voices" I hadn't heard before. On the last afternoon I zipped through 4 collections of drawings— just a rapid survey to find out what they were. Went to the Fish Division of the Nat. Mus. to see their c. 20 file cabinets of fish illus. from 19 cent. to present, active file for taxonomic work & publication. Whew!

Meanwhile, I really liked ███ family. I also spent an afternoon w/ my friend Rob who showed me his work at Voice of America, & took me swimming in a rushing Virginia River, & out to dinner at a Vietnamese Restaurant, all not under the glorious full moon.

███ & I went to the National Gallery & had a great time. He's fun to look at art with, although I have more energy for it than he does.

On the weekend, we went deep into the Maryland countryside— to their "farm" on a tidal creek— we had moonlight swims & sunset sails & a happy, well-fed out-door weekend. Except that ███ is very demanding & we had two fights. He is very possessive & insistent that I be completely transparent to him & always sympathetic. It can't go on, & fortunately he leaves next week for 4 days in Europe. What have I got myself into & how can I extricate myself & him? Oh well— somehow we manage, as you say. And otherwise emotionally I am more or less on schedule.

The very air + light have changed + with all of it - You gone back, ███ to California, apples coming into the stands, Summer ends. <u>At last</u>.

I miss you already, but we'll think about meeting in Philadelphia.
Carry on + Courage!
love,
Ann

6 Sept 78

Dear Sharon –

It looks as if I can't get to Philadelphia the week of Sept. 18. Reasons: schedule-coordinating among Lib. staff (read: Mary); a possible consulting commitment in the 2nd half of that week.

I'm going to try for the last week in Sept – or the first in Oct. Haven't yet been able to get hold of my friends there to even <u>ask</u> about staying. But I consulted my parents about whether or not I could "invite" a friend as well, and they recommended not to. So on all fronts it looks as if I'm not any help to you at all. I have to let you down. I've been counting on that week with you. And then I held onto the hope of a part of it – say Thurs. Fri. Sat., at least. I'll send bulletins about my plans, but don't let me mess up yours. Damn, I'm disappointed.

I spent Labor Day weekend helping my mother wrap up her Thesis. It was a crazy, disorganized, rushed, frenzied, flurried, emotional, exhausting few days. Oddly enough, I had a sort of good time. I was glad to be able to help, glad to be so thoroughly distracted away from my own problems. And I kept saying to myself– "I have a lot to learn from this experience. I may have learned to be organized, not out of discipline, but out of <u>Fear</u>! of what can happen…

Archives moves next week. This is a silly letter, it's mostly meant as an SOS about our lost plan.

A fresh letter will follow soon. I've been carrying this one for weeks.

24 October 1978

Dear Sharon --

Two days of Indian Summer had the effect on me of difusing my mind into the hazy light and heat that so took one's physical self by surprise, at this late date. Plus, getting very high to go see Ringling Brothers Barnum and Bailey Circus with a new friend and lover ▉▉▉ an ex-mime, clown, tightrope walker, now physicist, and soon to be student of ▉▉▉▉▉▉. (All of those credentials sound terribly exotic, but basically he's just a very sweet man.) But today a sudden cold snap snaps me back to attention and I'm mindful of how long its been since I last wrote to you.

You, last heard from, had accomplished two tasks, one the German exam BRAVO! and the good trip to Philadelphia. My trip there is still postponed still by library reasons, and I am somewhat frantic. To maintain an illusion of research I read up and down the secondary sources map-- mountains of books. (The Stanton book, Leopard's Spots is a shining example to us all of how to use primary sources, and how to write clearly and make the argument <u>fun</u> to read.)

On another front, I have started to take steps to find another job. I wrote to Polly for a letter of recommendation. and I asked Ruth Hill for one too. and I have talked to Helen Slotkin, Archivist at M.I.T. about some of the difficulties at M.C.Z. re: Archives. Its a major change of attitude for me and gives me a tremendous sense of relief. Oh, how I would like to have a long talk with you about it, over dinner, poor Sharon, always having to listen to my yarns. But the main thing is this: all these years, when the status of Archives was so tentative, I have felt like the flag carrier, that if I left that would be the end of the program. In spite of the lack of support, I envisioned a real archives, in the kind of records I accessioned and in the way I handled them. The two new developments are: that now the Archives has been incorporated into the Special Collections of the Library. so they are secure. (and I am free) but they will become subsidiary to the rare books, and be treated as a <u>manuscript collection</u> rather than as a live archives. And I could not bear the discouragement of that kind of curtailed expectation after the habit of a kind of schitzoid insecure but expansive thinking. So those reasons on top of the personality problems which when looking for new work it is important to keep very quiet about make it really a good time for me to start looking around.

Except for one major problem, that job hunting is very time consuming and I'm supposed to be writing a book. However, my father told me not to worry about that because I can always get an extension of the contract.

Oh well. and nevertheless, my spirits are very good I think i'm growing so accustomed to frustration that I'm not even aware of its presence any more.

How are you doing?

love,
Ann

Then realized that this must wait until after postal strike.

25 January 79

Dear Sharon —

Work needs attention, but I'm so clean + powdered, and sipping sherry and listening to the radio that I feel sociable.

How is your new life, I wonder. The city, the work, the new people, and your new lover. You and I are always talking about our main post-analytical issues - but you are a very together person, all in all. Now that the externals don't count, and I'm curious about your new situation.

It's been a long time since I wrote you, but I'm reluctant to go all the way back to - when? - my brother's wedding + Washington, for fear I'll get bogged down. Here's now, instead. This is my second week of dance classes - after a year + ½. At first I was so stiff I could hardly walk, sit or climb stairs. But from the first plié, all was instantly right with the world, and I felt like my old self again. The long hiatus was the result of being poor, and worse, the hold-over from ▮▮▮▮▮▮ of a lower back pain - so severe that I finally had to stop doing ~~your~~ yoga and resign myself to turning into a blob. Trouble's, lumpiness spreads to the brain. I can't express what a radical re-alignment it is simply to spend 2 mornings a week stumbling around in a leotard!

Another cause of my sense of imminent new life is that my lover ▮▮ is about to move out of town. Relief. In the past month we've been able to reestablish an agreeable existence together. But we didn't do so well for a couple of months. Problem no. 1; we almost fell in love, but didn't. My response to that was to withdraw; ▮▮▮ to lean rather heavily on me. Friction. Worse, we ceased to ▮▮▮▮▮▮▮▮. I pride myself a little that by being rather adult + objective about it all, and forcing a recognition of the state-of-affair, we managed to salvage something. Especially in relation to the reality of his moving away.... you can do anything if you know when it's to end. But basically, Sharon, my relation to the world these days is — no one is allowed to prevent me from flying at my chosen altitude. Independence is my winged hobby-horse.

My relation to the book is that I wish I were finished. And the only way to finish is to do it. I'm at a stage where I can't stop doing research + get down to it, you know. Philadelphia + D.C. were such euphoric weeks — solid, substantive, wonderful material. Today, those note cards + xerox copies seem already stale + trite — and haunting. I caught myself the other day, as I climbed my stairs w/ a bag of groceries, fantasizing about finding the key — the magical connection — the deus-ex-machina — that would organize the whole work. But that magical key is me, + hours at my desk — + pencils + paper, and crumpled up paper on the floor, and not being able to go outside, or out to dinner — there's some mental anguish + frustration on the schedule. Yuk. But ok really.

The library is yuk, too. Eva is ok now, I'm used to her, + she's not so afraid of me. Because she's got Mary to fend me for her. But ███████████. I spent last evening with my revolutionary friend George from Puerto Rico, and he explained to me my work situation in Marxist terms. I'm simply a wage earner who is of course getting screwed by management. And management will take the credit when my work goes well, and blame me when it doesn't. He was very sweet, and ███████████ ███. xxo. He's been in Puerto Rico so long his absorbed the cultural machismo. But I'm confident enough to make him accept my Yankee, Cambridge terms of friendship; and our meeting is a big contribution to my being so up.

I would love to visit you, but I'm so poor again that it's a matter of nickels + dimes. (At least until after I've paid my taxes.) I miss you, I love hearing from you and in between you are always a point of reference for many trains of thought. And having you as a friend is often a matter of pride + source of consolation.

    Love,
    Annie

16 Feb 79

Dear Sharon — your letter has given me so much pleasure that I want to answer right away — while I relax over cocoa, an orange + a cigarette.

I'm up today. Something really wonderful (potentially) happened. And not even something in my personal life, but a work thing. That I dreamed of but haven't had the confidence to explore. I have cherished the notion of lining up an interested sponsoring museum to do an exhibition of [the zoo?] illus., to travel around the country when the book comes out. Well, today, Dan Jones, head of the Peabody Mus. photo-archive, and former Time-Life photographer + ... well connected, called to ask if he could bring the Director of the Carter Museum of Western Art, Fort Worth, Tx. over to see the Alex Agassiz drawings on wood. Over they came. And we talked. And M. le directeur was very interested in the possibilities of an exhibition, for his museum, and he mentioned the Morgan Lib. + Berkeley, too, as other places. And interested in my book +, well, ... After they left I just flipped — its all very tentative, but nevertheless thrilling. And exactly the boost I needed to give fresh motivation to my work.

Then, another good work thing. This one, for M.C.Z. Archives. Mary Leeler recently spent an afternoon at MIT Archives with Helen Slotkin, Boston's hottest archival force. And under Helen's excellent influence, Mary now begins to see the importance + value of a real archival program, rather than a moribund subsidiary to rare books. Mary + I had our weekly meeting this morning + ████████████████████████████. Circuitously suggested (she is never direct + clear, ever) that she's ready to look at archives in a new way, to incorporate rather than shun my advice, + she vaguely explained why she behaved the way she did before — I don't care how she rewrites history, as long as she's taking Helen's advice, its going to be o.k.

So, on yet another bright + bitterly cold day, my spirits take a turn for the better.

I don't know if I wrote of this before, but the M.C.Z. Library is closing over the summer, and I have asked for a 3-month leave of absence. How I'm going to support myself I don't know. I talked to a loan officer at the H.U. Credit Union today. But Lord knows I need the time for the book, + I'll just wing it somehow.

On the heart front, I'm alone, + need it, + love it. And men make applications + overtures, but this woman is not interested. Sometimes I suspect I need to see a shrink to better deal with the anger I feel at men who put sexual pressure on me. I'll knock myself out for a friend, but I have little to give romantically. While I'm well aware of the history behind this, I just think I have to be as alert for confusion or syndromes or whatever as I can be.

Do come to Boston. Stay at Cook's if you want to, but I urge you to come stay with me if that appeals to you. The only absence from Cambridge that might come up is if Edw. Lurie invites me to a conference at Univ. of Delaware on Science + Art, scheduled for March, I think. In August he said he'd send an invitation + I recently wrote to him and brazenly asked him to. But no answer yet.

What's the issue your Thayer article is in? Once you're in print you can't hide anymore — it's a funny feeling. One has to come to terms with, accept the responsibility for one's work in a different way. Just thinking about it gives me butterflies.

Take care; work is painful, but enjoy yourself somehow. You sound as if you are —

love,
Annie

14 March 1979

Dear Sharon,

I have reread your article and I think its splendid. It flows, it develops, its perfectly serious but fun to read. Your quotes are witty -- if you're dissatisfied, then I have to imagine that the next thing you produce will only exceed this quality. You should be pleased. And you have reminded me that I can use a Thayer painting as an illusrtation in my book, and cite you as an authority.

Lurie sent me an invitation to the Art and Science symposium. Its the 20th of April. I plan to go but there are many ifs involved. If I get the Harvard Librarians' research grant, if I can get the time off from the library, I'd like to stay on in D.C. and do some research the week of April 23 - 27. That's about the time you were thinking of coming to Cambridge. Let's see what happens. You know from our frustrated plan of Philadephia last fall that library scheduling can foil my scenario.

Last Wednesday I had a meeting wiht my editor. He is such a sweetheart. Plus, he has great confidence in what I'm doing, he was encouraging, complementary, enthusiastic, charming...And I was euphoric afterwards. He told me that I should write the book I love, because not many people get to do that once in a lifetime. The truth is that all the nice things he said I wouldn't have beleived from anyone else. (except maybe Polly)

I had dinner last night with ███████ He is going through a sort of cosmic existential crises on several fronts. As a result, I felt for the fist time that that I had something to offer him, and that he perceived me in a way that's important to me, that other friends do, ...I felt like I could help him. An interesting role reversal.

ANyway, I am looking forward to seeing you here sometime soon.

Lov,
Anne

14 May

Dear Sharon —

I am so looking forward to your coming here. Sharon's arrival has become the harbinger of summer for me in the past few years. How I wish you could stay on!

In a very short time I will be finished with the Archives job when my 3 month leave of absence begins. I got the official form today: and that made me remember the incredible exhileration + liberation of the day I filled out my withdrawal form from Smith College — 10 years ago. (There is even a political parallel in the air. 10 years ago the anti-war movement was gaining strength, breadth + momentum, just as the anti-nuke movement is now. And I feel a sprouting optimism that perhaps the people can persuade the government to do a right thing.)

I spent the weekend in Maine, visiting David Lakari at the very beautiful farm that he manages. The views, the light, the beach, the sweet freshness of the air made me euphoric. Why don't I get out of the city more often? Because, I always feel behind on the book, that's why. But for once, those hopelessly-overwhelmed-by-work feelings are mitigated by the prospect of the summer of uninterrupted TIME. And also, still some of that good solid research feeling left from the Philadelphia trip.

I can't help remarking — and remarking on it in fact rather negates the pretence — that for once when I write to you some man is no where near the center of my concerns. Although I know that its still in reaction to all that went before, all this freedom + bouyancy after all that repression — still I enjoy it tremendously.

I'm eager to know what your plans are, and how you are —

with love,
A.

75 Hancock Street, 7 Cambridge Mass. 02139

13 June

Dear Sharon,

Its breaking with convention to type a letter to you but I do it as a symbol of my new life at home as a writer and proud renter of an IBM Selectric-- my home prose console unit. I have a fantasy that one morning I will be awakened by a clattering of keys as the sheets of paper miraculously slip into the amchine and the book writes itself, while I gaze in wonder and amazement at the illuminating perceptions and seamless text on Am 19th cent zool. illus. (thats illustration). I may even become before the summer is out a more accurate typist.

When are you coming? I could not bear to miss you by any contingency. I have ahd had a tentative date with Pantheon to hold the first design meeting some time x in June. We have delayed and delayed while I wait for the photographs I ordered in APRIL to finally be ready. They are ready, but the first batches from Philadelphia and from the Fogg Museum of Art no less are unbeleivably poor. I cant beleive that anyone would charge money for that kind of lab work. But I begin to understand that I have been spoiled by the superb copy work that Al Coleman at the MCZ has been doing for me. Anyway, the variable of the New York trip is not so much at this point the pictures as it is the due date of my editor"s wife"s baby. They are doing the father participation natural childbirth, and if my trip falls around the 12th of July, there's a very good chance that Tom will be "in labor" and not available emotionally or otherwise to look at my stuff. I love it that his work as an editor is built around this much more important event. He told me about this in February, and that's just one of the reasons I like him so much.

I'm beginning to get into the flow of this new life,; by which I mean that I have os- so internalized the pressure that the only releif is through working. I realize that I'm so used to missing you ka that its really imperative that we see each other or I'll axxxpt come to accept this state of affairs. love, Anne

18 October

Dear Sharon,

Glory Hallelujiah! I have mailed the MS to Pantheon, and one third of my task is DONE. More, of course there's more, always more, but I am just beginning to realize that I actually have submitted to the world a part of my writing.

I put the package into the hands of the guy in the mail room, and as I walked away I started to cry. I dont know whether it was from relief or a parting sadness.

I'm trying to relax. Just to sit with a glass of sherry. To read a little in The Ambassdaws Henry James. to listen to a little music on the radio. And to see a few friends, and to get back in touch with those who are too far away.

I havent had much life apart from the work. I hardly noticed when the leaves began to change, and it still seems to happen at a distance from me -- through an invisible shield. Men look interesting again, but I only have a few days to play before I delve back into the work again, and I dont have anyone on line for the occasion. But I did my laudry--mountains of it. Its truly humorous. I dont quite know what to do with myself to celebrate. Where are my old debauching partners? now, when I'm ready to have a little fling? The other impulse is to go out and spend heaps of money. But I dont have any, so that takes care of that. And the abstemious life had becmoe something of a habit.

Will I dry up into a little grasshopper? Or will little shreds of praise for my work replenish my vital fluids.

I suppose that this is how most people become workaholics. At least vis a vis my typewriter I know where I am.

Tempted as I am to tear out this page, crupple it up nad not send it, I think I should send it as a warning on the dangers of work.

On the other hand there is something reassuring about the phenomenon. Its interesting to have no expectations that some other person will rushin and fill the vacuum.

So htere is the weather report. As I type this I am smiling wryly and almost laughing. I guess I feel really good; I dont know, but I do feel amused.

Love,
Ann

5 nov —

Sharon —
life has been a little more normal recently. I'm afraid I've really been enjoying a sort of respite from the pressure of feeling behind the "vacation" is over. And I'm back behind the desk again. Meanwhile, however, it has been glorious — I danced all night at a party, had relaxed visits + long conversations w/ my friends. Wish I could see you —

love
Ann

20 November

Dear Sharon,

Yours of the somethingth inst. recv^d with pleasure. I think that you are so lucky, always aknowledging the hard work involved, to have a male companion while you float your skiff through the waters of allconsuming work. And I wonder why I cannot. On the subject of men, I still fell such anger that I sometimes wonder how it could still be there with so much intensity. For example, this morning I awoke in a rage ▓▓▓▓▓▓▓. This doesnt happen very often, and when it does, I am amazed. I wonder whether total candidness is possible between men and women. And when I meet men I like, my response is that I wouldnt want to visit my wrath on their presumed innocence. Oh well.

I am working out chapter 2. History of science got so much more complicated after 1835 that my biggest problems have been in organization. What proportion of concentration should I give to each individual and each issue? I think I have got the organization I want. But its one that is pretty hard to write, even if it does solve the problems of proportion. My working title for the second section is: The Education of Spencer Fullerton Baird. In the years before he finally became the asst. sec. at the Smithsonian, he corresponded and met with every mainstream American zoologist, geologist and collector and it was this personal network that was then translated into governemnt supervised sceince during his years at the SI. He had also met many of the artists who would illustrate the gov. sci. publications. The other problem that this tack solves for me is that of Agassiz. I wanted to see him through American eyes, and to continue to play the theme of American self respect in sceince versus the European dominance. The biggest difficulty with the Biard point of view is that I have to deal with people like SG Morton, Holbrook, Silliamn, Dana etc in seamlessly constructed flashbacks. It was exactly such flashbacks that gave me so much trouble in the part of the book dealing with Alexander Wilson. and I finally solved them by pulling them all out and constructing an introductory chapter. I just hope and pray that I have the writing skills now to work in the digressions from a straight chronolgy in a cohesive way. The only crit I have got so far on the first section is from my father, and he was very helpfull- he noticed that in some of the sections, I lost my track, and got diverted by side lines. Since my sin was on the side of too much rather than too little, it will be easier to correct-- shift topic sentences here and there, and condense paragraphs for a better flow. He also noticed that I seemed to get a little tired after a certain point. all words to the wise. I have been taking it all a little easier. And there is a degree of manic behavior that I certainly felt in the last days before sedding the MS away that I have a vivid fear of, and healthy reluctance to reenter. On the other hand I also saspect that it is only in that exclusive heat of monomania that I can truly crank it out. The double bind.

Oh Sharon, the little taste of normal life that I have had in the interval between mailing the package and now has been glorious wonderful delightful easy. What then will it feel like to actually finish the whole damn thing? For so long the idea of finishing has been one of a sort of dislocated future -- when all I now own would be worn out and long gone, when my life would have atrophied around me all except for the work. But then the other day, I was making a salad and I thought-- maybe the can of olive oil I now have on my shelf will be the same can I have when I finish. Maybe I'll still be using the same bottle of ahir conditioner. Maybe... I realized how close the dream is to actuality. (Notwithstandingthe tremendous amount of work remaining= especially the photowork and permissions...)

I am going to New Haven for thanksgiving. For a long time my sister and my father have been at odds, and so I wasnt planning to go, because I didnt think it would be good. But my sister has decided to try to bury the hatchet, so off we go to celebrate a holiday. I should stay home at the typewriter. And because I paln to take time away I have suffered various anxiety attacks in the past few days. I also plan to spend money I dont have and go into New York for the weekend. there is a show, travelling from the Smithsonian, now at the AMNH, on guess what -- american natural history illustration. Clearly a must on my list. I will attend, notebook in hand, and crane my neck over the towering shoulders of every child in NYC, all of them already ten inches taller than I will ever be, and take in what the Amercian public has been exposed to on my topic. I sk hope also to see something a little more contemporary in the way of art. I find that after this prolonged overdose fx of representatinnal/illustration, I hanker for the most abstract and painterly art I cna find.   linear

OK, here is the question. When can you come to visit. If I were to go away in January or February on a research trip -- a last loop around to make sure I havent missed anything -- could you possibly make xx use of my apartment for a week? And conveniently overlap with in time either before I wnet away or after. I dont actually have any but the vaguest plan for such a trip, but it is on my mind. And what else could I offer you that might attract you down here to this benighted city in midwinter.

In the meanwhile, courage, comrade in work, and

love!
Ann

AMERICAN SOCIETY OF ZOOLOGISTS

FOUNDING DATES: 1890, 1899, 1901

DIVISIONS: Animal Behavior, Comparative Endocrinology, Comparative Physiology, Development Biology,
Invertebrate Zoology, Vertebrate Morphology

28 July 1980

Dear Sharon,

Here I am several days into my two weeks away from the MCZ to write. As ever I am thinking of you as I work. I have been receiving a sprinkling of letters from Polly that indicate she is barreling along x in her wrok in her usual style. How I do envy her ebullience. I xxxix rarely if ever bounce as I write. Nevertheless, its going ok, slow but steady. I think I wrote you that ▓▓▓ is here for the summer. He had offered to be my reader -- and freindly taskmaster. His offer and my ability to accept seem to me a true mark of friendship -- his acknowledgemmnt of my work, his xssiii skills to help, my confidence to accept his judgements, etc.

His presence here has so far been very interesting. We are companionable, reaaxed, affectionate, candid -- even passionate. We were afraid to admit the sex, but could not deny it either. We are agreed to watch and see what it all means. Its a question that grows on me. And I am extremely wary lest any preoccupation with ▓▓▓ errode my independence, my enjoyment of being single. As an antedote, I sleep with other men -- that is, I continue my life as before. There are friendships, friendships with sex, affairs -- what I don't want is to find myself in a capital R relationship. Dont want means in this case, am most affraid of -- that emotional dependence. Or is it possible to stay free and still make a committment. Who knows, least of all me.

The summer has been really fun so far. I've had lots of house guests and oodgtimes with people. So now that its overdue time to dedicate myself to my work, I dont feel deprived at all am alone at the keyboard. Its were I want to be. I appraoch these two weeks as intense training. I've gone swimming every day -- pushing my distance and stamina. And feeling strang and disciplined doing x it. I love being wet -- horizontal movement in a benign medium. Sight and hearring counting for little -- just the ripple shadows on the bottom tiles and the sound of my own bubbles and kicking. Correcting my strokes for smoother motion. And glorious showers afterwards. Much as I love my qx quaint bath tub, these high-tech showers are a dream come true.

A copple of weeks ago I went up to Salem, Mass. for the day to talk with the ax curator of natural hsitory at the Peabody museum about my show. They want me to do a 19th cent. Am. Nat. Hist. Illus. show in the fall of /81, with my book as catalog. They are looking for a funding agency, but the museum is so solidly behind the idea that they will fund it anyway. We are talking abo-ut inviting other museums to collaborate with us, so the show could travel. The Peabody does a beautiful job mounting their exhibitions. John wants to devote part of the show to explanations of graphic techniques. He is a sort of pear-shaped, bouncy jolly fellowm, and I told him at the end of the day that id this was doing business, it was certainly my style. I felt do comfortable and relaxed about the "negotiahions." Especially compared to my overawed feelings when that museum director from Texas offered me a show a few years ago. I'm very pleased with the whole arrangement. Now all I have to do is finish the book on time. Oh, the Peabody will even pay me to be guest curator.

To change the subject, one reason I have you on my mind is a conversation I had with a friend recently. I think I'm learning something about how repressed men react to illness and death. My friends father is 84 and has just suffered a stroke. He needs to have a cardiac operation to prevent an imminent occlusion. Of course, my friend has been receiving midnight hysterical calls from his mother etc. And in general feels the reality of his father's age and nearness to death. To connteract the loneliness that his family situation has brought out (this is the man whose serious girl-friend has been away for a year, and whom I see on and off) reached out for affection, very naturally. But the expression that reaching out has been sexual. As if the sex both comforted and at the same time denied the death. This reminded me of one of your recent incidents.

Well, its time to attack that transitional paragraph again.

love,
Ann

25 November 1980

Dear Sharon,

There is a point on my route to work where I suddenly identify the real task of the day. This morning, I thought, as I passed in front of Gund Hall, the place in question, I must write to you. Hardly a task.

So much that is important to you has happened since I last answered a letter from you. I want to congratulate you on your divorce. Surely by now the trivial paperwork part has been accomplished? Its wonderful that you should have the injection of a sense of freedom at a time when you perhpas feel so very married to your thesis.

After I got your last letter I took ███ to task for not giving you enough support during your graduate student blues. But look at me, I havent done my bit either. I hope by now he has been in touch. He claimed that he had tried to call you and that you were never home. Its a fool proof claim, after all, no one can possibly refute it.

I can hardly believe that its Thanksgiving already. In fact, I decided to pretty much ignore it by not going home and not making any complicated plans for the holiday. I have had my own schedule for rest and recuperation, and it just so happens not to coincide with the national calendar. It all started one hot muggy day this summer when I said to myself, I jsut dont have the energy for the holidays this year. Not on top of everything else. And anyway, the things I want are all intangible--- like, to have finished my book, or relief from financial anxiety, or a better self-image...

A few w-eks ago, I sent some MS off to various readers and to my editor. (copy to Polly at her suggestion, and your reiteration). From my editor, at last, came approval. What a relief. I was down with a cold, the killer cold that has been making hte rounds, when he called to say I had turned the thing around since last year, and all systems were back to go. So I didnt mind the congestion, I just relaxed and took the opportunity to stay in bed and reread all the novels that I had enjoyed as a 12 and 13 yr old. Tale of Two Cities, Jane Eyre, Wuthering Heights, two Jane Austen's. I Had a marvelous time weeping and otherwise fully enjoying the romance and drama of the stories. Meanwhile, my ed. is coming next week, and we will discuss directions, photos, etc. Two of my other readers have sent some encouragement. Good editorial advice from a journalist friend, suggesting that I loosen up my prose, and other kinds of clarifying advice. Then, Ernst Mayr asked to read it. I blushed and shuffled and apologized for the juvenile level of my work, but he sweetly reminded me that we must all start somewhere, and he gave the MS considerable sttention -- gave me a reference for every remark he pencilled in -- and corrected a couple of howlers ∅that I left uncorrected and just sent it on to Polly as was.)

53

What else: I guess the principal change is that after a wretched and
depressed first couple of months of the fall, I am feeling better. The
issues I was unhappy about were all work related. I think that the
full impact of having lost that folder of manuscript finally got into
my blood stream -- mixed metaphor, but that's the idea. I felt that
I had nothing to show and had had no feed back to the point where I
doubted everything I had produced so far. The emotional climate that
these feelings created permeated every other activity. It was as if,
on a hot day, a neighbor's radio blared at top volume and there
was nothing you could do about it. Constant spinning of wheels. Trying
to write was just this awful impenetrable fog. And as I went about
the rest of my life I couldnt concentrate on or enjoy anything. Finally,
I just ranted and raved for a whole weekend, blew off some steam, got
a little help on some of hte MS, and got it together to send off.
By the time my editor finally called me back, I already knew that although
my work is far from perfect, there is plenty there to work from, and if
he hadnt liked it I would have argued.

Another hting, after I started feeling better this fall I had to recognize
that I had been in fact truely depressed and that getting depressed has been a
pattern and that it was time to start to give it all some serious consideration.
Its such a waste of time feeling that way. My parents, good academics that
they are, recommended during all htis that I read a new book by Maggie
Scarf, Unfinished Business, a book about depression in women's lives.
I found it very interesting, a had many recognitions and illuminations reading
it. Its not a self-help book . She describes a number of cases and
relates those specific women's experiences to current infomration in the field.
Somehow, it was clarifying.

And somehow, I do know that good things are happening. I am having a good
time with friends, and also controlling pretty well my sense of time and
space for myself and for my work. I am managing to balance seeing two
men and enjoying them both without feeling that I am off my center. Since
I started to calm down I have been able to concentrate on one thing at a
time, and go about my different jobs without worrying about where I am
supposed to be next., etc. And consequently enjoying things more.

And I caught myself thinking one evening that in fact, hectic and painful
as the first months of the season were, that in fact it had been a very
rich time.

So, let's see how long I can hold onto this relative calm.

Love,
Ann

12 Feb 81

Dear Sharon —

The day your letter arrived was my first day of painful withdrawal symptoms from going off caffeine. I tried to answer your letter but could hardly hold a pen and certainly couldn't penetrate the fog between my brain + the outer world. By the end of that day I decided that withdrawal was such a ghastly experience that I certainly didn't want to live through it ever again — so I decided I might as well quit cigarettes while I was about it. So, it's drug rehab. time. It's Day 3, and I do feel better, if still a little convalescent.

Sharon, I did not submit a title to JAS. It just would have been the last straw for this poor camel. January I devoted to centering myself — streamlining my schedule (I now have Fri-Mon at home to write) and discarding commitments that threw me off base. I'm still constitutionally unable to maintain a regimen such as you described. I draw up splendid rules + regulations, and fire up the old resolve — + then the first thing I do is play hooky, take a nap, — I suppose I really could have coped with speech making, but it also seemed like an obvious commitment to spare. I hope you I haven't let you down, + that you'll have plenty of other reasons for taking that badly needed break + going anyway, + that you'll visit me here in Cambridge.

Haven't heard a word from Polly. Does that mean she thinks it's so bad that she's unable to find anything nice or encouraging to say?

Right now I'm worrying more about money than the book. I have lost a reliable source of $100/month. Everything has just gone _up_ + its a close shave every week. Sometimes I can cheer myself by the philosophy of - oh well, it's only money. Or I scold myself by thinking that I'm just worrying about $ as an excuse to avoid confronting the Book. The book, meanwhile, gets _shorter_ + _shorter_. That's how I plan to meet my new deadline - Spring for this draft + Sept. for revised draft. Today I received, signed + returned a fresh contract from Pantheon giving me a Sep. deadline. Hooray!! for the first time in 2 years I'm not behind! on paper at least. Lord knows I'm slow + behind in reality.

My life has little variety. Tues - Thurs. is almost sort of my weekend. I work at MCZ, at other jobs, + don't even try to get to my own desk. It's mid-week that I try to see friends. Then weekends, its me against me. Truth + consequences at the keyboard. I'm so used to being bummed out that I've achieved a kind of steady, if mordant, cheerfulness. Sometimes a ray penetrates into my tunnel, + I wonder, what is normal life like - when you can take vacations, go on picnics, plan parties, go away on weekends.... I could weep for it.

I am looking forward to seeing you. Meanwhile, encouragement from the bottom of my heart -

love,

10 March 81

dDear Sharon,

It would be just wonderful if you came to visit. I feel better just looking forward to it. Because usually, as you said, life is so very xp predictable these days that often, when I go out or when I see a friend on the street, I just don't know what to say about myself. It seems like such a triumph to me that I can meet my schedule and in some way hold my own emotionally and even find ligtle islands of pleasure x from time to time -- but such is hardly the stuff of conversation. (My machine needs an overhaul, but I cant spare it until I finish this chapter.)

Yes, trying to finish a chapter. Itx seems ok one day and awful the next. I had to loose some time recently while making money. I read galley proofs for a Fogg museum catalog. In a way ti was x terribly anxiety producing to spend so much time not writing, but in another way, itxx was a sort of vacation from my own concerns. The catadog is of a show of Picasso drawings. The show is wonderful. The catalog stinks. I(and is about two months late. The museums concerned will be lucky if the catalog is in print intime to go to the second scheduled location.) Back to the catalog--never in my life Have Iseen such convoluted art history jargon and so much bad writing in one place. I feel like a Zen master of art writing after reading that. But at the same time I learned things from reading it. Especially about Picasso, although t o be honest, the parts I was frankly the most interesded in were the parts abouthim and his mistresses. But I was remindéd that it can be relevant to discuss certain artly details -- such as details of technique that helpp the reader get inside the artist's head a little. If its not done well it reads like mud. But mayb e I can do it well. Just save me from redundancies like "a hand-held pen".

57

I'm impressed that you will type your own thesis. I should think it would be very hard to finally say -- no more editing, no more changes, leave it alone and type it clean. I have the security of knowing that at some point my deathless prose will go through the mill at Pantheon and emerge in galley proof. Then, after I faint with horror at seeing my flaws in print, I'll just have to live with it ... and move to Brazil and change my name. (I'm pissed off at ▓▓▓ these days. I'm sick of his even less than perfunctory gestures of acquaintance. ▓▓▓▓▓▓▓▓▓▓▓▓▓▓▓▓▓▓▓▓▓▓ He ouwldnt have an inkling that I might a harbor such thoughts. He wouldnt notice.) Maybe I'm just over sensitive. I think I am in general, and that all feelings are exaserbated by the stresses and strains of writing..Sometimes I get flashes that I may be making it all harder than it need be. Isnt it self defeating to prefer to grind my teeth in solitude than to let saomeone comfort me. And then, when I have chased every one away, to feel hurt and angry when I think I'm neglected.

One of my private jokes, who else would think its funny anyway? is to recast the book as a childrens' book, á la: Bumpity bump, Auguste Sonrel's wagon clateered over the ruts. The big lithographic stones that had come all the way from Bavaria bounced behind him on the wagon bed. He hoped they wouldnt crack by the time he readhed ho me...Louis Agassiz xix beamed encouragengly," "What a fine picture you have made, my friend. Good enough to have your name printed on the title page along with mine, ha ha..." Dont worry Sharon, I havent really gone mad. Please 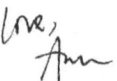come visit for as long as you like. I look forward to seeing you so much. until then,

love,
Ann

MUSEUM OF COMPARATIVE ZOOLOGY
The Agassiz Museum

HARVARD UNIVERSITY · CAMBRIDGE, MASSACHUSETTS 02138 · TEL. 617 495-2466

30 Mar 81

Dear Sharon —

Bravo! Congratulations. How splendid that you have a job. You're a star, of course. Very smart on Johns Hopkins' part, in my opinion.

Your visit plans sound great. Come. We'll celebrate. Bring your swim gear. I can bounce my chapter off your head a little. I'm so looking forward to seeing you!

Oh, what a lift to hear your good news. Bravo, once again. It'll be fun to hash it all over with you at length and at leisure.

Love,
Ann

MUSEUM OF COMPARATIVE ZOOLOGY

The Agassiz Museum

HARVARD UNIVERSITY · CAMBRIDGE, MASSACHUSETTS 02138 · TEL. 617 495-2466

13 May

Dear Sharon,

Just the quickest of notes to thank you for your letter and to accompany the xerox you needed. No trouble at all I assure to you find and copy these things.

Once again, I loved having you visit. Please always feel welcome to stay with me whereever I am and at any time. I enjoy your company -- and I love the way we have kept on getting to be better and better acquainted despite time and distance.

Today is one of those heady subversive intoxicating spring days when everything is so alive and beautiful. I want to be in perpetual motion.

Meanwhile, my writing does not go as smoothly as I might wish. I am still recovering from several distractions -- the worst was preparing to be on a panel of New England archivists. I think I acquitted myself with honor; I was certainly relieved when it was over. The occasion was a chance to go out to Amherst with a friend. We drove around in the countryside and explored. And revisited a favorite diner to enjoy a piece of famous diner pie.

I have to fly off now to the next MCZ errand.

Love,
Ann

MUSEUM OF COMPARATIVE ZOOLOGY

The Agassiz Museum

HARVARD UNIVERSITY · CAMBRIDGE, MASSACHUSETTS 02138 · TEL. 617 495-2466

15 June 1981

Dear Sharon,

Bravo for your tremendous thesis production. I hope Polly gives it back to you in tim e for you to revise it at a sane and human pace. In whatever breathing space you have in between, how are you coping with the impending move and job?

It was good to see Polly not too long ago. (also just dear how bouncy and cheerful Ruth Turner gets when Polly is here.) Polly was somewhat uneasy, though, about my MS. Although she apologized at least twice for not getting back to me about it, she volunteered not one single other word about it or about any idea therein. My worst suspicions are confirmed. If I had time to agonize about it I would be mortified. Fortunately or unfortunately, as the case may be, I just have to keep on writing without her help and barrel along into print only to get crucified by just such critics as Polly when its too late to do anything about it. Oh dear.

Meanwhile, I have just turned 31, a fine age to be I think. Somehow I do feel more grown up -- not responsible yet by any means, for I still need to live with the illusion that I could pick up and go without any incumberances at the drop of a hat... Summer is in full swing and the effects it has on my life are: melons for breakfast; cold showers after swimming; crime novels until well after midnight; rash moments of lust and equally rash moments of total indifference...

love,
Ann

MUSEUM OF COMPARATIVE ZOOLOGY
The Agassiz Museum

HARVARD UNIVERSITY · CAMBRIDGE, MASSACHUSETTS 02138 · TEL. 617 495-2466

8 September 1981

Ms. Sharon Kingsland
Department of History of Science
Johns Hopkins University
Baltimore Maryland 21218

Dear Sharon,

I was holding off answering your June letter that because of the postal strike didnt arrive here until very recently, because I KNEW that what I really needed was your Baltimore address. Congratulations on your 1) FINISHING the thesis -- bravo and hooray and my deepest admiration and 2) arriving at the appointed time in your new life-- that requires emotional stamina that probably event no.1 didnt leave you much of. What a double bill to fill, and how I hope that you are finding ways of sustaining your energies when probably all you want to do is sleep for a month. Of all the times for a Canadian postal strike when I really wanted to send you bulletins of support and encouragement and sympathy. Here they all are rolled into one -- !. I mean, there you are, living proof that it is humanly possible.

I need living proof these days too. I am running behind schedule and struggling to hold my own against the mounting internal pressure. Supposedly today is my deadline, that is, today my editor comes back from his summer vacation and the package of manuscript is supposed to be on his desk. It isnt. The summer turned out so differently from what I had supposed. The museum job took a tremendous ammount of energy and was in fact quite demoralizing. I was counting on my 3 weeks in August to get the bulk of the writing done but what I had failed to figure in was that I was pretty burnt out. I tried to combine relaxing and writing , but I'm afraid that both got compromised. By the time I was due back at the museum, I had worked myseld into quite a state. I'm calmer now and the chapters are ticking along, but all overdue. I'm just not able to handle overload. And what adds to the pressure, just as your knowing htat you needed to prepare courses added to yours, isthat I am just so eager and almost desperate to finish, to get rid of this package of by=now unbearable compromises that I have made in order to write the book in the first place.

So how is life after the thesis? All you dreamed? I promise that I will see you this winter one way or another. I picture us doing gymnastics on the waxed floors of your perfectly empty apartment. Or sitting in the middle of an empty floor having Camparis together, òr something unbelievably civilized, and to me at this moment in my life, unattainable. Morning tea is usually my last quiet moment of the day. After that, the internal voices are hard at work, sorting paragraphs, trying not to worry about money, nagging about overdue freelance assignments, etc. Once again, and forever, my deepest admiration for you having finished your task and begun another one so hard upon it.

love,
Ann

5 Dec 81

Dear Sharon —
 Thanks for your letter. I think this year I'll be up to the challenge of talking to an audience. I should have finished the book by April, so it should, in theory, be possible to put a talk together.
 In fact, I met with my editor at Thanksgiving. He's relaxed, I must say, + that makes me relaxed. He suggested we push the pub. date back to Fall '83. That gives me 6 more months to finish up. Relief. I had been sprinting since September, and it feels great to ease up a little.
 Easing up a little mostly takes the form of hustling up some free lance work. I've been so monomaniacal all fall that I haven't scrounged enough extra cash. So I've been dashing around town on free-lance errands. It feels great to be out + about.
 Don't be so discouraged about teaching. Everyone says it gets easier with practice. And also, you need a break, or at least a gradual winding down from your own thesis-finishing. You started the year behind in energy. The same thing happened to my mother — she flung the thesis at the typist on her way to meet her first class. And she said that her first semester was awful but the second one much better!
 On the subject of ▮ — there is nothing wrong with you. You should be pissed off — in fact, you should be so pissed off that you frankly don't care what you hear from ~~up~~ him.

He abused your friendship, not vice versa. He owes you an apology + you would be fully within the right to make no effort to get in touch with him until he offers one —

OR — to take your next opportunity when fate or whatever brings you together of giving him a piece of your mind, from A to Z. So now I've given you a piece of my mind.

On the subject of men in our professional lives — ▮▮▮▮ was in town but did not have time to see me. Nor did I expect he would.

I hope you'll get a rest between semesters. I know you need one, and it could make a world of difference in your outlook. The holidays themselves have sometimes in the past put me in a ~~foul~~ temper, but a little time off is always welcome.

Love,
Ann

31 December 81

Dear Sharon,

I hope you have had a pleasant holiday so far, and that you are not too burdened by blue-books to catch up on rest or fun or whatever you need most.

Probably this past semester was one of the most difficult things you'll ever have to do. My new year's wish for you is that it's easier from now on.

I'm still trying to reorient myself to normal life after a prolonged break for Christmas. My sister & I "gave" each other a few days together at my place before we went down to New Haven, and so I've done very little writing for almost 2 weeks. (I'm hoping that I can return to my work with fresh insights that permit me to problem-solve the wudgy little messes ~~two-ways~~ I left & despaired over.) Christmas in New Haven was really fun. All my family seems in good shape & we had ~~tots~~ lots of laughs. My brother seems especially well. As my father commented — it's been a good divorce for him. The prize for most classic comment of the season goes to a fellow guest at the neighborhood annual Christmas Carol party who greeted ~~asked~~ me thus: "And who are you married to?" The real & best Christmas present of them all was that my sister & father seem to have made a peace with each other — after over 20 years of disharmony (My personal pop-psych. theory is that the problem dates back to my sister's puberty when her emerging sexuality, so different from my mother's brand of womanhood, upset my mother + that my father took approach his wife's side of the conflict. Therefore, my sister was denied that all-important acknowledgement from my father — and the issue was only very recently resolved, when my sister telephoned my father and asked his advice on some problem she was having w/ her boyfriend.) Better late than never, anyway.

So, my resolutions for the new year — besides finishing the book, are: to live within my means; to take a real vacation; to figure out what to do with the rest of my life. (No matter if these resolutions are incompatible with each other.)

And I'll take advantage of the sentimentality of the new year to tell you that I value your friendship tremendously and that I think you're wonderful —

love,

Ann

THE LIBRARY
MUSEUM OF COMPARATIVE ZOÖLOGY
HARVARD UNIVERSITY
CAMBRIDGE 38, MASSACHUSETTS

"The Agassiz Museum"

18 February 1982

Dear Sharon,

I did not get my paper topic into the History of Science Dept. in time to be giving a talk at JAS. This was not the year. I think, also, that I'm just too chicken to get up in front of an academic audience and say my piece. Any psychologist would have no trouble at all figuring out my fears of academic judgement. I would rather publish my book and let it fizzle out quietly than stand up in a Harvard auditorium and talk about my research. So, I thank you for your encouragement, and for your suggestion that I submit my topic, but I'm just not up to it. Especially this winter when my work has been going very slowly and my confidence has ebbed all too low. I hope you arent too disappointed in me.

Since the new year my writing has just been a mess. I dont know if I've ever endured such a foggy period. Just cant seem to think or problem solve. I am trying to be patient and to work through it -- just by clenching my teeth and toughing it out at the typewriter. But its reached the point that I burst into tears after a round of working. This happens almost every morning now, for the last few weeks. The trouble is that this noxious state of affairs seeps into everything else, and to say the least I feel low. Never theless, I get out, see friends, go out to dinner, to the movies, go skating with the gang from work, take walks on the few and precious sunny mild days. (To spring of course I have an ambivalent attitude: on one side I think, how glorious spring will be, andon the other I panic and say, not spring already with the book not done...) I keep waiting for the internal weather to change and for that glorious morning when I sit down and slice through all the silt.

I'm sorry to send on such a gloomy report. But I dont know how long I would have to wait to send cheerier news, and I did want to stay in touch. Your last letter sounded so refreshed and energetic. I hope you've managed to sustain that. Maybe I just have a bad case of the winter blahs. I only hope they dont linger into the spring blahs. At the rate time is flying by, it wont be long before the JAS brings you here. I am so looking forward to seeing you. Will you stay with me? I'd love it; or are you making arrangements to meet with Paul. Do let me know.

MUSEUM OF COMPARATIVE ZOOLOGY
The Agassiz Museum

HARVARD UNIVERSITY · CAMBRIDGE, MASSACHUSETTS 02138 · TEL. 617 495-2466

17 march 1982

Dear Sharon,

Thank you so much for calling me not so long ago. Your encouragement really helped. I wish I knew what makes the very same situation one day (or month) look so bleak and then another time, seem perfectly satisfying. Fortunately, whether by fluke or through the good wishes of friends like you, my point of view is turning itself around. I just hope I can keep it turned around. The writing is going better. I´m picking up some free-lance work. And simply enjoying more the same things that not so long ago were so hard to carry.

I thought of you the other day when the Harvard GAZETTE ran an article about helping new teachers through the trauma of meeting those first classes. Wouldnt you know that Harvard would have a special program. But dont you wish that other universities did. The article didnt have any scoops on how to get over the problem; the advice took the obvious tack -- just keep teaching until you dont feel like a new teacher anymore. But I guess its value was in letting the participants know that they were not alone.

I am supposed to be putting together a little exhibit in the MCZ Library on the history of biology at the MCZ for the occasion of the JAS. At times like this I sometimes wish that the history of biology at the MCZ had been a little more glorious. Despite my loyalties, I feel a little ashamed to glorify such an intellectual backwater.

So, if its St. Patrick´s Day its almost spring. So far, no one from the Herp. Department has announced that the peepers are out yet in Concord. NOr have I seen anyone from Entomology wielding a collecting net. But the Red Soxs are in spring training and the MCZ softball team is beginning to talk about its season. Maybe we can even find another team bad enough to enjoy playing with us this year.

Once again, thank you so much for giving me a call. It was a real treat to have a chat. And I am looking forward to seeing you soon -- in April.

Love,
Ann

1 June 82

Dear Sharon, I am going to send this to the Institute on the off-chance that you'll get it while you're in Tonronto.

Thanks for your two letters. How did you get through this year? It was traumatic in just about every possible way. You clearly have tremendous stamina, so that even though you feel exhausted, you pull through. Try to remember that you actually made it through a year that you started by being exhausted, during which your relationship with your mentor was cruelly tampered with, and that you didn't miss a single class even though you probably wished you could, and through it all, you were in a new and strange town, among strangers, separated from your lover and to top it all, there was a true crisis in your family. I can't think of any other ways that its possible for life to be hard. Once again, congratulations. You are a champion. And although no one is going to let on that you have done anything more than they expected of you, nevertheless, I think you have really triumphed.

You deserve a rest. I hope this summer is restorative. I wonder if even some time to be with your brother will allay your worries; you may have even more to worry about knowing more about the situation. But I have found with friends who have breakdowns of various kinds that any time spent either during the crisis, or after, during treatment or recovery, is terribly important in cementing the bond. Most people treat mental patients like pariahs and avoid them. Attention and love during that time are very important. It may be very painful and frustrating to see your brother drugged up. And he might not seem immediately responsive to you and your attentions. But I am sure that the time you spend with him will increase his trust of you and maybe in the near future, he will turn to you more.

I loved your visit, hectic and all. You are very far from succumbing to the "▮▮▮▮▮ Syndrome" no fear. If I've said it once, I'll say it again -- I am delighted to have you for a friend, and it just keeps getting better as the years go by. I have often credited Polly with teaching me enough so that I could attempt a book. But the best outcome of my apprenticeship with her was getting to know you.

Now, here's what's happening in my life. I went ahead and promised my last chapter for the end of June. I don't know if I can make it, but why not try. It will be in rough form, not as complete (or as confused perhaps) as the other chapters. But I just have to get to the end one time. To round that marker. Then I'll be content to go back and revise. Meanwhile, just when I have allocated all my resources to writing, naturally my living situation goes crazy. My crazy neighbor is just too hard to live near. He has taken lately to smashing his apartment with sledge hammer and crow bar. As well as other things. I ahve called the police, but that's not a big help. Nor does it solve the feeling I have of being barricaded in my apartment, afraid to go in and out freely. To top it off, the building has been sold to the slumlord of Cambridge with a reputation for having his buildings burned. My building is such a bad fire trap that the last time the inspector came, he just laughed and said that the building should be evacuated immediately. However, the process of serving notice of fire code violations came to a grinding halt as soon a s the building was sold. Because the new owner pays off half the city government, apparently, to keep things his own way. Yuk.

I have decided to move. So long to a great apartment. But I can't handle the neighbor, or the tacky landlord. I'm going to move in with my friend Victoria, over in the ritzy end of town. She runs a gallery in NYC half the time, so half the month I will have the place to myself and the other half, the company of an old friend. (She and Nick's younger brother were in Athens the year Nick and I lived there, and then in our early days in Cambridge, the four of us lived together.) Don't think for a minute that this means you can't come to stay any more. Of course you can, any time. I think you'll like it, too.

So June is going to be quite busy. I will take two weeks off at the end of the month to write. And probably to move as well.

Despite all the pressure and hassles, I'm in good spirits and having fun. I wish you the best for the summer -- rest, refreshment, successful research and good times with Paul. After all, this summer vacation is supposed to be one of the best parts of the academic life.

love,
Ann

P.S. I've seen Polly only for seconds at a time. She looks great.

22 Oct 82

Dear Sharon,

Thank you for your letter; its great to hear from you. Was the summer good over all? Just to get away, be with Paul and so forth?

I don't know how to describe my summer. First of all, it seems such a long time ago. And then, my retrospecitve view falsifies it. Its been so hectic since September that those bright days of July and August take on a serenity that they didn't have at the time. I would say that this summer just blew everything wide open. At the end of June I moved and that precipitated all sorts of psychic disrupstions or accentuated those already under way. I am sure that a lot of what I've been feeling is the end-of-book syndrome. But immediately on moving suddenly I couldn't sleep. Many many white nights all summer. Midnight obsessions over book. Then, too, it was a summer of marriages, deaths, births, departures of old important friends. There was one week that I entitled "The Parade of Old Lovers." Events that dirupted or demanded emotional attention just didn't quit. Many were to be celebrated, but things got to the point where I could no longer distinguish between the pitch of emotion for gladness from that for mourning. To pique things a little more, I started seeing a man whom I like much too much for the degree of seriousness of the thing.

To be sure, work on the book continued, but its relative importance on the Cos-mic scale diminished. The on-going crisis of the summer was my realization that I was not going to finish the whole book by Labor Day. But I kept plodding away. One of the best things about the summer was having Polly here. We met at lunch and sometimes at 5 she drove me home, and these little seminars were wonderful for my morale. But such was the pitch of my life that I would get terribly excited about my work and history and science and all of it and just buzz out-- unable to turn off the brain at night. Of course we all sort of love those times when ideas are so exciting and life so electric. And Polly was very good to me -- giving me all sorts of advice that I'm sure was meant just as much for herself. I get so lonely in my work most of the timetime that just to have her here to talk with was wonderful. Bruce I saw only once and that very briefly. All in all, Polly seemed in great shape. Life is life and truly mysterious.

In September the pressure just went off the scale, or seemed to. My plan was to mail off everything to date the day after Labor Day. But at the edd of August, my colleague in Special Collections quit, and so the month from the start was distinguished by an increase in my Library hours and a decrease in my writing time. (Also in a loss of income for a while since I had to give up some of my freelance work to be at the Library and also had been laid off from another job over the summer.) The Labor Day weekend I marked from the start by having my hair cut very short -- to aerate the brain. I borrowed keys to get at a self-correcting typewriter and clean typed the Ms all weekend. I managed to maintain the disciplined work attitudd only becauseI had to. Because over the weekend, my sister called to tell me that she is getting married. That was it. Matters of Love took precedence over mere work, but without a doubt the system was overloaded. I sent the MS on schedule (minus chapter the last) and then just fell apart. Locked myself out of the house, risked not using contraceptive at the wronigtime and so forth... all leading up to the wedding and my departure of a dear friend the following week. Deadlines and schedule changes and extra obligations all continued to come due. My emotional life continued to intensify, and it all con tinues.

Some days I feel so emotionally naked that I can hardly believe I'm going to leave the house and meet my schedule. Other days I can't stop crying. And sometimes I jst just feel supersaturated and sort of numb. Is it my heart or my head? But at this point, what does it matter?

Maybe now I'll have a chance to pull myself together. Finally the new Book Assistant has begun in Spec. Coll. (But then, she is such a seemingly repressed and fragile person I am afraid that it could be a little difficult to work with her. She is the sort of person who seems to have spent her entire life with adults. We'll see anyway.) I am hoping not to negotiate for the return of some writing time. I have hardly had time or powers of concentration to ~~finish~~ write and the last chapter is haunting me. And to add to the stress, I still haven't heard from my editor about the last batch I sent.

On Thursday I had to throw in the towel at about 3:30 and go home from the museum. I had been crying all day, about what I couldnt figure out. Maybe just overload. I long for my old, prickly, centered, solitary mode. At least I knew those ropes and had developed a certain bravado. Now I assume nothing.

You sound pretty steady. Bravo. I will try to take you as my example. When I ther throw my I Ching, it says, that by maintaining firm correctness there will be progress and success but that this is a season of changes.

love,
Ann

P.S. Here's a little Bob Cook gossip. I saw him at a MCZ party, certainly he looked better than in recent years. He is now as you probably know the Program director at NSF and he told me that he had just spent his first million. Perhaps on the strenght of that, he greeted me with warmth and enthusiasm -- big hugs and kiss... I guess that prosperity makes him more generous to his old friends. That's OK I guess.

7 March 1983

Dear Sharon,

First: the title of the talk I'm giving in Texas is
         Charles Willson Peale: An Artist's Authority
The title comes from the quote from Rembrandt Peale's
<u>Disquisition</u> on the exhumation of the mastodon:

> "...for my part, my /scientific/ decisions are
> pronounced with no other authority than that of
> an artist... when <u>forms</u> and the right comparison
> of <u>lines</u> and <u>angles</u> is the subject of investiga-
> tion, I feel myself, as every artist must, per-
> fectly confident in the assertion of the truth..."

Now, if you do not feel that this is appropriate, we can
change it. But any talk I give is going to be about the
authority of the artist to contribute to natural history/
zoology. So I think we can drop the Peale part, but still
call my talk "An Artist's Authority." Please let me know
what you think.

I have given a dress rehersal of my talk to friends and they
gave me some wonderful suggestions. The biggest problem is
that I talk too long -- there is just so much to say . And I
am having some trouble cutting it down and still managing to
say anything at all substantive. Its an art, isn't it. The
best part about doing the rehersal is that I feel much more
relaxed than I did -- my audience liked it, and actually thought
the stuff is interesting. Wow. I get so saturated in what
I'm doing that I completely loose sight of what it's like to
see these amazing pix for the first time.

Buzzing along here. Having some trouble sleeping. March is
wild. Immediately on my return, I have to rush out to Salem
and write about 80 labels for the show, opening March 24.
It will be great to see you, under any circumstances. What is
spring without a good visit with you and Polly?

Rushed, but love til later --

21 April 83

Dear Sharon —

This is to thank you for your hospitality last weekend. Having such a friendly and comfortable place to stay definitely softened the strain of paper giving. I could never have done it without your encouragement — in fact — the whole thing was your idea all along, so I never would have done it if you hadn't brought me up to it. You do very well as impresario. And if I haven't perhaps slain the dragon — my fear of academia — I have at least wounded it. If you were anywhere nearly as tired as I was I don't know how you managed to go to Penn. on Monday. Next time you throw a conference, I hope you allow yourself some recovery time. It was fun, though, in that buzzed out way. And it was wonderful to see you.

I hope the end of the academic calendar brings you some rest and recreation.

Thank again for everything —
love,
Ann

July 9 83

Dear Sharon —

I mailed the last chapter to Pantheon on Tuesday, and have wandered around in a daze of fatigue and disorientation for days. Fortunately, there will still be plenty of work on the book — it's not gone + left me alone entirely. I awoke in the small hours on Wed. to obsess about re-writing the conclusion — something rousing about the end of the whole-animal era + thus of descriptive illustration... Thursday night, although I was heavy with fatigue, I couldn't sleep all night — tears + fears. What will I do next? What will the next Mission Impossible be? Why have I fallen in love with a graduate student who is about to move away? Friday, I regrouped around the first of my RISD assignments — made an apt. with Owen Gingerich for Mon. a.m. to discuss pre-Copernican cosmographies; ∴ must read his stuff over the weekend. It's like having homework + oh, my soul, it is so comforting. Sharon, I feel like last weekend I had everything. I worked all weekend to finish. I worked in the MCZ Invertebrates Dept. where my sweetheart dwells also. I had my book + my heart's desire. But Then.... on Wednesday I went to see

a movie called "Somebody Say Amen" — maybe you've seen it. Its about Gospel singing. From the first note I was flooded with the realization that there is so much more to life than work. That writing _is_ sensory deprivation. I still feel a bit convalescent, a bit lost + a bit sad. Call it the Blues, and sing it away.
I'm seriously in love + in excruciating suspense about what will happen with it. Well, life is life + happens all at once.

Meanwhile — I went to <u>California</u> for a weekend — for a wonderful wedding of my best friend from high school. Not bad, huh?, for someone who never goes anywhere.

How are you? Has summer heat enforced a little leisure on you? Or have you found yet more papers needing giving at a moments notice? Is Paul around? What an end-of-term ordeal you had!
Dolly was here last week. She is writing hard + looks great! + is in good spirits. She had enough to bestow on me all sorts of encouragement for my last sprint to the finish. She said: as of Tuesday when I marked the Ms. I should ~~it~~ consider that I have a PhD. Only she could say that to me + have it mean anything. Love, Ann.

18 July 83

Dear Sharon —

It's clear from your letter that your writing is flowing. Bravo. I envy you: my work seems so fragmented, bits + pieces of this + that, after the focus of writing. I'd rather sit down + start another book, or at least get on with my revisions. But I haven't heard from Pantheon yet. So I'm in suspense. Meanwhile, I'm flying around on the Dürer stuff. A morning at King's Chapel Archives, an evening working out a personal filing system for a photographer friend, an hour with Owen Gingerich on pre-Copernican cosmographical diagrams, another hour with Peter Mathews at the Peabody on illustrating Mayan hieroglyphics / all capped off with a look at my own DNA through Bob Woollacott's fluorescent 'scope! I used to love this kind of variety but now I feel homesick for my typewriter — the grass is _always_ greener, huh.

My biggest hurdle is going to be learning to make my own lecture slides. I've begun to fiddle with the camera. Frustration set in immediately. I must take the long view on this. At first I must expect failure — but if I can get some passable results this summer, enough to get maybe 4 or 5 lectures ahead of myself, then, later in the term when the crunch is _really_ on, I'll be better at the whole technique + can just crank out a roll of slide film on demand. My father assures me that by the laws of things, Pantheon won't get back to me with revisions until term begins.

Here are some notes from the lighter side of life: My tomato plants have fruit on them

My father is in the new Woody Allen movie. He plays himself, commenting on the central character of the film. As historians, should we all cultivate a career in film? I have also discovered that I can drink beer and work! This is a triumph + revolutionizes the working-weekend. Beer with a late lunch or dinner, (counteracted with a little bit of coffee) definitely smooths out the brain-jangles. Then the coffee puts a nice little buzz back in, and you're back at the keyboard ready to go! One word of warning — the brain is just a tiny bit slower + the fingers stumble a little. But it's worth it for the overall benefit to the inner self.

So, let those ideas pour out. I'm suffering a bit from the fear that I put all the ideas I've ever had into one book + that I'll never have another idea — They'll say - "she just writes the same book over and over again..." I think I feel like I've lost my intellectual credentials. Oh, enough of this.

Keep up your good work —

love,

Ann

Thurs 21 July
P.S. The last two days have been devoted to finding out that my mother has breast cancer. Full story on Friday. This certainly takes precedence over everything else.

22 October 83

Dear Sharon,

Thanks again for calling the other night. It was great to talk with you, in fact, it was a sort of relief to touch base.
After xeroxing the ms of my last chapter, I have made the mistake of re-reading it and now I am full of doubts and misgivings. It seems choppy and inexplicit, etc. etc. the usual criticisms of one's most recent product. But here it is, and I realise that I really do want some kind of constructive criticism from you, something from the very depths of your real, professional, historian-of-science knowledge and wisdom. And I realise that in wanting that, I really should wait until you have dispatched your MS in the winter before asking for any of your time or professional attention. But if I dont send this thing now I'll forget. Just promise me please that you wont use any prime working time on it -- just read it, if possible, for pleasure.

I am typing this on the machine in Invertebrates that I use on weekends. The nearest thermometer reads 52 F and my fingures make mistakes that my brain hasnt time to think of. Outside its a perfect October afternoon and some kind of football frenzy is happening, judging by all the tweeded personnel with blankets streaming through the Square. My biggest domestic problem of the moment is what to do and how to organize in order to have something hot at dinner time on these nippy nights. I came home to my summer staple cold dinner the other night and even inside my body the food felt cold.

I'll call you in a lttle while to find out how you're doing as your deadline approaches. Meanwhile I'll send encouragement and energy -- you're a champ and a trouper and an inspiration.

Love,
Ann

5 Jan 89

Dear Sharon, Thank you x 1,000 for your thoughtful + helpful comments on my Ms. I am overwhelmed that you took so much trouble while you were pushing on your own deadline. Congratulations! + Bravo on completion! I hope by now you have begun to recover from the fatigue + disorientation of the aftermath.

Happiness of wedding days on the 12th! I will think of you both as I fly on that day toward Puerto Rico. I'm going for 10 days of warmth and a preliminary look into the agricultural project I'm interested in writing about. RISD term begins the week after I get back. Help.

You said you'd send me a copy of your discussion of plenum. I'd love to see it if you can bear to handle the document. (There is that tender period when, for me, the fear that I will perceive only flaws + not strengths makes even peeking at the Ms. a terror. Then of course eventually I become less invested.)

I should give you a call when I get back from PR. I want a good long chat with you on all topics — more than we could cover in letters.

    Thanks again for reading my stuff +
      love, admiration + bestísimos (?) wishes
      for this year + always — Ann

10 September 84

Dear Sharon –

How was your summer, your trip to England? How are you? And what is next on your list of successes? And when will I see you next – are you planning to give seminars in this neighborhood any time soon? There is nothing I'd like more than a long chat.

Sharon, I have made the agonizing decision not to remain a _fringe_ intellectual any longer. I am going back to school so that I can emerge as a full-time egg-head. I am applying to U Mass Boston for January admissions – as a full-time undergraduate. Have to start somewhere, after all. The plan at the moment is to construct my own major – which they allow – in Am. Civilization – history of science, with maybe Latin American political sci. on the side. However, I am prepared to be surprised by new + fascinating subjects once I expose my mind to whatever... blah, blah... They have some good people there – it's a fine faculty in fact. In anticipation, I feel excited + also nervous. (I haven't yet made my plans officially public, so please, discretion.)

I hope to support the whole operation by teaching. This summer I taught advanced expository writing at the Harvard Summer School + there is a fair chance that there will be a position for me in the year program for the spring term. I like the idea of a teaching job at Harvard sponsoring a UMass education. Also I want to keep a Harvard affiliation for the library privileges.

All in all its been a good summer. My only regret is that I didn't get as much writing done as I usually do — because the accelerated schedule of the the teaching was so fast + pressing. But I took a real vacation in August + visited friends on Cape Cod, in Maine, in Vermont — spent most of the time outside, in water. Bliss. I feel rested, relaxed and pretty frisky. I'm hoping to get to D.C. for research this fall (the thing w/ S.I. friend now emphatically over — but my heart is quite whole + mended.) I miss you + often think fondly of my last visit. Best to Paul —
        love,
          Ann

5 October 1985

Dear Sharon, Just the other day I saw the advertisement for your book in the Chicago Press catalog, and then last night what should I find at home but the volume itself. It looks great. You must be very pleased. And I am honored to have an autographed copy. I guess it may be something of an anticlimax to you, that's what everyone says anyway about the physical thing itself, but I hope you are justly proud of it and can enjoy the well earned fuss that all of the rest of us can now make over it. I am somewhat embarrassed that it came before I had written to you. It was bad enough that Peter managed to send off yet another package and letter to you and I still hadn't sat down to send something of my own. And then the other night Polly called with a small errand for me to do for her upcoming Smithsonian talk (about the US Exploring Expedition, or some related topic) and there again was a reminder that I wanted to write to you.
I hope that by now Paul is in Baltimore with you and that he is finding something to do that interests him. I often think of your long wait -- the reverse of the typical immigrant story -- to import your spouse from the old country, but also, of the difficulty of coordinating place and work for two. Peter and I were so relieved that the MIT fellowship came through to solve at least for another year the problem of being together, but there remains the very real question about what next. And since for both of us the future is a complete unknown, how to plan it? I am sure that I want to continue my studies, but in what? I have not even declared a major yet, although I am concocting a mixture of political science and American studies. But do I want to go back to history of science? (It seems enough to have one of those in the house.) I find it is very difficult even to write my individual major proposal because of the many threads of interests that refuse to weave into anything that fits under one title. At the moment history of agriculture and American/Latin American studies compete for my attention. Anyone can easily see how they fit together in the larger picture but I cannot think of a title for it. This semester I signed on for a little too much in my effort to finish this undergraduate stage as quickly as possible. But until the going gets really thick (in about a month) I am enjoying a menu of anthroplogy of the Caribbean, comparative third world politics, American economic history, spanish, and a wonderful seminar in American immigration and ethnicity. I go out to school every day and it is beginning to feel familiar. Last spring I was always on the run with my own teaching to do and I never settled in to U.Mass. But now there is a little more time to go to seminars and other things that come up, and chat with new friends. One, my teacher from last spring for the Politics of Food class, recently suggested that I might be interested in a project she and some

others are trying to get going -- preparing á an agricultural policy proposal for Massachusetts. My mission, if I chose it, would involve an internship in the Department of Agric. (state department) that would also give me course credits toward finishing. This is very interesting to me as long as it doesnt involve number crunching or spending days at a time buried in records. What I would like to do would be something historical, but also personal, like talking to farmers. That was my favorite part of the research I did on cranberry farming last spring -- riding shot-gun with a cranberry grower who is the nicest, most voluable, conservative, free-market character -- sort of like my uncle the banker in western New York state. I have been trying to organize a return visit to see the cranberry harvest; we were to have gone today, but it's pouring rain, so the field trip is postponed until next week, which means unfortunately that Peter wont be able to go since he'll be talking to cladists in Miami.

Are you still going to that Marxist discussion group that you wrote aboutlast spring? The discussion group that Peter got me involved with has pretty much dispersed since its key person, Iain, moved to California to join his wife and daughter. Toward the end it degenerated into a series of scenes, as people who had felt disappointed by it, or by Iain, used the meetings to accuse the group of all sorts of sins -- sexism, lack of interest in them personally, hierarchy, whatever. There was also, and it still sputters on, an effort to motivate the group to engage in some larger project -- a cooperative building, was the one that Iain and another guy, an architect, pursued. Peter and I are less interested in a building than in organizing a series of discussions open to the public -- an Educational Association -- on topics such as Power, Seeing, Development (that's Peter's pet one -- theories of biological d.). I am interested in using some group like an educational association to do things like help with research on projects like the agric. policy proposal. The point it to break away from the academic and to work together on issues like teaching in a non-hierarchical way, in broadening audience, and so on. We are hoping to get this started next spring. Back briefly to the discussion group; I was at first reluctant to go because it just isnt my format to discuss things so abstractly, and often I found it very frustrating -- the discussion never seemed to get to the heart of the matter. But at the same time, I learned a tremendous amount, and alhtough I often didn't talk much, (my responses take longer than a moment, and the conversation would have gone on by the time I had articulated something) by and by I/came to enjoy the exercise. We continue to get together to read aloud once a month, something Peter used to organize, and that's great, but it is still up in the air whether the intellectual angle will keep on. Are you well, busy, happy, interested in what you're doing, glad to still be at Hopkins, or restless, planning a trip to Boston? It would be great to see you. love, Ann

15 May 86

Dear Sharon—

The good news, that I think you must already have guessed, is that Peter and I got married. On April 25 at Cambridge City Hall. My parents came with us. Joe Connarton, the city Justice of the Peace, was quite dressed up for the occasion, as were we in our favorite clothes, and he took us upstairs to the Barbara Ackerman Conference Room furnished in red carpet + folding chairs, where he read a statement we'd written. — I admit I giggled when I had to say "husband." Then the four of us went home for more snapshots + cake + champagne + later out to dinner. It was very nice. No matter how we downplayed the "event" nature of it — after all, this is an ongoing commitment — we were both actually nervous and extra-happy. The really funny thing is that we kept it so quiet before that now we have to tell people bit by bit. This gets easier as we grow more accustomed, more comfortable into the deed + the very real change that it works on us (both having dreams...). It is different being married. I do still get the giggles. Peter + "husband" don't yet seem quite the same person. And I certainly scarcely feel like a married woman. But as we tell people + absorb their responses it has a growing reality. And I think that at the time we were both feeling pretty worn down by the other events of the year — my semester's work, Peter's job interviews + choices, some hassles w/ Peter's father, a very interesting but very hectic week in Puerto Rico visiting friends during my spring vacation. It's not so much that things have eased up since then — we had a very frustrating experience at the Immigration + Naturalizat-

seeing you. We must plan a visit. love, Ann

Office; Peter is trying to finish another paper to send for publication (the one for Cladistics); I'm in the middle of finals. Rather, I think that with everyone congratulating us for getting married we do feel a bit feted or special, and also, we are getting closer to the time when my semester is over + we go on VACATION! To California + the southwest until June 21. (Unfortunately, I'll miss Polly's visit to Cambridge entirely.)

The whole school year has been an endurance test and even though I had over a month off in Dec + January, I felt tired when the second semester started. Then, because I had thought that a Spanish American Civilizat. course + one on the literature of the Cuban Revolution were going to be conducted in English (was wrong!) I found myself in 3 courses in Spanish + way over my head. But I hung in there + somehow survived; + my Spanish took a giant step forward. (There's still a long way to go, however.) It seemed that 3 out of 4 days a week I was up at 4 or 5 to finish a paper or an assignment. Peter has been wonderful, typing drafts into the computer as I cook them up beside him on the typewriter, and often helping me understand + interpret my Cuban lit. readings — one paper received 2 grades: one, perfect for interpretation, the other, less than perfect for grammar — and the interpretation was thanks to Peter. He is not, alas, any good at typing Spanish papers. That I have to do myself. This summer I'll be teaching at Harvard Summer School again + working as an intern at the Mass. Department of Agriculture (writing a history of the department + a policy for state agric. among other projects). I'll also start the research or whatever for my senior project in history of agriculture with Lou Ferlager, prof. in the Economics Dept whose field is American, southern agric, plantation economics. He taught the American

economic history class I took last fall; + he has vowed to discipline my thinking. It all should be good. I hear from Polly that you + Paul have bought a horse. Will you be painting all summer or will you get away for a while? Has Paul found something he likes to do? How did you survive your year? I miss

3 August 86

Dear Sharon, your May letter deserved an earlier response. It was so good to hear from you and there was so much in it to respond to — congratulations on your 1st grant, disappointment over your miscarriage. Even our more ordinary lives are such a rollercoaster I often wonder how we manage. By now I hope you have moved into your house; and perhaps you are at this moment in Toronto? (Speaking of which, Polly just breezed through here for her 25th high school reunion. She seemed very well indeed, although we had only the briefest visit.)

Our vacation already seems ages ago, but the highlights shine as bright as ever while the irritations fade. Driving west is a fascinating, somewhat hypnotic thing to do — miles pass + transitions evade definition. Somehow the flat, black rich + wet farm land of Iowa began to rise, become rockier, redder — the milk cows change to beef cattle, the corn to sage brush. From this perspective, each state stands distinct, but driving it, one slid into the next. I love the plains — they have so many variations — but for me the sparkling morning we drove from Nebraska to Wounded Knee + from there into the South Dakota Bad Lands was the best — the high plains in morning light, reduced to 3 elements — young green wheat, a white gravel road + blue sky! Everywhere we went, birds + other wild life provided endless thrills. Almost the entire breadth of the country there were red-winged blackbirds sitting on the fence posts along the roads — until one magic moment when they were replaced by the yellow-headed blackbirds — same song, same post... On the grassland that rims the Bad Lands canyons we saw buffalo, antelope, prairie dogs — all reintroduced since TR's hunting days. We became the geology equivalents of pop-psychologists — trying to determine the sequence of events that produced the wonders we passed through. Peter had never been to mountains as high as the Big Horns of Wyoming. We visited Old Faithful + the other hot springs of Yellowstone (where we saw more buffalo, elk + a sand-hill crane!

There was, of course, the trade off between exploring + spending too much time driving, so it was a relief to arrive in Berkeley + stay with our friends there. While in the area, we stopped at Davis so I could check out the history of agriculture people. (They seem a bit conservative.) Later, in the L.A. area, we visited my Hollywood uncle — talk, cool drinks by the pool, barbequed salmon steaks on the patio — etc. And my uncle, so like my father it's uncanny. We stayed in Claremont, east of L.A. with my best friend from high school + her husband — in their cabin up a canyon. And after visiting, + eating + drinking too much, we went home via the S.W. — a few days of hiking + camping in Utah + Arizona: Zion Canyon, Grand Canyon, Bryce Canyon — splendid geology, weird cacti — Bristlecone Pines — all wonders.

We got home just in time to teach. Peter's mother arrived + stayed for 3 weeks. We took her to meet my family over July 4th weekend. Some soon after that, another Australian traveller arrived. And just before Peter's mother left to go the rest of the way around the world, my friends from Puerto Rico came for a week. Throughout, we've been teaching; I've been going to the Dept. of Food + Agriculture every day (but not enjoying it — One internship is pretty much a bust: the Commissioner insisted that I do a survey + analysis of the state food processing industry before I work on a departmental history — so it's been a dull project + frustrating).

Now we're down to just the 2 of us, except for taking care of a dog, and we're trying to settle down to some work before Peter starts his commute in September. We'd love to see you (soon?) anytime you can come. We should just be careful that we'll both be here when you come, and that I haven't committed myself to a weekend in NY when you want to be in Cambridge. It will be great to catch up properly. I'm looking forward to it.

Best to Paul + love,

Ann

2519 Etna St, #3 Berkeley CA 94704
(415-644-2195)

9 Nov 87

Dear Sharon,

    I read your letter over and over again -- as if it were a snapshot of David and you. At moments when I'm not overwhelmed by school I have thought of you and wondered how you managed to change from one reality back to the university reality -- or irreality. Like Hopkins, Berkeley is very male and impersonal, a stark reminder of what most of academia is still like after my relatively utopian experience at UMass. Youre exactly right -- life is one hoop after another, and the Berkeley attitude is that it's up to the student to even find out what the requried hoops are. For example, there's an exam in my first field that I'm suppose d to take at the end of next semseter and no one has said a single word about it or what I will be examined on. The department has requirements for which it does not even offer the courses to fill them. And so on. There is very little during a given week that I actually look forward to. The courses I'm doing don't cohere -- I simply plod on burrowing through mountains of reading of probably parallel but seemingly unrelated topics and feeling very far from what I thought I wanted to be doing. I often remember that last spring after I told you and Paul what I hoped to do during my graduate career, you warned me that "They" would squash it out of me if possible. I get very discouraged every time I write a paper because it does not come together the way I would want; a new acquaintance, perhaps one day a friend, suggested that I feel this way because I'm not really committed to the topics I'm required to write about. I had been constructing all sorts of possible explanatoins but this one seems to have the ring of truth. The grass looks greener in the next semester; I'll take a research seminar and perhpas then I'll get into my subject and feel more oriented to a self-generated scholarkyship.

    Peter and I are relying very much on each other while we try to make new friends in this somewhat bizarre place. Neither of us can really believe that we now actually live in California when we stop to consider it. Then there is the added f disjuncture that California doesn't really seem part of the "west" -- nor does Berkeley nor SanfFranscio seem like part of the rest of California. Where are we and when can we go home? we often wonder. The flora isonly adds to the confusion: side by side stand ginkhos tress, some turning fgold and shedding leaves, some still green; neighborhood elm trees turn a sort of sickly brown and drop leaves while in the gardens, camelias are in bloom along with shrubs that would bdoom in a New England spring, like azaleas and rhodendron. The scraggly bourgonvillea outside our bedroom window is struggling into leaf and flower, while in the yard below the fruit on the orange tree is ripening. I'm confused. Then, in fashion as in flora. People dress depending on what time of day they got up and went out. On campus you see people in full fall fashion regalia with others in athuletic shorts and flip flops. (This only makes the 50 yr old male History professors in their Ivy League costumes all the more silly.)

    So in many ways we feel like visitors here; and yet in others we now have our work routines, and we move comfortably around our very pleasant sub-let apartment. We discover places to get incredibly good California produce; see how hot a hot sauce we can tollerate in our guacamole. And recently, we beetle around in our new pow-der blue VW bug, vintage '71. We got it from the first owner, the classic little old lady, who in 16 years had put less than 50 thousand miles on it. So my spirits rise and dip, depending on how dragged down I feel by school, while at the same time even little connections with the new community or a tree that looks properly autumnal will lift them again. We feel terribly far from friends, but it was wonderful to get your letter. (By the way, after I talked with you in the summer I never did anything on my book. Teaching two dourses took care of any possible spare time. Since then, an editor at Blackwell thought he wanted to look at it and then didn't; and now one at Princeton wants to see it, thanks to friends of mine making it sound like the best thing since sliced bread. I can barely stand to look at it but plan to send it on to UxP. and see what happens.) love to you all. Ann

21 September 1988

Dear Sharon,

This is a quickie. Thanks for your letter. I'm very pleased that Princeton was persuaded that you were the right person to read my MS especially for the last parts. I am going to copy the whole thing to have them send you, though you don't have to read it all. Still, I will especially appreciate your comments on:
-- the Baird/Agassiz chapter. It's too long and the evolution bit rambles in circles. It's fine with me it you say it needs work; I want to fix that part up.
-- the last chapter, which is essentially as you saw it before, and therefore still episodic. I told Emily Wilkinson that you knew about the project but I didn't tell her that you had already read parts of it and made comments. I don't think they would have sent it to you if they knew. So please don't say: Blum has made few substantive changes since I last read this or whatever...As I see it, I could develop the microscopy part almost into a separate section. The part about the influence of popular illustration on the peculiar genre of semi-popular/semi-professional natural history could also be expanded -- especially since it ties the book together in raising issues about pop vs. prof science, their early divergence and the late 19th-century attempt to bring them together again. Of course, this is where science fiction fits in, if you think I could do more with that aspect.

You don't need to rush off and study up on art. Your good sense, editorial acumen, and history of science will do fine. I plan to build up in my revisions the analytical framework re: "representation" and science, without getting trendy about Representation. Now that I have the chance of working with a university press, I don't have to be quite so narrative, and I can get a little more intellectual without alienating my audience. That is my main plan for changes. Charlotte Porter has given the MS a very careful reading and made countless little suggestions about details very much within her field -- such as, have I seen the child's notebook in the Phil Acad Nat Sci, and so on, or didn't so and so do or say this two years earlier... These are very helpful to me to get me back into the stuff in a scholarly way. But I also, as I said, hope to bring out the analytical framework more, rather than trying to disguise it in a narrative coating. You might encourage the author to do something like that.

Year 2 as a graduate student is much more relaxed than Year 1, although I still can't sleep the night before a seminar report, and I still read too slowly. I have built the year around making room for this book. It really threw me to have it come up so suddenly and interrupt my momentum toward a PhD in Latin American History. How to integrate my split life? I mull this problem over at length with a certain amount of toothgrinding at night. But for the semester, I have been as careful as possible to make room for both, with no distractions. I am taking a seminar on Brazil, to keep my hand in, and I am really enjoying being able to read in Portuguese ! after only two semesters of study. And I have arranged a reading course with one of the bosses of what I call the Lit. Crit. Mafia -- Tom Laqueur, who does 19th-century British medicine, and is one of the <u>Representations</u> honchos -- to look into the trendy representation stuff and see if there's anything there that will help me in my book, or whether I have come to the same conclusions without the lit.crit. jargon.

    Still no word on where our next baby is coming from. Peter and I are expanding our network for the search, but sometimes in the middle of the day, I realize that we could get word at any moment, oh my. But other times we forget to be in suspense, because meanwhile, we
are both trying to open up our books -- Peter to begin his and I to warm mine up again. How I would love a good visit with you. Are you going to be in Baltimore during the winter break? I plan to schedule archives trips to D.C. and Philadelphia after a Christmas visit to my parents (they have just bought a new condo and want us all home for a last Christmas in the old homestead). Perhaps I could spend some time with you while I use the S.I. materials? There are some compensations for the scholarly life if I get to see you in the process. Must go -- love to Paul and give my best to the small youth, it would be so good to catch up with his changes,

                                                  love,

                                                  Ann

Thinking about when we went to the trampolines on Cape Cod, and sang through the night

dearest dearest twin,

we travelled far to oceanside this past week, climbing up and down cliffs, scuttling through woods, taking too many pictures of miraculous views and amusing creatures and curious things. no matter where i am or what i do you are in my thoughts and heart.

your smile lights the universe. with raúl, with pamela, with me.

our holiday travel took us to sagres, whence the infante henrique launched the african slave trade and various colonial schemes. as you know i spit on his sarcophogus whenever i'm at the batalha cathedral. sagres was too bleak to even warrant summoning saliva, strangely void even of the expected fascist monuments. but! a crappy little very moderne statue of the prince lay on the ground by its pedestal. i doubt the downfall resulted from a political movement—as was the successful effort to topple cecil rhodes in cape town this past year. we marvelled a little about how the ships and ambitions launched from that spot produced the migrations, involuntary or not, that resulted in the 4 of us being there together contemplating the horror of it all, forever commingled by terror and love.

we're here for a little more than 2 weeks, returning stateside september 7. i'm missing the first week of school in order to participate in a little conference here on eurocentrism and racism. eurocentrism seems so quaint these days, but also apt—given the many crises concerning migration, islamic radicalism, greek (and spanish and portuguese) debt, and so on. what is europe? i revel in the fact that iberia broke off what became africa, the stone raft (as saramago put it) travelling on the molten sea until it fused with eurasia at the pyrenees. the myth of continents underlies the myth of races. but we keep battling, as though. as though.

i miss you all the time. i can't imagine how you feel, but send you everything i can through words and cyberspace and thought-transference and twinness. i was thinking the other day about when we went to the trampolines on cape cod, and sang through the night.

ask petah to show you craig's pictures from the alentejo coast if you would like to see the glory.

with all my love and more—there's always more.

RUTHIE
21 AUGUST 2015

94   Ann, Crane Beach © Paula Chandoha, 1978

1980s

Honorary degree in something like mind & body, music & dancing, sweet gestures, and bird pictures

Perhaps the only photo of the Blum nuclear family together

Ann, Tom, Pamela, Pam, John Blum before a wedding rehearsal dinner for a cousin/niece, Marritje Green (née Van Arsdale), 1981

Your big, alert eyes, full of curiosity and determination, followed closely by the lilt of your voice, gentle, animated, and strong

I can't tell you how sorry I am to read, in Peter's email, that the battle has not yet been won, in the first round.

Discouraging though this must be, I trust that in days to come you and your team will be able to craft a new plan of attack that will make this just a temporary setback.

Regarding Peter's lovely suggestion, my first thoughts are that I can't possible do the justice you deserve, nor do I wish to implicitly lend credence to any intimations of mortality, however insistent they may momentarily seem.

But, notwithstanding those concerns, let me share just a few of the things I love about you, and have every expectation of continuing to love for a good long time. For starters, your big, alert eyes, full of curiosity and determination, followed closely by the lilt of your voice, gentle, animated, and strong, both of which made a large impression from our first meeting one summer day thirty odd years ago at 7 Wright Street.

I have delighted in your probing, honest and perceptive intellect, your unconventional academic path and your intellectual scope, encompassing visual, analytical and ethical thinking, spanning both hemispheres of your formidable mind.

It was a great privilege to observe the brave and principled way you and Peter approached Vann's adoption process, and its beautiful fruition in the years since—and surely those to come—a story I have had many occasions to share over the years.

And on the subject of gifts, we too are reminded of you and Peter every time a bottle of wine is saved and reopened with the clever vacuum stoppers you gave us long ago, which we have assiduously managed not to misplace for all these years, and for an elegant triple-branched birch stem you gave us in honor of our girls, and for your gorgeous first book....

I look forward to building many more good memories in the years to come.

Love,
BRAD
19 FEBRUARY 2015

We feel like your fairy god-mothers

I am saddened to hear of Ann's death but heartened to know she was so vibrant even a few days before and that she was surrounded by such good love and care from you all.

You and Ann hold a special place in our hearts because of your having met at Macci's and my apartment in Somerville all those years ago; we feel like your fairy god-mothers.

Sending love to you,

BECKY JONES
30 NOVEMBER 2015

From Ann I first learnt to look at images with precision

I first met Ann in the Pumping Station days, soon after Gillian and I and toddler Hannah came to Massachusetts from East Anglia. At the time Ann was working at the MCZ library, and researching her first book then with—if I recall—the title 'Drawn from Nature.'

Whenever I describe myself, or am introduced as, a "social historian with a particular interest in visual culture," it is a silent tribute to Ann from whom I first learnt to look at images with precision, and especially at zoological illustrations. This has been a precious gift with an enduring resonance, a very personal gift because our family home in Norfolk is filled with the legacy and the lithographs of John Gould—the English Audubon, Darwin's colleague, and my brother-in-law Anthony's great-grandfather. I am working with Anthony on the treatment for a film about Gould and Darwin which will be dedicated to Ann's memory.

Ann was a wonderful teacher, with a deep understanding not only of the image world, but of the written word. In her writing classes she brilliantly lit upon the idea of using Christopher Hill's *The World Turned Upside Down* as a literary model. Thus her students not only learned how to integrate multiple quotations into their prose from a "master of more than an old Oxford college" (to quote the epigraph to Hill's book on *Paradise Lost*), but at the same time absorbed some history of the revolutionary decades of the 17th century.

After our years together in Cambridge and Berkeley, our families ended up living a continent apart, and I am less familiar with the fruits of Ann's research in the Mexican archives. But I do know how happy Gill was when their work and lives unexpectedly intersected again when Gill took on the task of conserving a fascinating cache of Mexican inquisition documents acquired by the Bancroft Library.

A few years ago Gill moved back to London to head the conservation lab at the Wellcome Collection which includes the National Library for the History of Medicine with its stunning collection of manuscripts and illustrations. In 2011 Gillian and I were part of a small group that founded the MayDay Rooms nr St Paul's, a safe haven for 'archives of dissent' threatened with loss or erasure in the current round of neoliberal enclosures and evictions, and as—one might say—an antinomian social space in the heart of London. Actually on Fleet Street, in front of Milton's old house, next to the press set up by Caxton's apprentice in 1500, and right across the road—currently—from Goldman Sachs.

The aim of MayDay Rooms is to help animate the past in order to ignite a future worth living in. Ann was—and is—an inspiration to us in that endeavour. When I came to Cleveland Street just a month ago, in our brief and precious moments together, Ann and I spoke about the importance of gathering and the spaces for gathering. In my life this has meant, above all, the Pumping Station, Retort, and now MayDay Rooms. I promised my dear friend there would be an Ann Blum scholarship to help young people explore the archives that we are intent on salvaging in order to weave and build a more ample life in common. From MayDay Rooms Gillian and I shall be asking you to contribute to that project.

In love and solidarity,

from Gillian in Bombay,
and
from Hammersmith,

IAIN
13 DECEMBER 2015

Joy of looking

I met Ann in the early days of Ann and Peter (1984?) via the Pumping Station, a dynamic reading/ discussion/ potluck group started by Iain Boal. Often the readings were dense, intense, critical and theoretical. One evening Ann brought a text that she read aloud. It was a recipe for some kind of game from an early edition of *The Joy of Cooking*.

She read it slowly like a story or a well cadenced poem. Then she did something that I found magical which has impacted me deeply to this day. Slowly she unpacked the recipe pointing out what kind of environment the sourcing of the game implied, what kind of equipment would necessarily be found in such a kitchen, what kinds of techniques and skills the cook would certainly have and how these might have been learned. She extracted an astonishing amount of context from the ingredients and the directions, but nothing that the text did not support. This was Ann magic: lucid, penetrating, intelligent love of the world in its small manifestations. Ann's skill and sensibility have been an inspiration to me as a teacher ever since that early time. Fast, too fast, forward to December 2015 and Ann is still teaching me how to see.

KATIE PLATT
11 DECEMBER 2015

Ann matriculated at UMB to find that she—already a distinguished author—was expected to take freshman English.

Ann was the life of my 8:30 a.m. section of Third World Politics.

She was very polite about my forgetting the name of Boston's basketball team.
Others went to the library to research their papers; Ann went to the field.
Then Ann and Peter went off to Berkeley
…and when I visited them there Ann taught me the secrets of the Hot&Cold Salad.

Ann and Peter moved back to Boston.
and found Vann (I may have this out of order) and learned lots about baseball and became ~~Celtics~~ ~~Patriots~~ Red Sox fans.
And lo! They both ended up teaching at UMB
…and raised dogs and flowers
…and tomatoes
…and snow

And went back and forth to Mexico and Portugal and Australia--you name it.
But they always somehow found time to rescue me—usually when I was moving
…and no matter how exhausting it got.
When Ann wasn't helping me get out of town, she made staying in town so much better.
And introduced me to Café Olé!

Once I got back to the USA, Ann and Peter visited my little house on the prairie.
Where Ann taught me principles of economy (aka secret recipe for molé chicken).
And taught me the authentic Mexican way to cut an avocado.
And she and Peter and Gilla took me exploring in The Woods together.

So Ann, I think of you
Every time I:

Hear the Red Sox won
　　　See a botanical illustration
　　　Buy, eat or cook cranberries
　　　Go to California
　　　See a golden dog
　　　Take a walk
　　　Open an avocado
　　　Open a packing box

And also whenever I:
　　　Pick up a seed catalog
　　　Go to a Mexican restaurant
　　　Come back from California
　　　Hear Spanish spoken
　　　Buy a rotisserie'd chicken
　　　Pull out the mole sauce
　　　Root for the Keltics

KATE HARTFORD
28 FEBRUARY 2015

Our ability to express these changes often lags behind the feelings that need expression

Found when looking for other documents: Ann and Peter's marriage vows, 25 April 1986.

```
                    MARRIAGE CEREMONY


     You have asked me to read the following, a statement of
what marriage means to you:

     For us this is a time to be reminded of commitments that
we have already made as our love for each other has grown.
     Early, we realized that our love would have to
accommodate expatriation for each of us at different times.
We live with an uncertainty about where we will be, and who
will be our supporting community.  And with this prospect, we
are learning to trust that we will make something valuable
wherever we are.  A home, but more:
     Astounded by our good fortune at having found each
other, and at the ease and fullness of our love, we committed
ourselves to learning how to extend and share this love with
others.  Since we began to make our home together, it has felt
most like home when friends and their friends have brought
their concerns and conversations into it.  We still have a lot
to learn about making our home open, for often, luxuriating in
our happiness, or else pressured by the demands of making our
```

individual ways in the world, we lose sight of our ideal. But we want to reaffirm what our ideal is: That our home is not merely a retreat, but a base for our action to transform lived reality. Within our home, within our partnership, we can ground the practice of cooperation, not just to meet our rudimentary needs, but to facilitate our most far-reaching work.

Such a commitment to change opens us to unpredictable experiences and feelings. We know that integrating new experience demands that we modify our perceptions of ourselves and others. And this can be hard because our ability to express these changes often lags behind the feelings that need expression. Each of us will need the other's patience, perseverance and faith, so that confusion and discouragement do not subvert the vitality of our commitment. Love does not shield us from the turmoil of our inner and outer worlds; love itself responds and changes.

Peter and Ann, Cambridge City Hall, 25 April 1986

Items that keep you in my mind and heart everyday

As I head out to the city to visit Jean, my Mom's childhood friend who is 93, I am swathing my neck in a gorgeous rust silk scarf/shawl, a gift from Ann. I realized that love of fabric, color, and texture is something we share and delight in.

Me being the lucky recipient of many well-worn favorites—an olive/taupe with navy and orange scarf, a cranberry shawl that reverses to a delicious dark brown (just discovered that it works wonderfully either way)...all remind me of you when I put them on. And then there are the baskets—another mutual love. While gifts to us all, I have commandeered all, primarily to hold in-progress knitting—something Tom surely enjoys from afar. Favorites are the woven package tape sturdy baskets that go to the Farmer's Market (when not full of yarn...). All items that keep you in my mind and heart everyday.

xxoo

NANCY
1 MARCH 2015

Cape Cod chowder and Central Australia

I just flicked through the Ann's Facebook timeline. I liked it

—11 photos in about 4 years; a link to a blog about photographer/ theorist Allan Sekula; and a few other bits and pieces.

I really liked the way it wasn't cluttered with stuff and so I wasn't overwhelmed by a Facebook plethora of images. Rather, it was a like a brief snap shot of Ann—a less is more portrait—some sense of who she was—her friends, her aesthetic, her passions and interests, a glimpse of a young John Blum in the navy (and an early memory of hers)—totally partial and incomplete but I loved seeing it all the same and getting this sense of Ann.

And things come out, on and between the lines – someone who was generous, kind, socially-politically engaged, curious, with a good sense of humour and a well-honed eye…

I am Peter's brother. Ann's brother–in–law. I don' t have the exact dates on hand of when Peter moved to the US, and when he met Ann in the Harvard Museum but Peter was at Harvard around the mid '80s and he met Ann around this time too. That's at least thirty years. Sadly for most of this time I have only known Ann from afar. She has been in the US (and Mexico). I've been in Australia.

Luckily there were a few times we got to hang out. The first of these was in the late 1980s—Summer 1988 to be precise. I was in my twenties travelling home from a trip to the US via a lengthy detour in Japan and Europe. The first Bush was running for the White House and Ann and Peter were holidaying at Cape Cod (there was no direct correlation between these events, as far as I am aware). While in Cape Cod, I met Ann's childhood friend Ruthie, and her partner (husband?) Craig. We ate clam chowder at a road-side stall famous for its clam chowder—when in Rome—and played beach cricket—when not in Rome (Peter, Craig and maybe Ann and Ruthie too, had just been reading a book on cricket and colonialism—CLR James 'Beyond a Boundary' (1963), and Peter and I explained something of the game to our American friends via a popular Australian beach-holiday variant of the game).

(Indirectly, through Ann and her close friendship with Ruthie, I got to meet Ruthie's parents too. They took me under their wing for a day or two. Ruthie's father played me some BB King and Ruthie's mother took me to a church where the Kennedy's used to pray—well, Rose did, at least.)

It is a blur where we stayed or how we travelled from one place to the next but, shortly after our Cape Cod sojourn, we travelled to Vermont. I met Ann's parents and played some croquet on the lawn. Ann took me to a favourite swimming hole and we checked out some tourist places nearby. It sounds like easy summer days—Cape Cod chowder, croquet, and swimming holes—and I guess they were. Now that Ann is not here, these memories seem especially sweet and precious.

I went to New York City for a week or two—the myth feeds on the myth; Peter and Ann returned to their home in Berkeley. Ann's brother Tom 'shouted' me lunch one day and I made some part-time money in New York working for a friend of Ann's—sorting out slides for a fashion photographer on the Upper East side (Maria Chandoha Valentino). (Ann was also a friend of Maria's sister, Paula.)

I made my way to Berkeley and stayed with Ann and Peter in their flat with the sunny balcony. Ann and Peter had their routines. There was no Gilla then but they liked walking in the morning, and walking and talking as well. Ann had discovered a packet miso soup she liked and this was her lunchtime staple and in the afternoon she liked a bottle of cold Becks beer. I did too.

I met some of Ann and Peter's friends—Raúl, who is a friend to this day, and a gentle, urbane couple from Buenos Aires—I have forgotten their names, but they were friends Ann had made in Berkeley. A theme Ann had at this time was a distrust of the romantisation of the American South West, especially by European artists *a la* Wim Wenders' photos of the SW and to some extent a film like *Paris Texas*. I could see her point, but I didn't quite get it. Looking back on this though, I imagine it was mixed up with her knowledge of American and South American history and how these 'romantic' images of the SW belied the complexity of what was happening with migrant labour, North/South; US/Mexican relations.

One day, Peter, Ann and I met up with my sister Sally and her first husband, Daniel. They were living in northern California in Lake County and we met in Marin County. I took some photos of the four of them in warm afternoon light. My mother has one of these pictures on her sideboard with an array of other family photos. I am a hoarder of images and last night I pulled out the boxes of old negs and prints from the time, hoping to be able to reproduce one of these images for this blog post. I found the packet from the Presto Prints, Telegraph Avenue Berkeley, but all the remaining prints and negs from this time have disappeared. Drats!

I do have some other more recent photos of Ann though. They are from a trip she made with Peter to Central Australia, as part of a family get-together/ celebration for my sister's 60th birthday. Of course there were some logistics to work out how we could all co-ordinate our lives to meet up at Alice Springs (approx. 2000 miles inland and West from Sydney). And there were a few dramas in getting there, but essentially it was a great holiday. We walked some desert trails and were able to hang out and cook and eat. Even just after the holiday, it seemed special that we were all able to make the trip and spend time together. Now, particularly so.

There were four Taylor siblings and our mother, Gilly, and partners and my then 14 year old daughter, Odessa. Ann was easy gracious company, even after the 25+ hour flight from Boston to Alice Springs. It was great to be able to catch up on her news about Vann and hear bits and pieces about her work and role-playing games she worked into her Latin American history classes. I liked her humour and wry asides too. Ann got on with us all but 'bonded' with my partner, Georgia. Towards the end of the trip they retreated to a bar to drink white wine and talk books and life (and swap tips on 'taming the Taylor'). In Central Australia, Ann told us about the good parties thrown by the Zoology department at Harvard. And we were able to joke how 'nerdy' it sounded, her first meeting Peter in the Museum of Comparative Zoology. So nerdy it is also cool too. And there's something mythic and fateful about it—like a meeting of minds and bodies that was meant to be.

Early this year, my sister Sally and I were speaking with Peter via Skype. Ann came on the line and told us of her decision to not have further chemo-treatment. (She said she didn't want to, but it wasn't really an option given blood cell counts and other factors.) We were somewhat taken aback but she seemed very sure and resolute in her decision. I thought she was incredibly brave facing up to life and death in this way—and she was—but I understood her decision and resolve.

Sorry my thoughts and memories are so long-winded, but I hope these add to the matrix of Ann Blum memories past and into the future.

ANDREW
1 DECEMBER 2015

Ann in New Harmony, Summer 1985

Ann, Craig, Ruthie, Andrew, Cape Cod, Summer 1988

Central America Then and Now

I think last time I saw Ann was at LASA 2012 in San Francisco, when she organized one of my favorite panels ever, a 25th reunion of our interdisciplinary Central America seminar we had organized with Margarita Melville at Berkeley in 1987.

Our career paths intertwined—Berkeley, Boston—but also pulled us in different directions so that we never got to know each other as much as I would have liked. After Berkeley, I think the most time we spent together was when I was outside reviewer for her Latin American and Iberian Studies program at UMB. And then this panel:

> 394 // HUM - 7630 - Workshop - Friday 10:30 am - 12:15 pm, Pacific Suite ER
> Central America: Then and Now
> Organizer: Ann S. Blum, University of Massachusetts/Boston
> Chair(s): Linda B. Green, University of Arizona
>
> Participants:
> Aviva Chomsky, Salem State Univ.
> Linda B. Green, University of Arizona
> Sheila R. Tully, San Francisco State University

Ann pulled us all on board and wrote the description for the panel:

> This workshop addresses the legacies of the Central American conflicts of the 1980s from multiple perspectives. Participants were part of an informal working group on Central America in 1987 and 1988, and the workshop will explore how that moment informed their development as scholars. Discussion will address themes such as: activist scholarship, then and now; intellectual work on capitalism

and violence as a political project; 1980s Central America as the laboratory for current structural adjustment and anti-labor politics; social justice and the visions of the poor in research and teaching, then and now.

Although Cindy Forster did not appear on the program, she also participated in the workshop.

It was a wonderful moment in our harried careers to pause and reconnect and think about those Berkeley years.

I will miss your presence, Ann!

AVI
30 NOVEMBER 2015

Pamela and Ann, Missouri, 1988

1990s

Peter, Ann, Vann, Vicki, Nedra, January 1990

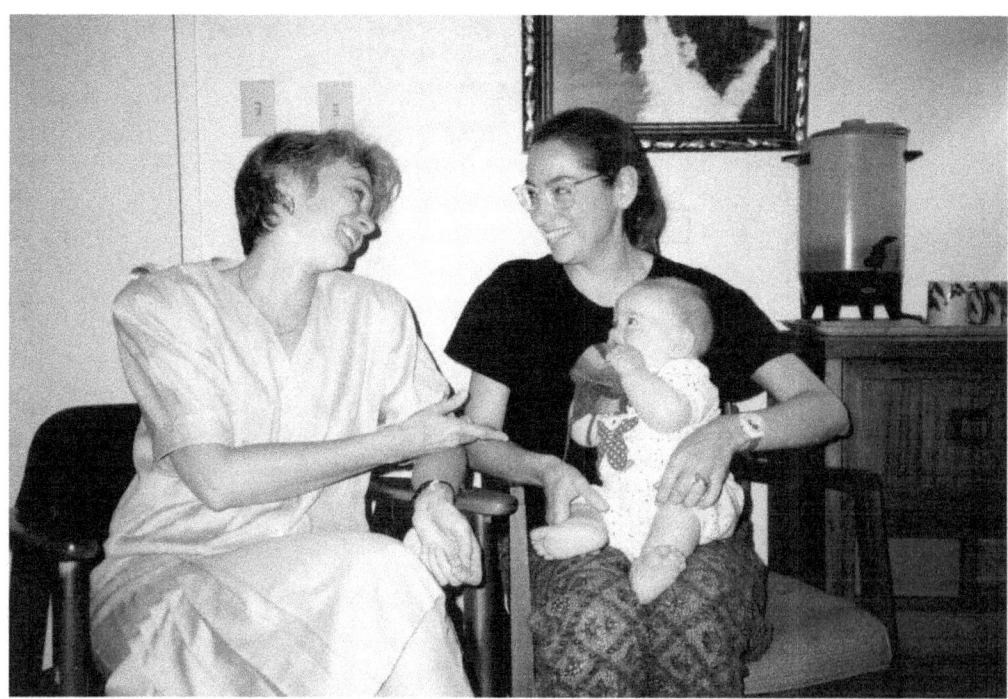

Candace, Ann, Vann, Spring 1990

Vann, Ann, Cheryl, Petaluma Fair, Summer 1990

Vann, Ann, Ruthie, Berkeley, Summer 1990

Vann and Ann, Vermont, August 1990

Vann and Ann, Mariel and Carol, Swarthmore College, September 1991

Ability to take life's challenges and move on

I looked all through our photos because I know I have some great ones from Berkeley when Vann first came on the scene. One especially that I will find and send of Ann's mom holding Vann on Ann's birthday, if I remember right, in a Berkeley park.

There are two events that come to mind and capture that resolute part of Ann that I will miss so much, and that stay with me still. One, when we were walking the High Line in New York in 2012. (Wish I had gotten a photo of Ann that day, but we were following Peter and Matt!) You had come down on a bus from Boston to spend the day with us while we had a weekend there. Ann was limping, but shrugged it off when I asked her about it. Described it in a straightforward way, but then moved on. Man, she was not one to complain or be interested in her own physical complaints, at least at that point, when they could be managed.

The other, when she came to spend time in Wisconsin and we had some valuable time together. The trip ended for her in disappointment, but, as I drove her to the airport, while I assumed she was still processing it, she was already there. That ability to take life's challenges and move straight on, not holding grudges or dwelling on what could not be changed is an inspiration to me still.

One other thing about Ann. It didn't matter who she was with—our kids for one example, even in their adolescent stages—she took them seriously, and took great interest in whatever they were interested in. Not holding the line on having only conversations of the highest order, but elevating even childish concerns to that level.

She was a rare and special friend and a gift to me, and I will try to honor her by holding myself to her standards, a tough challenge.

Love,

BECKY MAY
6 MARCH 2015

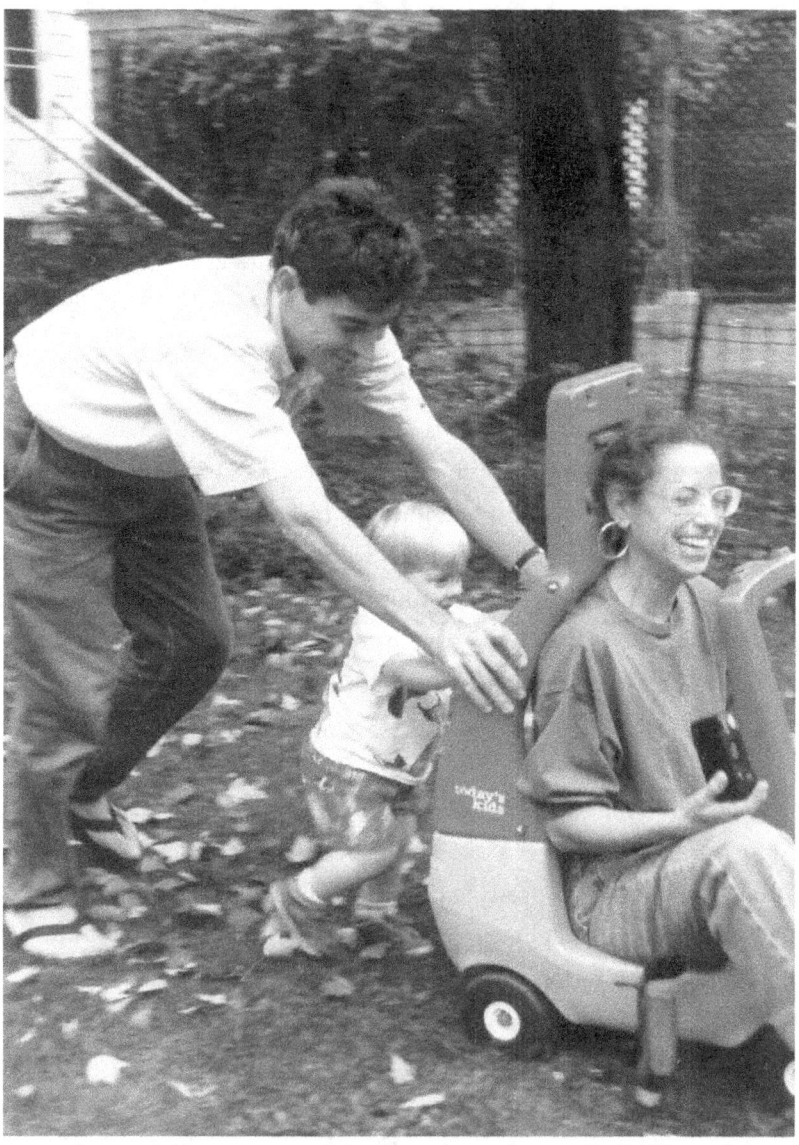

Peter, Vann, Ann, Ithaca, Fall 1991

To my dear friend and comadre

Our incredibly beautiful connection started with 5 words that you said to me that I will never forget. I'm sure that I have shared this with you but I want to tell you again now.

It was my first Mother's Day and you and Vicki were coming to see David and me. I have to admit it was not my first choice of how I wanted to celebrate this day! When you looked at David with your beautiful smile and open arms, I murmured in a slightly sarcastic voice, "I know, he looks just like Vann, right?" You said to me "He looks just like David." In those 5 words, you gave me the reassurance I needed to feel the entitlement to be David's mom. In those 5 words I sensed that our unique bond would deepen and that I loved you.

Thank you for being my "mother guide." I have turned to you for advice and comfort on so many occasions. As we are family now and have always shared our boys, I will always be one of Vann's comadres.

I would love to see you Ann, and would be there in a heartbeat if you have the energy to see me. I also understand that this is your time for spending the time as easily and comfortably as you can, and this may mean quietly with Peter and Vann and close friends nearby.

I send you love across the miles of deserts, and mountains and rivers and feel you close in my heart always.

ALISON
22 FEBRUARY 2015

Ann and Peter, Ithaca, c. 1992

Wrapped up in a gritty conversation about orphans and homeless teens and...

Ann and I first met in the Archivo General de la Nación in Mexico City in the summer of 1992, when we were both starting our dissertation research. Over the many years since then, I have been extraordinarily grateful for her warm friendship, generosity as a colleague and scholar, mischievous sense of humor, and down-to-earth humility.

I remain amused and appalled that one time over lunch at the Mexican restaurant in your old neighborhood we were so wrapped up in a gritty conversation about orphans and homeless teens and sex workers in Mexico that another customer came over and chided us, asking, "Do you even KNOW how your conversation sounds to other people?" And I will certainly cherish the many things Ann taught and shared with me—from insights regarding the politics of labor and reproduction to how to brew a stellar cup of coffee in a less than stellar Oaxacan hotel room.

Abrazos,

KATHERINE
3 DECEMBER 2015

Ann and Raúl, Tepotzlan, Summer 1992

Strong sense of line and of simplicity and of material

As Gail was tapping away, I was wondering what I would write about and my mind wandered to interior architecture, as it so often does when I think of Ann.

(And I notice that Gail has also written about your old house.) So often when I look at something in our new house, I think, Oh, Ann wouldn't like that very much (the old fashioned built in lamps above our bed…..). Ann has such strong sense of line and of simplicity and of material. I remember your house in Ithaca, and it seemed to me to be too bare then, but now I understand you better after seeing what you have done in Boston. We had a dear architecture friend in Ithaca (Carl Pancaldo, died a number of years ago) who also loved simplicity, and his signature is horizontal lines and openness. Always a pleasure to be in his houses. But you can get it wrong, even if it's simple. I think Ann always gets her interiors right. (And I was going to add that Peter has a tendency to make a bit of mess in them, but I realize that this not (quite) right!)

We are thinking of you all specially now.
Love,

ZELLMAN
23 FEBRUARY 2015

A Farewell Picnic, 1996

A Farewell Picnic
for Ann, Peter and Vann

Vann, age six, has made up a play,
and under his joyous direction the children
dash across the lawn waving sticks,
plastic cups, a fire chief's hat.
Ashley's long hair's afloat, Liam
tumbles and crows, Nick runs the fastest.

The uncomprehending parents applaud,
seeing the children against a backdrop
of massed purple and white Rose of Sharon,
behind it the tall hemlocks beginning
to blur with evening, and back of that,

in the next yard, a box elder hovering.
How lush it all is, and not one child
crying, even the baby in his sling chair
cooing. We glance over the tops
of houses, where evening is turning rose,
a color we swear we've never seen there.

"These are the great days," Harry says,
a minute before it couldn't be said:
we fold the blankets and put away food,
calling the children. Above us hangs
a splendid silver maple, a tree

notoriously weak-wooded, vulnerable
to wind; but here it is, still,
swallowing the last of the light. A while ago
four of the men went off and came back
struggling under Vann's playhouse,
ours now. They set it down in front

of the deep hemlocks: spray-painted red,
yellow and blue polkadots on white,
and a crude rainbow. The children swarmed;
one almost got crowned by the trapdoor;
the house became part of the play.

From our window, when everyone is gone,
the playhouse becomes beautiful, almost
glowing in the near-dark-this childish
assertion, dwarfed by the gathering curtain of trees.

ELIZABETH HOLMES
(FROM THE PLAYHOUSE NEAR DARK, 2007)

The day you and I walked in the neighborhood where you grew up

We are sitting on a French train, on our way from visiting friends in the south, including a composer I hadn't seen for thirty years. They live in a village where there are no cafes, no restaurants, just pretty old houses.

There was something a little grim about the quiet village, but they are warm people (he's Australian, she's French) and they have a large ginger cat who owns the house.

We are thinking of you and Ann, particularly, and the hard days and nights you are living through, and remembering fine times we had together.

Ann, I think of the day you and I walked in the neighborhood where you grew up and saw that your old house was for sale. We were able to go inside and you were moved to see the rooms you knew so well. Then we walked and talked for what seemed hours. I don't remember much of what we talked about, just the pleasure of easy conversation about children, family, Mexico. It always seemed when we met that we were able to pick up the conversation where we left off a year or two earlier. I remember, too, when we rented two houses in Cape May Point and the children played on the beach while we grown-ups did nothing in particular (Peter was always playing with the kids, but we were happy to walk and talk).

I have pictures of them together, Zoe with a gypsy skirt, the boys quite small. There was nowhere to shop except that little store, reminding me of holidays in Australia when I was young. What did we eat? I don't remember food at all. You always seemed better organized than we were and probably brought suitable provisions. Zellman must have brought wine. He is seldom neglectful of his two drugs—coffee and wine.

All my love to you three.

GAIL HOLST WARHAFT
23 FEBRUARY 2015

A wonderfully perceptive listener

Dear Peter, We have never met, but Ann always spoke so lovingly of you and Vann. I met her more than ten years ago in Mexico City where I now live.

From the beginning I felt her joy when she talked about her family and her work. But what I will always remember the most is her incredible gift of empathy. She was a wonderfully perceptive listener who could respond to others and engage them in ways that were so honest and natural to her. Whenever we connected, I instantly felt her warmth and vibrancy and her deep kindness. The sense of profound loss that I feel cannot compare to yours, but I wanted you to know how much she was respected and cherished by so many of her friends in the Latin American history community.

SUSAN DEEDS
30 NOVEMBER 2015

Ann and Vann, Christmas, New Haven, 1999

2000s

I knew already of your great skills as a mentor

First I want to thank Peter for sending this update on Ann's well-being. I'm sure I am like everyone on your list, spending a lot of time thinking and worrying about you both. It is good to know that there are some good days for Ann and that the bad episodes can mostly be helped with medication.

Besides sending my love and best wishes, I have a small anecdote to share that I hope will bring a smile to Ann's face. A couple of days ago, a familiar-looking woman whom I could not place greeted me in the 4th floor hallway of the McCormack Bldg. It was Sandra Haley, who had taken Ancient Mesoamerica with me a dozen years ago. I was so pleased to learn that she had gone on to do an MA at UMA and is just finishing her PhD in History at Brown. When she told me about her dissertation topic—on the lives of indigenous domestic workers in Oaxaca after the Revolution—I immediately thought of you and what an excellent prodigy of yours she is. Sandra told me how much guidance you have given her over the years, including serving on her dissertation committee.

Ann, I knew already of your great skills as a mentor, for we have shared that role with Elizabeth Newman. Elizabeth has told me countless times what an inspiration you have been for her. I would not be surprised to learn that there are several other accomplished or aspiring Latin Americanists out there with similar stories. It is a great legacy to have—not only the tangible books and papers attesting to your life's intellectual work, but also the generation of teachers who, in turn, will pass on both knowledge and a mentoring spirit that they learned from you.

Our lives are enriched by knowing you.

Fondly,

JUDY
24 SEPTEMBER 2015

Being bad girls in academe

Good Morning Dear, I am thinking of you as I sip my coffee in my PJs.

I am reminded of many hotel rooms in the early morning.... reading, writing (usually me) and editing conference papers and enjoying being bad girls in academe!

Abrazos from across the miles,

SHEILA
16 SEPTEMBER 2015

When as parents we don't live up to our own professed standards

There are so many times parents don't live up to our own professed standards. Ann, you probably don't remember a conversation we had about 15 years ago. We were in the kitchen at the Cornell Street apartment.

I must have mentioned feeling bad-mom guilt about letting my picky-eater daughter live almost entirely on Annie's Macaroni and Cheese—augmented with nothing green whatsoever. You laughed and said something like "Oh, you wouldn't believe the things I let Vann eat just so we could get through the day!" Bologna or something equally nutritionally incorrect may have figured in the details of your reciprocal confession. Whatever it was, such an admission from you (one of my role models for living well!) has given me permission to let myself do what needed to be done during many trying parental moments.

MARGERY
20 FEBRUARY 2015

Brings a sense of calm, warmth, and touch of frivolity into the room

Hey Peter, What a beautiful photo! Thanks so much for sharing. Don't know why, but it made me flash back on our wonderful time on the Cape together with the boys, eating clams, oysters, and wandering the windswept beaches together.

That in turn reminded me why I so enjoy spending time with Ann. She always brings a sense of calm, warmth, and touch of frivolity into the room—perhaps why so many of us are drawn to her.

I will be thinking of you both, and sending best wishes and positive energy as I start a three-day hike into the Grand Canyon this morning.

Much love,

KEVIN
7 MARCH 2015

Vann, David, Kevin, Ann, Peter, Seder on Cape Cod, 2001 (Photo by Alison)

How do I miss thee? Let me count the ways...

And when do I miss thee? Yes, that, too...

Every day, while I'm in my kitchen, I see a little scrap of paper stuck to the cabinet that says: elote: cocer en agua hirviendo cinco minutos. That's to remind me how not to overcook corn! That I learned from you, my dear friend! I also think of you, maybe not with every breath I take, but surely with everything I eat. Why? Because I love my Paul Revere tableware, and thanks to you, I have all that I need!

And when for some strange reason I think of hankies, not disposable tissues, I remember you looking for linen ones on-line for your mom.

And when now that I no longer wear contacts but have glasses, I'm reminded of you-- and, yes, of my auntie Harmony, who used to do the same--every time I peek over my glasses to read small print.

And when I think of all my friends, I think of you, of what a special friend you are! I think of how we always manage to stay in touch, despite the distance and the seasonal character of our time together. Summer equals school's out equals research for all the profs equals Ann's coming!

Do I miss you? Hell, yes!

Love,

HERZONIA
20 OCTOBER 2015

Glow with a special sort of meaningfulness

Ann, you may remember the time when you and Peter and Vann stayed overnight here, and Peter had to catch a god-awful early morning flight from Stewart Airport the next day to attend a conference. I got up with you both, and I have the wonderful memory of the 2 of us talking on the ride back.

I remember most how the intimacy of driving on that dark empty road made even the ordinary subjects we talked about glow with a special sort of meaningfulness. ...and then the cheery breakfast with Pamela and Vann when we got back (...unless of course Vann was still asleep).

Much love,

RICHARD
19 FEBRUARY 2015

It may have been over a year or much more yet it is as if we talked every day

Dear PETE & Ann. I am thinking countless times a day in so many various ways of the great variety of happenings----- of such warm connectedness --- the real conversations that stay in my memory & give such assurance & help reignite hope when my supply is dwindling I will give just 2 tiny almost everyday fortifications of my gratitude

If ever I ring & you PJ are not home I have this great conversation with Ann-- sometimes it may have been over a year or much more yet it is as if we talked every day----- I feel such friendship & concerned care & a wisdom that goes beyond the very real high intellect to an ability to speak truth
------ the 2nd small island of specificity & certainty is Pam gave me a small silver jar with lid that I keep tea in & use each morn & feel such gratitude at having formed such a bond with my extended family ----This is fortified +++ when I frequently read 3 or 4 v. special detailed cards from Pam ---about Vann & appreciation Of your parenting - & concerned care for each other
I thank you for the way you told me the news & gave me a direction to follow I must go & dress now as Paul my home help is coming —on his 90min visit- once a fortnight--today with more than normal material to be put away before vacuuming
love EJ.

GILLY
18 FEBRUARY 2015

Frequent conversationalist on the fourth floor of McCormack

...I always valued her as a colleague and a frequent conversationalist on the fourth floor of McCormack, and she will be missed.

I wish you and your family the best during this difficult time.

STEVE SILLIMAN
3 DECEMBER 2015

Vicki and Ann, High School graduation for Vann, 2009

2010s

Summer in Vermont 2010

HI Peter and Ann, I was looking for some photos on my desktop and found these wonderful pix of you in 2010 when we visited you in Vermont.

We had a fun time visiting you and having dinners together. Thank you. I am so glad we had that summer leisure time. With love and appreciation for all we have shared together.

Hugs and woofs,

PAULA AND REAUX (FROM THE OTHER SIDE)
27 SEPTEMBER 2015

Capturing the delight you sisters take in each other's company

Well, dear Annie, one of the most enjoyable things about you has been your relationship with your sistah.

And as inevitably intrusive as a camera may be, it has for me captured the delight you take in each other's company. You've seen these before. Maybe it's good to send them once more.

Much love,

RICHARD
22 FEBRUARY 2015

Pamela and Ann, Arlington, 2011

Poster for 1992 conference on the collection from which Ann's research on men's diaries drew

Intimate Histories

Fatherhood and Family in Private Memoirs, Mexico, Late 19th and Early 20th Century

Paper presented By Ann S. Blum on panel entitled: ¿Me lo dices o me lo cuentas?: Discursos autobiográficos en la (re)presentación del yo mexicano y US latino. XXX International Congress of the Latin American Studies Association. May 23-26, 2012. San Francisco, CA.

The autobiographies that I will discuss this morning were written during the late 19th and early 20th century by men from all walks of life and regions of Mexico.[1] All of them are part of a collection formed after a 1992 conference that was organized by Mexico's Instituto Nacional de Antropología e Historia to bring together individuals who had in their possession family records in a variety of formats: official documents; account books; diaries; memoirs; correspondence; photographs; deeds; genealogical charts, and so on. Many participants granted permission to the INAH to photocopy their family documents and make them available for scholarly research.

Today I will discuss a group of diaries that record births, baptisms, marriages and deaths, and emulate with varying degrees of fidelity the format found in a variety of official documents such as parish registers and the admission registers of the orphanages that I examined for my previous study of working-class families in Mexico City.[2] The earliest examples of these diaries were begun in the 1870s and the latest was initiated in 1919. Thus, the authors belonged roughly to two overlapping generations. All the authors of the diaries were aware of the format or conventions of the genre, despite their class, ethnic, and regional diversity and varying levels of literacy. One of the earliest examples I have found was written in Mixcoac, then a still-rural *pueblo*, now a *colonia* close to downtown Mexico City, but the later diaries are mostly provincial. These characteristics suggest that I have seen a small sample of a fairly common practice.

Although my focus today is the diaries, I would like to point out a few of their differences from the memoir genre, which is closer in form and intent to autobiographies written for publication and a broad readership: principally, the author is the protagonist of the narrative. In contrast to the diary writers, who focused on family and community, the authors of the memoirs created cosmopolitan narratives that draw from an array of models, including novels, film, and sometimes, confessional genres. (Remember that Mexico's most widely-read novel during the 19th century, Fernández de Lizardi's *El periquillo sarniento*, was a "confession" supposedly penned by a father for his children and describing his youthful transgressions to exhort them to follow appropriate models of filial behavior.) The memoir authors also belonged to the same generational cohort – roughly, the generation following the dairy authors, and, indeed, the memoirs recount similar coming-of-age stories of rural and/or provincial childhood and youth, with the transition to adulthood marked by a journey that frequently carried the eager protagonist to Mexico City, the nation's political center. This is, of course, the grand narrative of 20th-century Mexico, the collective national journey to urban modernity.

Yet for all their significant differences, both the diaries and the memoirs share two central characteristics: their authors wrote as fathers; and they wrote for a readership of immediate family, primarily their children. Those characteristics account for my interest in these documents. Examining these works as a historian of the family and private life, I explore the intersections of family life and identities with community and national narratives. I am interested particularly in the ways that familial relationships and identities shaped the narratives, whether, as in the diaries, the authors portrayed themselves within a world defined as local and bounded by family and immediate community to construct intimate histories, or whether, as in the memoirs, the authors drew on the panoramas and tropes of prevailing national narratives to construct a platform for inserting the themselves as protagonists into a more public "history."

To support my claims that these diaries be taken as autobiography, I am guided by the notion of "relational" identities and narratives proposed by Paul John Eakin.[3] Eakin argues that, "*all* identity is relational," that "narrative is a – if not *the* – principal mode in which relational identity is formed and transacted," and that the "definition of autobiography… must be stretched to reflect the kinds of self-writing in which relational identity is characteristically displayed."[4] The concept of the relational self or relational identities is most closely associated with women's life writing and feminist contributions to the study of the autobiography. Feminist scholars of the genre have expanded the variety of life writing forms now considered to be autobiography. Yet Eakin sees a "polarization by gender of the categories we use to define the life of the self," with the female characterized as collective, relational, nonlinear, and discontinuous and the male characterized as individual, autonomous, narrative – and patriarchal. The diaries that I will address today nicely complicate the picture. They could certainly be seen as documents of patriarchy: their authors wrote precisely because they were fathers and heads of households, and this social position was strongly reinforced by civil and penal codes and the growing realm of printed mass media. But it bears noting that those identities or selves could only be constructed in relation to immediate kin, who were, simultaneously, actors in and the audience or readership for the diaries' narratives of family and community.

Relational Histories

The diary genre consists of a succession of usually brief and fairly standardized entries recording major events in the family cycle and immediate community. In this genre, I contend, the author's identity is relational: grandson, son, father, husband, godson, *compadre*, neighbor. The opening entries of the diary of Enrique Haas of Juchitán, Oaxaca, exemplify this relational self.[5] Haas began his diary with an entry recording his grandmother's death "of old age" in September 1881. The following entry recorded the birth of his first child, Daniel, on the last day of that year. The first two entries frame the generational position that establishes the author's own passage to a new stage of his adulthood, defined in terms of family passages: his elders die, his first children are born. Of course, Haas probably assumed other adult roles such as earning a living, years before. But by starting his diary in that year, he defines his adulthood and self as writer based on his status as a father and head of a growing household: it is this status that bestows on him – and the other diarists—not only the authority but also the responsibility to create a written record.

The diary also positions the author in networks of *compadrazgo* and community. Each entry recording a child's birth, for example, also records the baptism, with equal weight given to naming the child and naming the baptismal godparents, *padrinos*. As you know, compadrazgo, the practice of fictive kinship, creates relations of mutual albeit asymmetrical obligation between compadres. A young couple would typically ask older, more established, sometimes higher status members of the community to serve as baptismal padrinos for their children. The request put the younger couple in social obligation to their compadres for the favors that would presumably be conferred on the godchild in the future. Ideally, in time the younger couple would achieve the same respected status that their elders had held. Haas enlisted married couples as his children's baptismal padrinos. His choices reflect his own respectability and their acceptance of the role reflects the respect he enjoyed within the community. In this vein, Emilio Montero Guzmán, of Mixcoac, began his diary with an entry recording the baptism of his godson in May 1884, a decade after his marriage. Notably, serving as baptismal godparents established Montero and his wife had attained mature and respected membership in their community.[6]

The emphasis on compadrazgo throughout the diaries as a genre illustrates the ways that their writers saw family relations as inseparable from their relations within the community. The diary of José Vázquez, resident of the *barrio* San Martin, town of Huizquilucan, in the state of Mexico, provides a telling example of this connection. Vázquez wrote for only a year or so, from 1885 to 1886, and he mingled records of his own family events with those of his neighbors. Indeed, it seems that at times his neighbors asked him to do so, such as the entry in which Vázquez proclaims himself the record-keeper of the betrothal of Isabel Nava to Agustin Rueda: "and that is why I make this record I José R. Vázquez. Huisquilucan today's date."[7] So, if family relations compelled diary keepers to write, and bestowed on them the authority to write, writing can also be seen as fulfilling their obligations created by their community relations.

Why Write?: Historical Imperatives
The two earliest diaries I have found to date were written by men whose lives spanned the mid to late 19th century: these two documents point to possible origins of the genre. The diary of Hermenegildo Dávila (b. 1846 d. 1909) of Nuevo León, a lawyer, poet and historian, represents the upper end of the social scale. Like other diarists, he recorded the family cycle, although his diary is distinguished from the others I have seen to date by its literary flourishes. It is, however, similar to all the others in its purpose: the author writes as head of household, husband, and father. Dávila begins his diary with a record of his marriage in May 1870 and includes the same information that a parish register of marriages would include: names of the parents of the bride and groom; the names of the grandparents on both sides; and the names of his marriage *padrinos*, a recently married couple. Yet Dávila also adds an extended reflection on his

own and his wife's character that in turn becomes a prayer to the "Lord of Creation" for virtue, honor, charity, resignation and fortitude in the face of the life's vicissitudes.[8]

Dávila's marriage prayer echoes the famous 1859 epistle on marriage by Melchor Ocampo, a leading founder of the Mexican liberal state. Ocampo's epistle delineated the separate responsibilities of husband and wife and their shared obligation to raise honorable citizens for the republic. Mexico's liberal reforms of the late 1850s and early 1860s removed the rites and recordkeeping of birth, marriage and death registration from the authority of the Catholic Church and placed the family cycle under state, secular oversight. Historians of the family in Latin America have made much of the advent of liberalism and its implications for family ideology and practice. Some have focused on liberalism's redefinition of private property and the implications of that redefinition on inheritance law, especially the new primacy of inheritance by legitimate offspring. Others have focused on the long-term secularization of the family, set in motion by legal reforms like Mexico's.

Can the new republican imperatives linking state and family explain in part the appearance of this diary form? All the examples I have seen fall within a historical period more or less defined by the advent and rise of liberal ideals and implementation of a legal apparatus informed by liberal notions of the individual and their evolution – and eventual corruption – during the 30-year presidency of Porfirio Díaz that famously ended in that convulsion of liberal renewal known as the Mexican Revolution. The contextual implications are intriguing. It is clear that all the practitioners of this form of family narrative knew the conventions of the genre. Yet I have not seen any examples of an earlier date. Did this practice emerge within this specific historical period in response to changes in concepts of fatherhood and paternal authority, a change significant enough to prompt fathers of that era to record their family and community relations in this manner? Could these documents be a family-based practice that reflects the ideals of citizenship and community that historians have called "popular liberalism"? There is some evidence for such a connection. Dávila, for example, named one of his sons Isaac, after a close friend who had died before a French firing squad during the wars of the French Intervention of the early 1860s. Dávila hoped that "patriotism would be the virtue that ruled" his son, and "his siblings also," and added, "I pray to God that my children will be worthy of their parents and their fatherland. The family is virtue! The fatherland is justice!"[9]

But patriotic invocations of this kind are rare in the diaries. Rather, the diaries collectively convey a sense of the responsibility to create a record of family history in a variety of written formats. Emilio Montero of Mixcoac belonged to the same generation as Dávila. Montero's diary is a compilation of elements, some written directly into a small notebook and others enclosed in it. When Montero began the diary in February 1874 he entitled it "Book and Record of my Marriage. And birth of my children." His earliest entry describes the events that led up to establishing his conjugal household: his courtship; the date when his *novia*'s parents gave their consent; the reading of the bans; and the date of the wedding. Although in this extended entry Montero does not name his novia-then-wife, he names the priest who celebrated the wedding and the *padrinos* of the wedding ceremony, and notes that after the ceremony, the wedding party "went to eat."[10] Subsequent entries record the birth of his children, their baptism and baptismal padrinos. Montero marked the entries recording deaths with a cross, including the deaths of three of his children. In these ways his diary resembles parish records.

But Emilio Montero was not the sole author of this diary nor are all elements in the standardized diary format. Enclosed in the diary are two courtship letters penned by another hand (a local scribe?), certificates of burial of family members – including Montero's own burial, and certificates of merit, some signed by President Porfirio Díaz, awarded to Montero's children as they progressed through the public school system. These documents, together with the diary, suggest that Montero was of solid middling social status: he married in the church before his children were born and he took pains and pride in educating his children. All the pieces of this cache of papers are needed to tell his own and the family story – and status.

As historian William French has observed regarding the circulation of love letters in northern Mexico, documents of all kinds gained increasing importance during the late 19th century and early 20th century. Love letters could be used in court as evidence of a promise of marriage.[11] By the late 1800s, new elements were needed to reinforce the centuries-old importance of land titles and deeds establishing the family's claims to property and often their means of livelihood. The family cycle intersected ever more intricately and legally with a growing state and local bureaucracy. Individuals needed documents to prove relationships and legal identity. New laws on inheritance favored bequests to children of legitimate birth, hence the importance of recording the day, place and witnesses to a parents' marriage, or of the children's baptisms as a stand in for a birth certificate. The litany of standardized diary entries provided the family's "copies" – if you will – of exactly those facets of the domestic and civic life. Manuel López of Chulula, titled his diary, begun on December 1, 1919 "Notebook to record ages, births and burials," and signed the title page, "Property of Manuel Lopez Family." In that regard, each diary entry reiterated the family "charter," the relations among the members and the rights, obligations and identities that flowed from them.

Affective Worlds
In addition to births, baptisms, marriages and deaths, Enrique Haas (of Juchitán) also recorded his employment in his career as a bandleader, his positions in local government, the construction of his house – including the cost of the materials, as well as his children's schooling and later their employment, engagements, marriages and the birth of the next generation. In these ways, his narrative not only provided the kinds of evidence that the family required to document its personhood and civic rights, but also knit together an affective world of intersecting networks of kin, fictive kin, and community bonds. In José Vázquez's diary, betrothals and deaths, first communions and marriages mingle with the building of the kitchen walls and weaning a child.

Towards the end of his notebook he summarized the arc of his affective life in a single extended entry: his birth in 1853, marriage, the birth of his first child in 1878 and subsequent children.[12] Manuel López of Cholula, state of Puebla, noted the emergence of his son's baby teeth a year before he and his children's mother married. While his diary focused on births and baptisms when his children were young, he later turned his attention to strikes at the textile factory that employed many of the men in his community worked and also recorded in detail the frequent earthquakes that shook his community and the automobile accidents that occurred near his home.[13]

Historians of the family sometimes define the family as the bridge that connects the private and public spheres. The writer-narrators of these diaries wrap a thickly woven fabric of family and community life around themselves: it is this fabric that establishes their identity as writers, as autobiographers. Yes, regardless of their place, level of literacy or ethnic identity, all of these diaries were written in dialogue with normative paternal roles, which defined honorable masculinity and the authority – private and public—that derived from those roles. In these ways, these authors also constructed an idealized space where intimate and national narratives of self, domestic authority and social responsibility intersected. This is a space that would become the object of nostalgia – and conversely, the norm to challenge—in diasporic memoirs and autobiographies that have sought to redefine self and reader or to forge new relationships with the past. Yet at the same time, these diaries challenge us, today's reader, to articulate the difference between patriarchy and fatherhood and to reassess the affective bonds that compelled these writers to tell their family stories.

BIBLIOGRAPHY
MANUSCRIPTS
Acervo Histórico de Testimonios Familiares, Instituto Nacional de Antropología e Historia, Dirección de Estudios Históricos, Biblioteca "Manuel Orozco y Berra," Tlalpan, México, D.F.
PUBLISHED WORKS

Blum, Ann S. *Domestic Economies: Family, Work and Welfare in Mexico City, 1884-1943*. Lincoln: University of Nebraska Press, 2009.
Eakin, Paul John. "Relational Selves, Relational Lives: The Story of the Story." In *True Relations: Essays on Autobiography and the Postmodern*. G. Thomas Couser and Joseph Fichtelberg, ed. Westport, CT: Greenwood Press, 1998: 63-81.
Hirsch, Marianne. *Family Frames: Photography, Narrative and Postmemory*. Cambridge: Harvard University Press, 1997.
Holden, Philip. *Autobiography and Decolonization: Modernity, Masculinity and the Nation State*. Madison: University of Wisconsin Press, 2008.
Shelton, Laura M. *For Tranquility and Order: Family and Community on Mexico's Northern Frontier, 1800-1850*. Tucson: University of Arizona Press, 2010.
Smith, Sidonie and Julia Watson. *Reading Autobiography: A Guide for Interpreting Life Narratives*. 2nd Edition. Minneapolis: Minnesota University Press, 2010.

ENDNOTES

[1] All documents discussed in this paper are part of the Acervo Histórico de Testimonios Familiares, Instituto Nacional de Antropología e Historia (hereafter INAH), Dirección de Estudios Históricos (hereafter DEH), Biblioteca "Manuel Orozco y Berra," Tlalpan, México, D.F. See: Delia Salazar and Juan Matamala Vivanco, *Guía del acervo histórico de testimonios familiares* (Mexico City: Instituto Nacional de Antropología e Historia, 1994).

[2] Ann S. Blum, Domestic Economies: Family, Work and Welfare in Mexico City, 1884-1943 (Lincoln: University of Nebraska Press, 2009).

[3] Paul John Eakin, "Relational Selves, Relational Lives: The Story of the Story," in *True Relations: Essays on Autobiography and the Postmodern*, G. Thomas Couser and Joseph Fichtelberg, ed. (Wesport, CT: Greenwood Press, 1998), pp. 63-81.

[4] Eakin, "Relational Selves," p. 63.

[5] The Haas—or Haaz—family in Mexico originated with Charles Haaz, who came from Alsace Loraine in 1850 to work on the Isthmus of Tehuantepec railroad. See the Haaz family genealogical website: http://www.haaz.mx/ 10 May 2012.

[6] Emilio Montero Guzmán, "Recuerdos muy memorables que tuve en el pueblo de Mixcoac," 1884-1921. INAH Papeles de Familia, 46.

[7] José R. Vázquez, "Cuaderno memorial," 1885-1886. INAH Papeles de Familia, 125.

[8] Hermenegildo Dávila, "El diario del Abuelo," 1870-1904. INAH Papeles de Familia, 84.

[9] Dávila, "Diario del Abuelo."

[10] Montero Guzmán, "Recuerdos muy memorables."

[11] William E. French, personal communication.

[12] José R. Vázquez, "Cuaderno memorial," 1885-1886. INAH Papeles de Familia, 125.

[13] Manuel López. "Cuaderno para apuntes de edades, de nacimiento y hinumaciones [sic]," 1919-1944, INAH Papeles de Familia, 86.

Home: The Color of Memory

Paper by Ann S. Blum for panel: "Visions of Parenting and Childhood in Colonial Latin America"

Rocky Mountain Council for Latin American Studies, Santa Fe NM, April 3-6 2013.

To begin his autobiography, Maximino González recorded his memories of his childhood home in Guanajuato, not in words, but in a carefully detailed pen drawing. The house and its stone patio nestled into the folds of a hill and were enclosed by a wall topped by a row of potted plants. At the center of the patio stood a tree and a bright sun shone down on the scene. Remembering the house where he was born in 1879 and spent his childhood, González then described the expansive view from the patio and the exuberance of the flowering plants and their fragrance during the rainy season and wrote "Oh, how my heart is overcome with feeling to recall those times and those things gone forever!"[1] (76)

The notebook in which González recorded his life story, which he titled "Recuerdos íntimos," is filled with such sentiments. Indeed, before he began to write his memoirs he transcribed into the small volume scores of poems on themes of love, separation, loss and memory, some written by 19th-century European poets such as Victor Hugo and Ramón de Campoamor, but many by the author himself. With the exception of his idyllic childhood memories, the life González described in his memoir was one of hard physical labor and a series of personal setbacks. He had little schooling, started work at age nine, and labored most of his life as a builder, painter, plasterer and carpenter. "My children will know or whoever reads these poorly written lines will see, that my life with very few exceptions has always been a constant struggle." (108) By 1931, at the age of 52, he achieved a modicum of stability and was able to purchase a small property to establish a permanent home for his wife and children in the Federal District: there he wrote his life story.

González's themes of memory, distance and loss echo those of other fathers and heads of household from all walks of life and regions of Mexico who recorded their life stories for a readership of immediate family during the early 20th century. On the surface, these themes are perfectly understandable: in telling their life histories these writers also recounted the deaths of siblings, parents, and frequently at least one of their own children. Yet what caught my attention in reading these autobiographical accounts is that, in contrast to the attention, detail and feeling that the authors invested in recalling their own childhoods, most of them wrote very little – often nothing! – about their home life as partners and fathers. Why, I wondered, were intimate family relations and domesticity a compelling subject only when they were in the past? In particular, I became interested in how gender influenced the ways these writers depicted their early affective worlds, and how gender created or defined the distances, ruptures and losses that separated the adult writers from their childhoods. I propose that one way to answer these questions is to see childhood or the childhood home as the foil to the expectations of masculine adulthood, especially in metaphors of distance traveled along the life course. Indeed, it is through a gendered geography both real and symbolic—a relational distance—that these men revisited the affective world of their childhood homes through their life writing.[2]

Generations and Geographies of Life Writing

The life accounts that are my focus today resemble autobiographies written for publication and a broad readership: that is, the authors positioned themselves as the protagonists of their narratives. Each writer created his own form for telling his story and wrote for a specific audience of close kin: some referred to those readers by name and suggested who could supply for the others details that might take too long to write.[3] Yet these private works share certain core characteristics. Written in mid to late life by men with little formal schooling, these works are strikingly cosmopolitan narratives that draw from an array of models including novels, film, and sometimes, confessional genres. (Remember that Mexico's most widely-read novel during the 19th century, Joaquín Fernández de Lizardi's *El periquillo sarniento*, first published in 1816 and considered Latin America's first true novel, was a "confession" supposedly penned by a father for his children and describing his youthful transgressions to exhort them to follow appropriate models of filial behavior.[4]) Additionally, all the memoir authors belonged to roughly the same generational cohort born in the late 19th century. Indeed, the memoirs recount similar coming-of-age stories of rural or provincial childhood and youth, with the transition to adulthood marked by a journey that frequently carried the eager protagonist to Mexico City, the nation's political center, where he navigated the shoals of the urban economy and formed a new household. This is, of course, the grand narrative of 20th-century Mexico, the collective national journey to urban modernity. These writers were simultaneously participants in this story and also wrote it into being.

The memoir form was not, however, the only model available to fathers and male household heads for telling their life stories. I am also working with diaries produced by two overlapping generations slightly older than the autobiographers. The earliest examples of the diaries that I have seen were begun in the 1870s and the latest was initiated in 1919.[5] One of the earliest examples I have found comes from Mixcoac, then a rural *pueblo*, now a *colonia* close to downtown Mexico City, but the later diaries are mostly provincial. These personal accounts recorded births, baptisms, betrothals, marriages and deaths, and emulated—with some leeway for individual embellishment —the format of official documents such as parish registers (and also of the admission registers of the orphanages that I examined for my study of working-class families in Mexico City).[6] All the authors of the diaries were aware of the conventions of the genre regardless of social class, ethnic identity, region or degree of formal education. These characteristics suggest that I have seen a small sample of a practice that was fairly widespread during a specific period of time. The shared elements of these diaries, especially compared to life writing of a younger generation, suggest ways to historicize personal or individual memory.

Besides generation, one principal difference between the memoirs and diaries is that of geographic range. The diary writers stayed rooted in their communities and kept their accounts closely focused on family and spiritual kin. In this genre of life writing, home and family were the lived center of the writer's affective world throughout adulthood. Indeed, the imperative to write stemmed in part from the formation of the writer's own conjugal household, a defining event of adulthood. Many of the diaries ended only when the writer died.[7] The personal, intimate milestones of children's lives, such as cutting the first tooth or taking the first steps or the first job, were as worthy of record as the major life events of baptism, betrothal or marriage. The home was treated almost as a living extension of the immediate family. Many of the diary writers recorded in detail the costs of materials and family labor for building and furnishing the home, room by room.[8]

I wish to call particular attention to the connection that the diarists made between the lived arc of their affective lives and the family home—physical location of their adult lives—because it suggests a way for us to rethink gender and domesticity. We historians of family, women and gender, and I include myself, have focused so intently on domesticity and maternity in constructions of feminine roles and identities that we have largely written men out of the picture. Indeed, these diaries offer us a masculine and paternal rendering of domestic space and family life.[9]

In contrast to the diarists, the younger generation of writers embraced autobiography or memoir as the narrative of mobility and migration. They begin by describing the birthplace, but as I have already noted, many of them crafted their accounts as coming of age stories in which leaving the childhood home was the requisite first step towards adulthood. Crossing that threshold usually meant that the writer-protagonist had begun to work, which marked the end of childhood as a life chapter. That transition also meant leaving the immediate protection and company of the writer's mother or other female caregiver. From that point on, the writers took their stories on the road to describe new terrains – geographic, economic, political, social and emotional—in which they must find their way. Some took pains to recount episodes when their lives intersected with public figures and events of their times.[10] But in contrast to the older generation of diary writers, few of the autobiographers described their adult homes and family lives: instead, they invested their childhood homes with profound emotional significance and at the same time, reinforced the gender trope of home as a feminine space.

The autobiographers recalled their childhoods and childhood homes from a number of distant vantage points. The moment of departure from the feminine space of the home into the masculine world of work offered an opportunity to reflect on the writer's relationship with his mother. They also looked back across a distance in time, including distance along the life course, chronological age, the generational shift from son to father, and, for some, public constructions of historical memory. By the time they wrote their memoirs, the deaths of close family members heightened the feeling with which the autobiographers remembered the childhood home. They also wrote from a significant geographic distance from the birthplace, both real – in kilometers—and symbolic, such as the distance between rural and urban perspectives.[11] It was as migrants from the hinterland to the capital that they looked back on their rural origins from the city of letters.

Home: The Color of Memory

Today, in the interests of time, I will discuss only two of the memoirs. The first, by Adalberto Mendoza Ruvalcaba, is the longest of these autobiographies. Born in 1885 in the state of San Luis Potosí, Mendoza spent his entire adult life working on the railroad. In 1938, resident in Mexico City, he began writing his life narrative so that his children would know him better.

Mendoza had idyllic memories of his rural childhood. He described the family farm in Guayabos as "a corner of Paradise" located in a "tropical zone of extraordinary beauty," bathed by an "abundant river," and producing a cornucopia of tropical fruits. (20) The view from the house was an "enchanting landscape," with a river winding between the trees, cane fields, and distant sugar mill. (v. 1 21) He recalled that, "to me the characteristic murmur of the river seemed divine." (v. 1 22)

Mendoza's childhood was punctuated by a series of departures from and returns to these pastoral scenes. His father held a legislative position the state capital for twelve years. That extended sojourn exposed the boy to the urban modern world of train travel, electric light, and school. The landscape near Cárdenas, where the family moved on leaving the city evoked Mendoza's strongest sentiments, closely associated with his mother. "My good mother was in her element and told us that the time there was the happiest in her life. We children also found the environment perfect for our play and for leading a simple and wholesome life, each according to his sex and age." (v. 1 33) He recalled that he and his sister ran across the hills collecting fruits and flowers and swam in the streams. (v. 1 33)

At the age of eight, however, the boy was removed from this environment when his father sent him into town again for schooling. This was his first experience of separation from his mother and the break caused him great pain. "I cannot escape the emotion that it causes me to remember that period of my life. My troubles began ... at that point. I have never understood why my father separated me from my mother." (v. 1 43) He felt abandoned and was allowed home only during vacations and weekends. Over time, he pondered the reasons for this forced separation: "I know well that my father loved me deeply and I cannot understand what he was thinking to impose on my such terrible suffering in my childhood." Addressing his readers, he warned, "Now you will see what more I had to suffer." (v. 1 48)

These words closed the first volume of Mendoza's memoirs. The second opened with his memories of his last vacation with his mother, a rural idyll of swimming and hunting.[12] His mother nurtured and encouraged his transition from childhood games to "virile country sports," gave him money for powder and shot and praised him when he returned home with his catch. These bucolic recollections were deeply colored by hindsight: Mendoza's mother would die the following year.

Mendoza already equated separation from his mother with abandonment and with leaving the countryside for the city. Her death marked the end of his childhood and left him emotionally homeless. "Oh sweet memories of the few happy days of my tormented childhood! They were like moments spent in a welcome oasis, on crossing the inhospitable desert of my adolescent years." (v. 2 n.p.) He described his life after her death as a dangerous sea voyage away from the safe harbor of her care: "I carry engraved in my memory the sweet image of that sainted woman who even after death was my guide, the beacon that kept on course the weak bark in which I set out on my life voyage across the tempestuous sea of my existence." (v. 2 n.p.) Mendoza portrayed the rural landscapes of his childhood as Paradise, with the end of childhood representing eviction into a life of suffering. Indeed, he represented his childhood and the landscapes of his childhood in the profoundly gendered terms of a garden or a harbor, fixed in location in relation to his real and symbolic movement in time, place and life course, and revisited through the lenses of separation and loss.

David Martínez Becerril looked back on a childhood home that he had scarcely known. Born in 1911 in San Miguel de la Victoria, state of Mexico, he was raised from toddlerhood by his widowed grandmother. His father, a tailor by trade, lost to drink the land, animals, house and furnishings he had inherited from the writer's great grandfather. As a young child Martínez may have visited the property; he described the house, its three bedrooms, salon, dining room, parlor, room for servants, kitchen, corral and stable. But the description may have been based on his mother's memories: he wrote that she had danced under the tree in the patio on her wedding day. Thus the bitterness he conveyed about the lost home could well have been learned from his mother: by the time he had reached the age of 7, he recounted, "the earth I walked on did not belong to me." (10)[13]

It was this crisis that propelled the boy across the threshold marking the end of childhood. He left the care of his grandmother and accompanied his mother and siblings to Mexico City, where his father had gone to seek work. Hunger dominated his memories of that time in the capital.[14] Unemployed, his father would visit people from their region who were resident in the city to ask for a loan as if, wrote his adult son years later, he were begging for alms. When he would arrive home from these missions in the late afternoon with *masa*, the children would finally have food calm their "ravenous hunger." (11) Defeated by the city, the family returned to San Miguel de la Victoria and made the return 100-kilometer journey on foot. Back in the relative safety and comfort of his natal *pueblo*, Martínez Becerril recalled, they still "suffered from hunger," but it was "more tolerable" being near family "because there was always someone who could give us a tortilla." (13)

Martínez expressed his feelings about this abrupt life transition through the details of his narrative rather than the language of sentiment. His father's alcoholism and inability to provide for the family destabilized the generational positions and relations between father and son. His father, the ostensible head of household, had failed in his most important adult masculine role – supporting and protecting his family. The failure of his father to fulfill these responsibilities represented a parental betrayal and form of abandonment. We can surmise from the narrative attention that these issues received in the account that Martínez felt them more deeply than his placement with his grandmother before the age of two.

Martínez attended school in part because his father became a schoolteacher. Despite receiving a significant portion of his students' fees in goods rather than cash, the father drank away half his salary. Hunger remained a constant in Martínez's life. So did involuntary mobility. His father often sent the boy on errands requiring long hikes to nearby *pueblos* or *ranchitos* to ask the teachers in those communities for loan of a few pesos or corn. (18) At age 11 he left school and began working to contribute to the family's subsistence: these jobs usually required him to live away from his family. On the occasions he stayed under his parents' roof he slept on the floor in the kitchen with the dogs. When Martínez reflected on reaching adolescence and beginning work – in his own words, as a "peon," (21)—he described that passage as the end of his "triste infancia."(18)

Clearly Martínez did not enjoy what I have called in other contexts a protected childhood, that is, an early life protected from physical harm and adult concerns and devoted to play and school.[15] By the age of 21, when he left his birthplace to his own fortune in Mexico City, he had been working for ten years in jobs that required hard labor and had been living away from his family for most of that time. Yet despite these hardships, he turned to the language of sentiment to describe his departure from "beloved native soil ... filled with recollections" of childhood and youth, a leave-taking that moved him to the "depths" of his soul. (38) His account emphasized the sacred filial rituals: fear that he would never see his parents again; kneeling before his mother for her blessing; his parting kiss to her forehead and hand; her tears; and a sense of fate leading him forward—"it was the decisive moment of departure, there was no looking back."(38)

We can never know whether this account is a true record of the event, and it does not matter. What is clear is that memory charged this particular departure with heightened significance, even though Martínez had already left his parents' home many times to work and had made his first trip to Mexico City in search of work eight years before. It is certainly possible that the details of the emotional *despedida* between mother and son were colored and rearranged over time by similar scenes in the popular media. Tellingly, however, Martínez invested no other scene in his narrative with this intensity, not even his account of his courtship of his future wife. Indeed, marriage and family life are completely absent from his memoir, although he described in detail his career as a traveling salesman for a pharmaceutical company.

How can we interpret the author's recreation of feeling and gesture in this particular farewell? I would suggest that the remembered moment condensed and encapsulated the key elements of the gendered relations and symbolic geography of distance and loss. Like Mendoza's reconstruction of his last idyllic summer with his mother and his eviction from paradise at her death, this farewell combined a major transition in the writer's life course and in the trajectory of the masculine coming-of-age narrative with a definitive step in the protagonist's physical journey away from his "native soil" and toward the capital city and his initiation into the modern urban world.

BIBLIOGRAPHY
MANUSCRIPTS
All documents discussed in this paper are part of the Acervo Histórico de Testimonios Familiares, Instituto Nacional de Antropología e Historia, Dirección de Estudios Históricos, Biblioteca "Manuel Orozco y Berra," Tlalpan, México, D.F.

PUBLISHED WORKS

Blum, Ann S., "Bringing It Back Home: Perspectives on Gender and Family History in Modern Mexico," *History Compass* 4:5 (2006): 906-926.

-----. *Domestic Economies: Family, Work and Welfare in Mexico City, 1884-1943.* Lincoln: University of Nebraska Press, 2009.

Blunt, Alison, and Anne Varley. "Introduction: Geographies of Home." *Cultural Geographies.* 11:1 (2004): 3-6.

Eakin, Paul John. "Relational Selves, Relational Lives: The Story of the Story." In *True Relations: Essays on Autobiography and the Postmodern.* G. Thomas Couser and Joseph Fichtelberg, ed. Westport, CT: Greenwood Press, 1998: 63-81.

Holden, Philip. *Autobiography and Decolonization: Modernity, Masculinity and the Nation State.* Madison: University of Wisconsin Press, 2008.

Legg, Stephen. "Memory and Nostalgia." *Cultural Geographies* 11:1 (2004): 99-107.

Rama, Angel. *The Lettered City.* Translated and Edited by John Charles Chasteen. Durham, NC: Duke University Press, 1996.

Ralph, David and Lynn A. Staeheli. "Home and Migration: Mobilities, Belongings and Identities." *Geography Compass.* 5:7 (2011): 517-530.

Salazar, Delia, and Juan Matamala Vivanco. *Guía del acervo histórico de testimonios familiares.* Mexico City: Instituto Nacional de Antropología e Historia, 1994.

ENDNOTES

[1] Maximino González [Ramírez], (1879-1949), "Recuerdos íntimos," 88 ff. Acervo Histórico de Testimonios Familiares (hereafter AHTF), Instituto Nacional de Antropología e Historia (hereafter INAH), 139. All documents discussed in this paper are part of the Acervo Histórico de Testimonios Familiares, Instituto Nacional de Antropología e Historia, Dirección de Estudios Históricos, Biblioteca "Manuel Orozco y Berra," Tlalpan, México, D.F. See: Delia Salazar and Juan Matamala Vivanco, *Guía del acervo histórico de testimonios familiares* (Mexico City: Instituto Nacional de Antropología e Historia, 1994).

[2] Alison Blunt and Anne Varley, "Introduction: Geographies of Home," *Cultural Geographies* 11:1 (2004): 3-6. I am also interested in the relational concept of life writing. See Paul John Eakin, "Relational Selves, Relational Lives: The Story of the Story," in *True Relations: Essays on Autobiography and the Postmodern*, G. Thomas Couser and Joseph Fichtelberg, ed. (Westport, CT: Greenwood Press, 1998): pp. 63-

81. See also Stephen Legg, "Memory and Nostalgia," *Cultural Geographies* 11 (2004): 99-107.

[3] Adelberto Mendoza Rivalcaba, "Autobiografía de A.R. Mendoza," 10 v., AHTF, INAH 49.

[4] Angel Rama, *The Lettered City*, translated and edited by John Charles Chasteen (Durham, NC: Duke University Press, 1996): pp. 42-43.

[5] Emilio Montero Guzmán, "Recuerdos muy memorables que tuve en el pueblo de Mixcoac," 54ff., 1873-[1921], AHTF, INAH, 76: Manuel López, "Cuaderno para apuntes de edades de nacimientos y hinumaciones," 121ff., 1919-1944, AHTF, INAH, 86.

[6] Ann S. Blum, *Domestic Economies: Family, Work and Welfare in Mexico City, 1884-1943* (Lincoln: University of Nebraska Press, 2009).

[7] Hermenegildo Dávila, "El diario del abuelo," 132ff., 1870-1910, AHTF, INAH, 84.

[8] López, "Cuaderno"; Enrique Haas, "Memoria desde 1881. De los más notables sucesos de la familia y su ligera cronología," 18ff, AHTF, INAH, 30.

[9] Ann S. Blum, "Bringing It Back Home: Perspectives on Gender and Family History in Modern Mexico," *History Compass* 4:5 (2006): 906-926.

[10] Philip Holden, *Autobiography and Decolonization: Modernity, Masculinity and the Nation State* (Madison: University of Wisconsin Press, 2008).

[11] David Ralph and Lynn A. Staeheli, "Home and Migration: Mobilities, Belongings and Identities," *Geography Compass* 5:7 (2011): 517-530.

[12] The descriptions recall early chapters in Jorge Isaacs's novel, *María*, first published in Colombia in 1867 and widely read throughout Latin America. Although he described himself as an indifferent student, Mendoza became a voracious reader when he began to work as a railroad telegrapher.

[13] David Martínez Becerril, "Apuntes biográficos," 131 ff. (3 vols.) 1989, AHTF, INAH, 137.

[14] Ibid.

[15] Blum, *Domestic Economies*.

The family is key to our understanding of politics on intimate, national and global scales

Good afternoon. It is very gratifying to be celebrating the official opening of Rita Arditti's archive as a research source.

I would like to say a few words about the importance of Rita's work on social movements and human rights and the work of the Grandmothers of the Plaza de Mayo within the field of Latin American Studies – and beyond.

Latin American Studies, like other area studies fields, emerged from Cold War imperatives to investigate regions considered strategic to U.S. policy. Latin American governments responded to U.S. geopolitical motives with terrifying creativity and used them to justify national politics by any means. During the 1960s, '70s and '80s Latin American governments carried Cold War logic to horrific extremes. It was National Security Doctrine that provided the supposed rationale for Latin American governments to wage war against their own citizens whom they labeled subversives. In Uruguay, Argentina, Chile and Brazil, the victims of those dirty wars were mostly young adults and many were adolescents. It fell to the surviving older generation to confront their children's torturers and murderers and their grandchildren's abductors.

Rita made profound contributions to celebrating the people who found the courage to confront those horrors. First, as both a scientist and a humanist, she engaged with and gave ongoing support to the Grandmothers of the Plaza de Mayo of Argentina and their campaign to discover the fate of their young-adult children, to locate their grandchildren, abducted and concealed by Argentina's military regime between 1976 and 1983, and to restore their grandchildren's rightful identities. Out of that engagement came Rita's enduring book, Searching for Life, illuminating the Grandmother's quest for justice and the myriad forms it took – from the famous weekly marches circling the Plaza de Mayo, to their pioneering work in forensic genetics, to their contributions to the United Nations Convention on the Rights of the Child.

Rita was neither the first nor the only scholar-activist to study and celebrate maternal activism in the Southern Cone. But the importance of the topic and of Rita's approach cannot be overestimated. Her work combined key strands of inquiry in pioneering ways to highlight the connections among: the complex political and human legacies of dictatorships; what came to be called "new social movements"; an approach to activism and scholarship on human rights that focused on gender and childhood; and her particular stamp – the connections with grass-roots science initiatives and the application of science, forensic genetics in particular—to human rights. In recent years, these areas of scholarship have helped transform the field Latin American Studies—and redeem it – from its Cold War origins.

My own area of research is family history. Students and other scholars sometimes ask me why I study the family when there are other far more important, more political topics. Rita's activism and scholarship provide a ringing rejoinder. The family is political and it is key to our understanding of politics on intimate, national and global scales. Rita's work with the Grandmothers centered on family. Her study embraced the complex interactions among three generations as family relations were projected onto national and international politics. The Argentine military regime was brutally astute: they made state terrorism a family affair. After torturing and murdering the young activist parents, the regime concealed the family origins of their victims' children and placed many of them with the parents' torturers to raise surviving children lost their parents. The loss of their children and grandchildren inflicted searing emotional pain on the elder survivors. Rita's scholarship spotlights the ravages brought about by the deliberate politics of targeting the institution of the family and depriving the state's political opponents of the life-giving satisfactions of family bonds across generations. The inspiring courage of the Grandmothers of the Plaza de Mayo, acting first a caregivers to their children and grandchild and later as nurturers of the nation's conscience, was to expose that brutality, to seek justice for its victims, and to seek an end to impunity for the perpetrators.

I would also like to say a few words about Rita's contributions to Latin American Studies here at UMass Boston. Every year in my introductory course I teach Rita's book, Searching for Life. I teach her book because it is accessible to students at the introductory college level, because it is a way to teach about gender and social movements, and because it is a way to transcend prevailing cultural stereotypes about the Latin American family. I also teach Rita's book so that new generations will know what happened and will not forget.

Rita was unfailingly generous to our department and our students. She never declined an invitation to speak to students about her book and its larger context, whether in a small classroom setting or a larger forum. She came even when we could afford no more honorarium than parking and lunch. She and her partner, Estelle Disch, helped bring representatives of the Grandmothers to campus to speak to our students. The last time they came, young and articulate members of HIJOS, the organization formed by restituted grandchildren, accompanied them. I am proud that UMass Boston awarded the Grandmothers an honorary degree in 2000.

For today's student, 2000 was a long time ago: the 1970s are ancient history. Rita's work makes those issues present and urgent. Every year I encounter a former student who, without fail, speaks of the powerful experience of learning about the Grandmothers of the Plaza de Mayo. Thank you, Rita. When I teach your book, I feel like you are teaching by my side.

For these reasons, the collection we celebrate today will quickly become a valuable source for students of Latin America in many fields: scholars of new social movements; of gender and family; of the politics of late 20th-century democratization; students of literature, life writing and testimonial writing; scholars of social studies of science. It was Rita's vision to understand that these fields converged in the work of the Grandmothers. It is Healey Library's vision to make these records accessible to the world. I cannot think of a better way to honor Rita's contributions to Latin American Studies or to honor the work of the Grandmothers in global human rights.

And for her acute awareness of these strands of meaning, there could have been no better transcriber of these important documents than Doris Cristóbal. Doris has a personal and astute first hand insight of the complexities of the gender and family politics in the Southern Cone. She dedicated her great intelligence and fine sense of language to the process of transcribing the interviews with the Grandmothers. Thank you, Doris, for your invaluable contribution to making these records publicly available. Thank you also to Joanne Riley, University Archivist, for undertaking this transcription project; to Daniel Ortiz, Dean of University Libraries, for supporting the project of making this archive available for research; thank you to Sandra McEvoy, Associate Director of the Center for Gender, Security and Human Rights, for suggesting a brilliant transcription system; and always, thank you to Estelle Disch, beloved colleague and inspiring teacher, now retired, for arranging the donation; and thanks also to María Cisterna of the Latin American and Iberian Studies Department for facilitating it.

ANN BLUM
LATIN AMERICAN AND IBERIAN STUDIES, COLLEGE OF LIBERAL ARTS

INAUGURATION: ARCHIVES OF AN ACTIVIST: CELEBRATING THE DONATIONS OF RITA ARDITTI TO UMASS BOSTON: HEALEY LIBRARY APRIL 22 2013, HTTPS://VIMEO.COM/64758505

Ann in garden, July 2012; Sarah's zinnias in foreground and her hand on far right

Our chats when we were in the desert

Ann—It's raining here today, the end of summer—and, miles away in Marrickville, we're all thinking of you.

I often recall our chats when we were in the desert—particularly when we let the more able-bodied go on with the bush walk around the gorge and we went and sat by that waterhole. We talked of aging parents, menopause, teenage children and all the stuff of life at this age. I remember there was a family camping and they had a child who was swimming in the water. It was so quiet there, and you could hear her calling out to her dad. The sky was cobalt blue and the water a deep green.

Sickness is a strange time, where you separate out from the rest of the world. I so hope you come through this much more quickly than you expect, returning to all the other stuff of life soon. You are in my thoughts often.

With much love

GEORGIA
19 FEBRUARY 2015

Ann sitting up enjoying her French roast and reading in the quiet morning hours

Dear Pete and Ann, When I picture you both in my mind's eye it is in warmer climes.

The image that comes to me is when we shared a room at the motel in Uluru (Ayers Rock in the centre of Australia). I woke up in the morning and rolled over to see Frans sleeping next to me, Pete sleeping in the next bed and Ann sitting up enjoying her French roast and reading in the quiet morning hours. It was a warm fuzzy family feeling—happy that we are of the generation where we could share a room together and prepare our meals and eat communally on our balcony with Andrew and clan rather than capitulate to the restaurant. I always am grateful for that holiday and especially to Ann for coming such a distance to join the Aussie outback adventure,

Much love to you both

SALLY
2 MARCH 2015

Our time in our little theater of two

I send love and love and love.

I drove up through the California mountains north of L.A. yesterday.
HUGE deluge up in the mountains.
And then sun as I drove through miles and miles of cherry trees in rows and rows and rows.
OH this is where those California cherries grow!
Then up again over green green mountains; like velvet rumpled blankets.
Cottonwood trees shaped like broccoli.

Such beauty here.

Now in Palo Alto.
Will drive to San Fran today and set up my 3rd show in a row.
La Jolla and Santa Monica were sweet and swell.
I hope for more tomorrow night in San Fran.
SOOO much swell of feeling to do the show in this city which means so much to our generation of gay men.

OHH. I want to meet the meaning. Like a Pilgrimage. My story added to the City of Gay Men's Stories.
Oh yes: tales of the city.

OH, dear Ann, thanks for our time in our little theater of two and the darling pooch.
Very helpful launch for this California Dream Tour.
I hope you have seen my Facebook photos sent back from the Full Spectrum Spring Color here, dears.

Always ALL WAYS,

Love and Hugs and Support and LOVE AND LOVE,

STEVE AND JASMINE
26 FEBRUARY 2015

It has been my encyclopaedia for drawings from Nature

Pete --just to let you know how much Ann's book is inspiring friends -this is just one eg LOVE

- must go as Sal & I are going to lunch with Frans & AGT---EJ.

Dear Gilly

We came home late last night after the film on Stephen Hawkins 'The theory of Everything' to your sad email. I wish you and Pete all the best and hope that you will achieve the strength you will both need during this passage of time.

Co-incidentally, Ann had been on my mind all of yesterday.

After reading that John Ruskin said that he would 'rather teach drawing that my pupils may learn to love Nature than teach the looking at Nature that they may learn to draw'…I thought I would draw my shell collection, so I spent 4 hours in the studio yesterday, drawing one shell. While drawing, I was thinking all along that I would have to refer to Ann's book "Picturing Nature" to find out about that shell. Last year I did 4 images based on some diagrams and studies in her book. It has been my encyclopaedia for drawings from Nature.
Ian and I share your deep concern for Pete and Ann.
….

Lots of love

ENID
21 FEBRUARY 2015

When I hear Spanish on the streets of NYC

Ann...

I think of you when I hear Spanish on the streets of NYC.

TOM
22 FEBRUARY 2015

Multiple roles as a health caregiver

The primary caregiver for someone who has a serious illness may be one person, but that person has multiple roles.

While there is research on caregivers having multiple roles (e.g., working, looking after children, etc.), the literature that one is provided in healthcare settings does not seem to discuss the different caregiving-related roles or the challenge of moving between roles that call for a different kind of presence and attention.

Medical
1. Care in the present, especially pain management. (Includes learning from homecare visitors to do care well when they are not around.)
2. Participate in medical decision-making—conversations, explorations, debriefing after new information, medical advocacy (especially when in hospital).
3. Preparing for the dying process, which includes conversations in advance about expectations of the caregiver when the medical takes center-stage.

Living
4. Bringing life, projects, and people's news, with their spirit of continuing into the future, into the day to day.
5. Recollecting and savoring what has been lived, together and separately.
6. "Before I die" (i.e., helping get affairs in order, having the conversations, making the trips, etc. that the ill person wants and that the caregiver might regret not having made possible).
7. Making/practicing changes that the ill person would like to imagine continuing in the future.

Facilitating and empowering others
8. Go-between (in communication with others and arranging visits, virtual as well as in person).

9. Noticing and caring for the feelings and responses of others, including taking time to be with callers and visitors, being open to unexpected, in-the-present expressions, giving thanks.

Arranging
10. Financial, legal and healthcare wishes and paperwork.
11. Domestic (cooking, shopping, laundry, dog walking, snow shoveling, trash, keeping order, repairs, thinking ahead, tackling extra tasks [e.g., ice dams]).

Personal
12. Self care (stay fit, sleep, eat well so as to be present in the moment, judge well, recover from slip-ups, avoid distractedness given the inevitable unmet responsibilities outside caregiving).
13. Making space for one's own feelings and learning (including sadness about what the ill person will miss out on seeing, "I don't want to regret").
14. Envisaging the future.
15. Arranging coverage for responsibilities outside caregiving and for certain caregiving tasks (e.g., under #11) so as to have space for all the roles.

—-

Notice that most of these roles are difficult to delegate to others (despite the frequent offers of "let me know what I can do to help"). One approach to the demands of multiple roles might be to try to do one thing under each role each day. Another approach is to use quiet time before others are up for the Personal and for the Go-betweening (#8) so as to be more mindful and wholehearted in other roles during the day.

PETER
2 MARCH 2015

I think of you when I smell a Pinyon wood fire

TOM
1 MARCH 2015

Another time I think of Ann

Ann... I think of you when I read the news from Mexico.

TOM
8 MARCH 2015

I don't drink retsina often

I think of Ann when I drink retsina. (I don't drink retsina often, but when I do, I think of Ann.)

TOM
17 MARCH 2015

Green chiles on the menu

I think of you when I see green chile or sopapillas on the menu.

TOM
23 MARCH 2015

When I see peaches at the market

Ann... I think of you when I see peaches at the market.

TOM
3 APRIL 2015

When I drink Turkish coffee

I think of you when I drink Turkish coffee (just don't tell a Greek).

TOM
14 APRIL 2015

Always, we come back to chat and sit together to compare notes, respectively, of our recent journeys

Thank you for all you shared in our last visit, my dear friend. I think of you every day.

I keep going back to the quote from the explorer, John Charles Fremont (c. 1857, writing to a close friend, while following the Santa Fe Trail.). To me, it speaks of the depths of friendship and exchange possible with colleagues, friends, mentors.

> I am very far from either forgetting you or neglecting you, or in any way losing the old regard I had for you. There is **no time** to which I go back with more pleasure than that spent with you, for there was no time so thoroughly well spent; and of anything I may have learned, I remember nothing so well, and so distinctly, as what I acquired with you."

I think of our friendship, Ann, when I read it. I smile when I remember our friendship started and continued over dinners together as well as through our individual travels like Berkeley and Cornell, Paris and New York, which created long absences between us. And always, we come back to chat and sit together to compare notes, respectively, of our recent journeys.

As ever now, as in the past - despite distances of any name - our friendship continues. I appreciate it. And, I love you.

I am here for you. Call me anytime. I am close by.
Love,

PAULA
22 JULY 2015

Wonderful to hear your voice yesterday

To Ann, kindness of Peter. Ha, how many people know the latter phrase? (Thank you, I guess, Babou.) And who would think it would show up in an email? Well.

It was wonderful to hear your voice yesterday, but I could hear you work for breath. So, I think I'll keep up a bit more frequently by reviving some short emails rather than leave you breathless from chit and chat. I guess the theme is around "think of you when" or "thinking of you."

It's been quite a year to think of you when I read the news from Greece. "I shall wear the creditors' loathing with pride," said Yannis Varoufakis. Indeed.

When

Wolfgang Schäuble say Varoufakis does not understand his dream for the Euro

William Cohen says Robert Reich does not understand Goldman Sachs's role in re-financing Greece debt, or similarly

Jamie Dimon says Elizabeth Warren does not understand what's wrong with Glass-Steagal

You can be sure all of them perfectly understand, the reason Wolfgang, William, and Jamie fear and hate them.

Love,

TOMMY
29 JULY 2015

The square of Babel

Thinking of you each weekday going to and from my office just north of Times Sq.

Every morning and evening you can hear a Babel of languages and accents, Spanish, German, occasional French, Korean, Japanese, and some Australian. (I can pick up on some Australian.)

Some colleagues find the tourists tiresome, but I enjoy the swiveling faces and excited chatter, particularly of agog, say, 7 to 11-year-olds and thrilling packs of teenage girls and there oh-so-seen-it-all boy companions.

With much love,
mi hermana, su hermano--

TOMMY
1 AUGUST 2015

Aesthetic Tyrant, for Ann

Your mother was an aesthetic tyrant
you said to excuse your despotic taste.

I watched your slow descent to inspect
the new stair-rail. The carpenter stood

waiting, pleased with his work.
A moment is all you needed

to say *no, it'll have to go*.
Useless to ask you why,

since the stairs are too steep
for you now, this matters so.

Everything's wrong, you sigh
settling your bird-thin bones

among the cushions. *He didn't show me
the final drawings.* Control

is hard to come by these days.
Your body flouts the rules

you made, the garden's out
of reach, but still you know

each bed and row
planned in Spring has grown

into a flawless arrangement of color
and scent. Like the bowls you brought

from Mexico - a malachite flower
splashed at the bottom, careless

and practised as calligraphy. *You see
the hand that made it,*

you said. And the eye that chose it
has left its fastidious mark on me.

GAIL
4 AUGUST 2015

Morning thoughts, walking the dog around the Middlebury College campus

Here it is, the beginning of August, and already I can see the summer slipping away. The light has changed/is changing.

The trees are slightly less lustrous, their green is not fading (yet) so much as flattening out, and here and there little patches of yellow or brown are starting to show around the edges. They might represent nothing more than noshing insects or wind damage, but there they are, forerunners, seasonal intruders.

The grass is yellowing. Dandelions have long since passed, replaced by clovers and some little yellow buttercup-type blossoms whose name I do not know. The grass is getting tough and wiry, with some broadleaf growths that make me think of aquatic plants and some seed-bearing spikes thrusting out of the surrounding blades. Occasionally I discover a wild strawberry or two in my lawn. In Sweden, walking through the pasture surrounding an old farm-settlement that's now a national heritage site, we came upon copious wild strawberries, which we ate by the handful, notwithstanding the proximity of cowpies. To which I could only say, with a glance upward to make sure that Ingmar Bergman was watching, "Of course."

It's still dark outside at five o'clock when I get up, let the dog out, and sit at the end of the couch with my coffee and the Burlington Free Press, which was delivered to my doorstep a couple of hours earlier by a woman driving a beat-up Toyota, who's probably doing this as a second job. It's my favorite time of the day, the peaceful time when there's no exigency pressing at me, no one and nothing trying to get my attention. A little before six, I'll make a cup of chai and take it, along with the newspaper, upstairs to Emily. An hour later, I'll wake the boys up for school. Make that the boy. Make that ... wait a minute.

Only a few weeks ago, you could see the sky begin to lighten and hear the birds waking up at around three-thirty, then four, then five. Now they're sleeping in, almost till six. One by one or all at once, they check in, announce themselves. They seem to be mostly robins, either because they're the loudest or because they're the closest to the house. This summer there's been one particularly distinctive, really strident robin whose call I've come to anticipate, which I hear as something like, "Dickybird EATIT!" over and over, which never fails to make me smile. It's so insistent, so cranky.

And then.

And then, this morning, I slept in until just past six, when the light started to arrive. I lay there, listening, and heard nothing, no robins. Off in the distance a few cheeps and twerps from the smaller fry, and now and then a crow's call, but no "EAT IT!" The robins have gone, just like that, headed off to that place in New Jersey or the Delmarva Peninsula or for all I know Belize where they all go in the winter. They'll be back at the end of March, beginning of April. The ground will still be frozen solid, probably with a few inches of snow on it (though we don't seem to be getting nearly as much snow as we used to), and the birds will shiver in the trees without the strength or will even to be cranky about it. I think of them as tourists who booked the discount package at the off-season rate, though by now you'd think they'd know better. Don't get me wrong, I like the robins and I'm always glad to see them when they come back, but I find it hard to respect their intelligence. Or is that what they mean by Bird Brain?

So the season's change isn't always gradual. Sometimes the page turns and the next chapter arrives all at once. I turned seventy-five this week, which feels like a significant number, and I guess it's making me thoughtful about things like time and seasons. Visiting you last weekend pulled me right into the present; you radiate the focus of the moment. Yes, radiate. I bask in the warmth of you, Annie, even as you dwindle in flesh and fiber; it's in your eyes, which refuse to dwindle. Be comfortable, seek peace. I love you.

ALAN
9 AUGUST 2015

Ann-ness

Ann, thanks for sending your note via Peter. I have been thinking about it for a couple of days.

First of all, I am so sorry to hear about your mother! It makes me think of all the talking we've done about families, including your mother--how much we talk about them shows how much they matter, no matter what we are saying when we talk about them.

And the second thought I have been returning to is related: you have said that you are becoming much weaker. This, of course, is distressing to all of us who love you. But—not sure how to put this, so I am going to invent a word—your *Ann-ness* is not weaker. I could point to several things even in the short note that demonstrate this. It makes me feel so happy about the talks we've had.

Love you, sister,

RACHEL
17 AUGUST 2015

I am thinking of you

Dearest Ann.. Have been on the road visiting my dear friends in Marquette (Upper Peninsula of Michigan) and Beloit, WI and now headed to Cincinnati to see my mother and sisters and kids.

What a shock to hear about your mother's passing. My second thought—after imagining your shock and grief—was that I was glad she was spared dying after you. I can't help wondering how you are dealing with this news in the context of your days and nights right now.

I am glad you are being so clear with your needs and wants. And so I will send you a note.

You are constantly on my mind, dear Ann.

I am thinking of you as I hike up to a glorious view of Lake Superior.

I am thinking of you as I wade into the cold waters of the same lake, baking in the sun on a rock, like a lizard or a turtle.

I am thinking of you as watch a thunder and lightning storm roll across the prairie of southern Wisconsin.

I am thinking of you on the road as I listen to endless hours of podcasts, gazing at miles of cornfields peppered with McDonalds billboards—and the occasional fanatical pro life message [guaranteed to piss me off every single time].

I am thinking of you as I eat grilled veggies purchased from a soft spoken ponytailed farmer at the farmers' market.

I am thinking of you as I settle into a different bed every few nights, struggling to find sleep and listening to Thomas's breathing, wondering how long I will have the privilege of hearing it.

I am thinking of you when I get angry at Zoe—frustrated by something she is or is not doing. Finding myself NOT appreciating that I have her in my life. And catching myself.

I am thinking of you as we drive toward my sisters and 87-year old mother preparing myself to be open to them, to cherish them, to listen, to laugh, to share food, to trade stories. And to suppress the other companion—terribly familiar—impulses to focus on the negative.

I am thinking of you and what your living and dying are teaching me. And trying my best to be present with you—with as much of your rich and meaningful life as I know it—seeing you as endlessly beyond these impossibly hard months, weeks, days, hours while holding them, too.

In solidarity, and with love.

CHRIS
19 AUGUST 2015

I think of you every day

Just to remind you that I think of you every day!

You know I love my Oneida tableware, and I always think of my dad—who bought my first set for me when I was settling into my third story attic apartment in Milwaukee—and you, who so diligently found more Paul Reveres for me!

Love you and miss you,

HERZONIA
21 AUGUST 2015

Compassionate intelligence

Thinking of you and Ann today. We came home from Seattle to dahlias blooming in our yard and luscious tomatoes and corn from the farm stand nearby.

I hope your garden is prospering and that Ann is able to enjoy it still. I remember when I first met her with you and saw how well the two of you suit each other. When I think of her, she always comes to mind with her beautiful smile and her bright sparkling eyes that reflect her compassionate intelligence. I also hear her laughing at me for describing her in such a way.

LIZ TAYLOR
23 AUGUST 2015

Emma para mi querida Ann

Querida Ann, las dificultades del trabajo no me permitieron ir a verte en persona, pero tengo a un maravilloso mensajero a quien le he pedido te haga saber lo siguiente:

Las personas tienen muchas formas de sellar un afecto duradero. El rebozo que me regalaste es para mí este sello de una amistad verdadera de dos mujeres adultas y que dura a través del tiempo, traspasa la diferencia del idioma y la geografía.

Con este rebozo me envuelvo al levantarme de la cama y en la tarde para refugiarme durante una hora en mi propia intimidad y meditar, antes de dar la cara al nuevo día y antes de que la noche me encuentre con su silenciosa y fresca oscuridad. En mis cursos de meditación es compañero fiel durante días, horas, minutos. Su hermoso color oscuro armoniza con el tronco de los árboles.

Si hace frío o necesito sentirme protegida también lo tomo y siempre tengo en mente que no me regalaste un rebozo sino un refugio de lana que me protege, da calor al cuerpo y consuelo al corazón.

En mi rebozo te quedas mi querida Ann y al envolverme nos abrazamos sin importar la distancia.

Dear Ann, the difficulties of the job do not allow me to come see you in person, but I have a wonderful messenger whom I asked to tell you:

People have many ways to seal a lasting affection. The reboso [shawl] you gave me is a mark of a true friendship of two adult women and lasts over time, the difference goes beyond language and geography.

Wrapped in the reboso I get out of bed and in the afternoon take refuge for an hour in my own privacy and meditate before facing the new day and the night before I meet her silent and cool darkness. In my meditation courses it is a faithful companion for days, hours, minutes. Its beautiful dark color harmonizes with tree trunks.

If it's cold or I need to feel protected, I always take in mind that you gave me a reboso, a wool shelter, that not only protects me, it warms the body and comforts the heart.

You get in my reboso my dear Ann and we hug wrapped together regardless of distance.

EMMA
25 AUGUST 2015

Cackling in my heart with you

my beloved twin, it's already september. the light has shifted and there's a little chill here in azorean high region of the eastern atlantic.

rachel herzing came for a brief visit. we took a day trip south of lisbon to explore salt ponds along an estuary and peninsula that's now a vast park and bird sanctuary. we saw lots of flamingos padding through salt ponds. somewhere beyond an undulating rice paddy some shotgun blasts rousted about 100 storks. i never knew storks flock. my entire experience of them had been in relation to their immense nests—on power pylons, church steeples, and any convenient roof. later, while we wandered through a village some storks returned to their neighborhood of assorted nests. we stood listening and watching them clack their bills in long & intricate evening salutations. who would think these creatures are mute?

i'm reluctant to go back to the states even though i'll be happy to see my students and continue to explore our new neighborhood. the war between the people and the police will only get worse for the forseeable future.

my fall schedule is—as ever—overwhelming but also exciting. we'll be in cambridge sept 24-26 for a brief seminar at harvard. no sweat this time; walter johnson asked me and my dear friend and mentor cedric robinson to comment on a manuscript by a postdoc at walter's center. (talk about luxury!) we'll comment in viva, and then withdraw to hang out with our beloved partners and comment amongst ourselves.

cackling in my heart with you. the storks' clacking is a kind of cackling, or so i tell myself.

with all my love,

TWIN
3 SEPTEMBER 2015

Craig and the twins—Ruthie and Ann, September 2015

The honey and yoghurt remain wonderful

Hello my dear Ann and Peter. It's election day in Greece, so things are unusually quiet in the city. People go back to their towns and villages to vote.

I always think of you in Greece Ann. But this is not the Greece you and I discovered many years ago. Still the honey and the yoghurt remain wonderful.

You are in my thoughts every day
Much love

GAIL
20 SEPTEMBER 2015

The last heirloom tomatoes of the season

To Ann, kindness of Peter

Thinking of you eating the last heirloom tomatoes of the season.

TOM
6 OCTOBER 2015

Bananagrams

Rebecca, my niece, was here last weekend, visiting from Oaxaca. Had I told you that she's moved back there?

Will probably be in Mexico for at least two years, working with an NGO called Puente a la salud. She's heading a project that has to do with the production of amaranth.

She took an overnight bus and arrived Saturday morning, and went back on Sunday night, to be in Oaxaca on time to go to work! Enjoyed her visit, as usual. We caught up, went out for breakfast with friends of her parents who were visiting the DF, picked up stuff for her from my friend Juan's house on Bucareli, and thought of you as we played Bananagrams!

The rainy season seems to have tapered off. We had some very wet, grey days but now it's been quite warm and sunny. But as you well know, you never know; Mexico City weather can certainly be, as Novack used to say, sweater on, sweater off.

So just wanted to let you know we missed you while playing Bananagrams!

Love,

HERZONIA
7 OCTOBER 2015

A few thoughts on returning to a geographical place that purports to be a state of mind

Last week I traveled to San José/Sunnyvale to meet with a group of investors from Hong Kong.

My last foray into California was over ten years ago when I also met with investors trying to save us from closing the organic tilapia project in southwest Brazil. Then everything was closer in to San Francisco—now Silicone Valley.

It did not seem so desert-like then. Very disheartening to see California from the airplane and then to look close up at cement front yards, succulents around the houses, green established trees, but everything else shades of brown. I saw one squirrel. Maybe it has always been thus, but I don't remember it that way.

Of course, I guess that that has to be offset by the bicycles, fresh food, laid back business style, and those things that make California attractive to an East Coaster. Perfect weather—of course, no rain.

But what can you really do with a one-layer society. That is everything radiates from strip malls, all housing one story, car an absolute necessity and those roads and traffic jams—the envy of Puerto Rico's development model. Even our 30-year drought this year seems to be copying.

There was a convention in Silicone Valley and I finally found a room in a 1958-built motor hotel in Santa Clara. I was plainly in Korea-town and had to pass through Thailand and Bombay to get to Sunnyvale. As I looked for the omnipresent Mexicans, I was just amazed by the ethnic diversity. Made for good eating.

I think the Hong Kong group will finally finance our aquaculture/ microalgae project. This coming week will tell.

think of you often.
All my love,

JORGE
1 NOVEMBER 2015

What I see here

For a relative in the very early stage of diagnosis and treatment for a serious illness and for their family as caregivers:

• My here is quite some distance (=understatement) from your here.

• Autumn is coming to an end, today was rainy and cold, the last leaves are being stripped off the trees, it is dark by 5pm. We are heading into a second winter with Ann's illness. Time has many cadences. Who knew it would not all be over by now? But who can imagine that Ann will see another autumn? Sometimes so much changes so quickly; sometimes illness progresses so slowly.

• Almost everyone has had a close experience death, dying, cancer. So I ask—and Ann insists—not to be seen as something special or heroic or….

• One thing I do end up conveying to visitors and other inquirers, who commiserate about the sadness, is that I, as caregiver, have a different position—I've got a job to do, day to day, and I don't fast-forward so much to the sad (or scary) future.

• At one point, perhaps just before Ann's curative treatment stopped, I wanted to empower well-wishers, asking them to write about what having Ann in their life has meant. But Ann was not so interested in this—"no eulogies yet" (not while she's alive; indeed, not when she's dead). Savoring the life lived, Ann might now say, is asking her to be ready to say goodbye to her life. I support her in resisting that, while at the same time knowing that I have to support her as she moves towards becoming prepared for that.

• For nearly nine months we have been under hospice/palliative care, which frees us from the noises, proddings, waiting, and disruptions of the hospital and clinic. We have autonomy, control, quiet. We have one person, Karla, who visits frequently, who has experience with other people in similar situations, who can provide perspective on the ups and downs, the cycle of good days and not so good. This is a wonderful relationship and sharing of the weight.

• When I can I think and write, trying, as is my bent, to make ideas fit together in the various areas I think about. I do this in part because it helps me not feel ground down, and so I can keep being a more or less attentive caregiver. But I also do it because I imagine that, if I were very ill, I would feel some urgency in getting my ideas out on paper. Ann, however, reads mostly junk books—it is too tiring to do anything more. She knows her day-to-day focus has to be on keeping as healthy as her illness allows.

• One of my little thinking-through projects was to define the multiple caregiving roles of caregivers, a blog post I only now have made public [see p. 181]. (This is different issue from saying that caregivers have multiple life roles, such as holding down a job, coaching the soccer team, and so on.) It takes mindfulness to shift among caregiving roles and, especially when tired, I have missed making shifts and misread cues. Oh well.

• One of the roles is "bringing life, projects, and people's news, with their spirit of continuing into the future, into the day to day." Vann is great at this.

• As a caregiver, especially when I look after my health and wellbeing (which I mostly do by taking Gilla for a walk and being outdoors twice a day) has the shadow of knowing that I will be the survivor in this journey with Ann. I can be a solid support, but I'm not with the patient all the way. Then Ann interrupts this survivor's guilt by making clear that the most important part of the job I am doing is to be there, for her to be reassured that there is a reliable companion in the journey, someone she knows she can hold on to. We both miss that holding on when, on some Tuesdays, I go to campus to teach for the evening. Which I did last night and so am very short of sleep. I will edit this now and send it in the morning if it stands up to the light of a new day.

• With deep love—and understanding that your here and nows will unfold in their own way.

PETER
11 NOVEMBER 2015

Reminding her and us of the unexpected friendship

Dear Ann, This photo is Margarida and mini-Gilla, the little plush dog you gave her in 2012

that is still present in her life today, reminding her and us of the unexpected friendship between a child and a dog living so far away.

We send all our love to you and your family and friends.

PATRÍCIA
27 NOVEMBER 2015

Sad news

Dear friends & family, Ann died this morning, simply stopping breathing around 7.

On Thursday she'd made the first toast—with thanks and love, to life—at our small Thanksgiving gathering. She savored every flavor and bite, from the prosecco to the Mexican mole on the Turkey to the pumpkin pie.

Yesterday she weakened and slept a lot and, in the evening insisted on being moved back to our bed, out of the hospital bed she'd used for just three nights. A patient and caring hospice nurse organized the transition and taught us—her sister, Pamela, had arrived—how to care for someone who might be in bed for longer than was, alas, to be the case.

We have had a wonderful mix of primary support during the 16 months since her diagnosis of ovarian cancer and have been buoyed by the regular notes and emails about life, work and families, past experiences and future hopes. Ann insisted on a pot luck party—no speeches, but it is important to me that everyone is able to acknowledge what it means to have had Ann(ie) Blum in our lives. Stay tuned for arrangements. (The party will probably be on Sunday 13th.) For now I'm looking at some quiet time to reflect and eat down a well-stocked fridge. Vann, Gilla, Pamela, and husband Richard will be around; I won't invite phone calls and visits just yet.

love,

PETER
28 NOVEMBER 2015

A great team of caregivers

Karla, the hospice nurse; Pamela, the sister who visited for a couple of days each week; Grace, who came for the evenings twice a week in the fall.

Karla, Pamela, Grace—Caregivers extraordinaire to Ann, December 2015

Remembering

In the rising of the sun, and in its going down, we remember her.

In the blowing of the wind, and in the chill of winter, we remember her.
At the rebirth of spring, at the blueness of skies, and in the warmth of summer, we remember her.
In the rustling of the leaves and in the beauty of autumn, we remember her.
When we are weary, and in need of strength, we remember her.
When we are lost and sick at heart, we remember her.
When we have joys we crave to share, we remember her.
When we have decisions that are difficult to make, we remember her.
When we have achievements that are based on hers, we remember her.
So long as we live, she too shall live, for she is now a part of us, as we remember her.

A Jewish prayer, sent by

RACHEL
28 NOVEMBER 2015

Some immediate threads on www.facebook.com/ann.blum.7

Ann was one of those people whom you describe with memories rather than adjectives.

One of my favorites is the relish with which she discussed the less-than-scholarly relationships among the 19th-century paleontologists Cope and Marsh. We had similar tastes in fiction, but Ann also read much more serious stuff than I. When I heard the news, I realized that I had always expected to sit and talk with her again.
MAXINE SCHMIDT

i was 21 when i started working there. Ann was 30. i remember her being thrilled when she got carded. i remember how graceful, smart, artistic, and funny she was. i remember feeling lucky whenever i was invited to hang out with you two. i remember how lovely her hands were and how she used them to talk.
MARA SIEGEL

At conferences and research trips to Mexico Ann always took time to grab a delicious meal, a coffee, a glass of white wine or an amazing limonada to catch up on life and our research.

Thank you for sharing so much of your time and wisdom with me.
I will always remember that smile and laughter- we shared so much of both over the last 12 years. During our visit together this past May, we laughed, reminisced and looked toward the future over a Sancerre Sauvignon Blanc. We said all the things we needed to say to each other. We said goodbye. I feel blessed to have had her in my life, both personally and professionally. She will be missed by all whose life she touched. As I said when we embraced in the kitchen that sunny morning in May, "I love you my friend."
MARÍA L.O. MUÑOZ

Ann and Bill French really were a dynamic duo in Oaxaca. One of my favorite memories with her (besides early morning walk/runs and just her fun, kind, energetic spirit) was going into one of the archives in downtown Oaxaca and deciphering some of the colonial documents. As a modernist, I don't work with the older materials, ever. I loved doing that, and will cherish that memory. It made me realize how fortunate I was to be there, with her, looking into the mind and rationale of someone who had written the words in front of me centuries before. Fantastic stuff, beautiful experience. Thank you, Ann.
KELLEY CASTRO

i have so many memories of working with ann in Oaxaca—in seminar, on our morning walks on the cerro del fortin almost every day, in coffee shops, restaurants, searching for the perfect frutero--she made me see things in my work in different ways, she modelled how to treat everyone with respect, warmth, and great caring, she inspired me to try to be better, and she enriched the lives of all who took part in the program—i'll always have our conversations from those walks—so glad we could share so much in Oaxaca.
BILL FRENCH

Ann was a uniquely generous scholar and human being.

She always had time to sit down for a coffee or a meal and listen, really listen, to what was going on in one's academic and personal life. She would furrow her brow in intense concentration as she took in what one said and then, kindly and quietly, offer advice. Often she would explode into laughter and an easy smile at life's little quirks.
GABRIELA SOTO LAVEAGA

I am heartbroken, but more grateful than ever for Ann's mentorship, which saved me in grad school and my early career. She leaves a legacy of generosity and integrity. And I will always swoon over the precision of her prose!
ALEXANDRA PUERTO

A marvelous historian of adoption and childhood in Mexico.

Her work has contributed a great deal to how I think, but more, I will always remember her as an archive-friend in the long days in the periodical collections at UNAM. We would have lunch together every day, talking endlessly about the history of children in Mexico, our work, and our lives. Above all I remember her laughing—hard, without reserve, full of joy and amusement at our collective absurdity.
LAURA BRIGGS

She did have a great laugh, and a wicked sense of humor.
MAXINE SCHMIDT

¿Cómo no estar triste? ¿Cómo no llorar su pérdida?

Pero ahora mismo me tomo una copa de jerez en su memoria porque la alegría que marcaba su cara con una gran sonrisa era uno de sus rasgos característicos y el que quiero recordar! Qué viva Ann!
EFRAÍN BARRADAS

Hemos perdido un ser humano de integridad, valores excepcional y luchadora incansable en su vida academica y personal. Tuve la suerte de trabajar con Ann en varias capacidades… Ann viene de una familia de academicos y fue una alumna ejemplar del recinto que amo: UMass Boston.
DANIEL ORTIZ ZAPATA

Obituary from UMass Boston

Dr. Ann S. Blum, Associate Professor and former Department Chair of the Latin American and Iberian Studies Department (2007 – 2012), passed away on November 28 at her home in Arlington, MA, 16 months after being diagnosed with ovarian cancer.

Professor Blum received her B.A. in American Studies at UMass Boston in 1986 after working many years as an archivist in the Museum of Comparative Zoology (MCZ) at Harvard University, teaching writing classes, and freelance editing. While at the MCZ she wrote a first draft of what became her award-winning book, *Picturing Nature: American Nineteenth-Century Zoological Illustration* (Princeton University Press, 1993). She went on from UMass Boston to complete a Ph.D. in Latin American History at the University of California, Berkeley (1998), and returned to our University in in 1998 as a Lecturer, then in 2000 as an Assistant Professor of Latin American Studies in the Department of Hispanic Studies (now the Department of Latin American and Iberian Studies) where she developed and sustained an exemplary career.

She often described herself as a social historian yet Professor Blum produced a scholarly body of work of broader scope moving easily across institutional, political, and economic methodologies. Her research examined childhood and adoption, connections among the urban poor and their children, family-oriented public policies and institutions, family practices and class formation, social reform, and nation formation. Her work has been published in multiple articles, essay collections, and monographs. Results are impressive when high-level scholarship is informed by a deep compassion. This kind of fusion lent a special weight to Professor Blum's work on working-class families and explains why it commands so much respect from her peers. Her ideas were fully developed in her second book, *Domestic Economies: Family, Work, and Welfare in Mexico City, 1884-1943* (University of Nebraska Press, 2009), which received an Honorable Mention at the 2010 American Historical Association Conference on Latin American History for the Mexican History Book Prize.

Her subsequent research concerned the intersections of family life and identities with community and national narratives in Mexico. Using a rich collection of men's life writing, she began to explore the "intimate histories" of authors' daily work, social roles, childhood and affective lives within a world bound by family and community. She was seeking to elucidate masculine and paternal renderings of domestic space and family life.

Since 1999, Professor Blum served as a faculty member in the Oaxaca Summer Institute, a month-long graduate seminar on modern Mexican history and culture held in Oaxaca, Mexico. As her involvement with the seminar grew, she became co-director of one of the institute's major components dedicated to gender history, history of the family, and life writing. She had a lasting impact as a role model and mentor, influencing the ways in which dozens of graduate students conceptualized their research and developed their professional identities as students and later as faculty at various universities.

At UMass Boston, Professor Blum amassed an equally stellar teaching record. Her success and dedication are reflected in the courses she taught: "Latin America: Contemporary Society and Culture," "Food, Culture and Society in Latin America," "Latin American Popular Cultures," "Latin America Before 1800," "Reform and Revolution in Latin America," "Latin American Film," "Hispanics in Urban America," and "Modern Mexico," among others. Her skills as a teacher and mentor are evident in the high value students placed on her teaching, in the labor-intensive approach to student-centered teaching reflected, and her deep commitment to student advising.

On campus and beyond, Professor Blum was an exemplary colleague, generous with her time and ideas, and a model of supportive and critical engagement with the work of peers, students, and administrators. Her service record is a model of excellence and integrity. At UMass Boston she was widely known and respected as a firm defender of faculty governance, and of students' and workers' rights. She was often called upon to serve on complex and crucial committees: NEASC, General Education, Salary Anomalies, administrators' reviews, AQUAD reviews and all types of promotions. One of her major contributions was the reconceptualization and the academic and administrative transformation of the former Department of Hispanic Studies into a new and innovative Department of Latin American and Iberian Studies, where students approach the Latin American and Iberian world guided by scholars of different disciplines (history, translation, anthropology, literature, and linguistics). To help establish and support the newly created unit, Professor Blum mentored junior faculty, modeling and encouraging thoughtful service, solid teaching, sound advising, meaningful research and, above all, strict professional integrity.

Professor Blum's generous spirit, calm demeanor, gentle tenacity, unfailing integrity, courage, compassion, and sense of humor are ingrained in the fiber of the LAIS Department and are an indelible part of our institution. She will be deeply missed by all who knew her.

Ann Blum is survived by her husband Peter Taylor, her son Vann, her sister Pamela, her brother Tom, and a wide circle of family and friends. A public event to honor Dr. Blum's life and work will be held in spring 2016 at the University. Reflections that capture some aspects of having had Professor Blum in our lives can be viewed and contributed to at http://bit.ly/annblum.

The Department of Latin American and Iberian Studies is establishing a scholarship to honor her memory. In lieu of flowers please send a charitable gift to the University of Massachusetts Boston c/o "The Ann S. Blum Memorial Scholarship in Latin American Studies" to University Advancement, 100 Morrissey Blvd., Boston MA 02125, payable to "UMass Boston."

CLARA, EFRAÍN, REYES, SHAUNA, SANDRA, PEGGY, SUSAN, MARIA, BILL, AND PETER
2 DECEMBER 2015

Her work stands as foundational

As we both know, we were so fortunate to know her, to have her smile and positive energy in our lives.

I had just spoken of her last week at the History of Science Society meeting to a student interested in the history of scientific illustration. Although she left that field so long ago, her work stands as foundational.

But most of all, I feel such sadness of the loss of an especially wonderful human being. But I take consolation knowing how lovingly you accompanied her down this path and were with her until the end. That is the way to share the end with those we love. Not easy, but the only way to do it...

PAM HENSON
3 DECEMBER 2015

How graceful and freshly pretty she was and how lucky you were

Words are scarce in a moment like this, when one loses the lifetime partner, your sweet Ann.

I haven't had the opportunity to know Ann better, except for that one time in Coimbra when she visited you and Gilla, where you both offered us a lovely dinner. I had the chance to talk to Ann in my slow and bad spoken english, which she was kind to patiently listen with a smile :) I remember to think how graceful and freshly pretty she was and how lucky you were :)

I'm glad, in a way, to know that Ann was full of love and her dearest friends around her in her last days, and, from the messages and your letter, I see how she touched indelibly her dearest friends and everyone who knew her.

May she continue to be an inspiration to you and all those she held dearest...

MARTA
3 DECEMBER 2015

To be near Ann was to feel the warmth of her

Ann with her gentleness and her fabulous sense of humor. Her infectious laugh.

She was a world of ideas and convictions and she seemingly led from so deep in her heart. I was always grateful to be in conversation with her whenever our paths crossed.

That I feel so much right now, after not having crossed paths with Ann for quite some time, once again reminds me that when we are thusly touched and moved, we carry that within us always. Thank you Ann for touching my life.

My heart grieves too.

I send much love and light especially to Peter and Vann and her siblings and to all those so very fortunate to have been so close to her.

Abrazos,

SHAARI
3 DECEMBER 2015

Supportive connections you two were continually building

Thank you for your account of the last gathering and of Ann's final days and decisions. I was grateful for it, as I have been for all of your state-of-the-clan reports through the years.

The scenes it describes are just what I would have expected, knowing your family; the supportive connections you two were continually building with such care and sensitivity were clearly a comfort in the end.

You and Vann are in my thoughts, as are those others who must be feeling her loss most acutely. I'm glad she had you all around her.

Love,
SUSAN OYAMA
3 DECEMBER 2015

On covering suitcases

It's Friday last, early evening. Ann has slept a lot after a Thanksgiving day of toasts and tastes.

Awake, she insists on returning to our bed, out of the hospital bed of the last few nights. "Now I can focus on strengthening." She repeats this.

Soon it becomes harder for her to talk; the phrase "I need..." is begun several times but not completed. I am able to respond to "Water," to "Breathing" (a request to adjust her posture so she can breathe better). But then, she looks directly into my eyes: "I need to cover the suitcases." To calm her, I reply: "It's OK, I've done that." She pushed firmly back: "No you haven't."

Interpretation is open, but looking back at these, her last full sentences, I favor "cover" as "hide." In hiding the suitcases, she wasn't ready to leave us. And she was advising me, her restless partner of 30 years, to appreciate where I am—not seeking to move on to something/where else.

PETER
5 DECEMBER 2015

Brilliant and loving human being

I absolutely thought she was just an incredibly brilliant and loving human being.

I will never forget first meeting the two of you with Ray outside of your home that summer day in 2012. You both were and continued to be so thoughtful and generous with me. I am so sorry for your loss...

SUE HARRIS O'CONNOR
6 DECEMBER 2015

Her stories and conversation was always a pleasure

Ann was surely a special person and one of my favorite clients to have sitting in my chair.

Her stories and conversation was always a pleasure, I truly enjoyed her company. She always seemed to be so happy in life and that is really more important than longevity...

HAMID
7 DECEMBER 2015

So warm, so gracious and so centred

It is really hard to appreciate that such a life force as Ann has gone. We have such happy memories of time spent with you both, and having you at our wedding in 1985.

I am looking at the photo of that event now, with Ann elegant in a black and white skirt. She was so warm, so gracious and so centred....

With all our warm wishes and love,

HILARY AND CHARLIE
7 DECEMBER 2015

Living under constraints, less emphasis on death and dying

※

This blog post was not made public at first because it seemed too definite, too sure about the generality of its view of caring for someone "living under constraints." Please read it as one facet of a crystal that continues to shift its shape.

To speak or think of "dying" is to keep the focus on a seriously ill person being dead in the foreseeable future. Looking ahead to the person soon being dead shapes what others—the caregivers (or other visitors)—do (unless we want to rely on there being life after death). A different view and different practice follows once we insert the category *living under constraints* into the picture and separate this from looking ahead to a time when the person cared for is dead.

Under this category, the caregivers provide the best support for the living that is happening day by day, with its ups and downs, of the person cared for. The person experiencing this consistency of support gains a rock to hold on to until the end—especially towards the end. One part of this support is to help the person cared for *not* to be asked to say goodbye to their life and, at the same time, helping them become prepared to do so at some possible point in the future.

For the person cared for, living under constraints comes unavoidably with frustrations at those constraints. It is not surprising if depression follows. That can be readily mixed together with sadness about the loss of being part of the future that caregivers (and other survivors) will have. The person cared for won't be there to hear of their highlights, accomplishments, reflections, or to be depended on in times of others' needs. Yet, instead of dwelling that impending loss, the person cared for can enlist the efforts of caregivers to put things into place that the person would like to envision being in that future, from having a tree seedling planted to caregivers getting into healthy habits (such as consistent exercises to reduce back pain). The emphasis is on living.

Does living under constraints mean missing out on making opportunities for important conversations and interactions, which might set up the person cared for or the caregivers to be regretful? For example, the person cared for may be less anxious about their decline if they've had a chance to reminisce and appreciate what they have done in their life. There may also be things the person cared for and caregivers need to say to each other—hopes, instructions, confessions, forgiving, reconciling.

Perhaps. But, alternatively, the person cared for may need to reminisce only if that was what would regularly happen in conversation anyway, that is, before illness entered the picture. People could decide to say the needed things as part of living, without waiting for illness to move them into roles of person cared for or caregiver. Indeed, that's one thing that the person cared for would like to envision in the future—before as well as after they are dead.

Seeing that living under constraints can be well supported is a significant lesson for anyone who lives past the death of the person cared for—it is possible to *live* under constraints.

PETER
8 DECEMBER 2015

Ann and Gilla

A sweetie pie yellow lab named Gilla found an amazing family with Peter, Ann, and Vann. They hired a dog walker in Feb 2006. That was me.

As many of you know Gilla is the best pup and much of the credit goes to her wonderful family. I loved stopping by and having a chat with Gilla's owners when I picked her up for a hike. Ann had the warmest smile and the greatest hugs. I was always amazing how such a petite woman could light up a room. We would chat about Gilla's adventures, her travels, and writing topics. So many years and so many everyday conversations. I will miss that.

Every year for Christmas I would receive a Panettone Bread; it was tradition. Ann made arrangements before she passed to make sure I received one. It was waiting for me when I came for Gilla. I didn't get a chance to say thank you and goodbye. I'm so thankful Ann, Peter, Vann, and Gilla came into my life and Ann will always have a special place in my heart.

JEN
11 DECEMBER 2015

Memories from far and near

Peter: What I want to do today is give people a chance to reflect or share a simple story or just an idea about Ann. Not a eulogy, not everything about Ann. Just something that captures how having Ann in your life has influenced you. I will start.

Ann and I have always shared our study. There would be phone calls that would be taken when we're in the same room, and I'd often hear people ask Ann how she is, or how the semester is going. I would know about various strife that was going on, and Ann would never mention that. She would zoom right in on what was going well or well enough to focus on. So there was no sharing of what the downers were. It was always the sharing the things we could celebrate and appreciate and build upon. And I think that's had an influence on my life.

Zellman Warhaft

I'm Zellman Warhaft and sitting beside me is, Gail, my wife. We got to know Peter and Ann in Ithaca, I can't think when now. I just have a few little things that I want to add. First, that I saw Ann twice in the last months. Once in the summer when I visited, and once just a few days before she died, just before Thanksgiving. I think of both of the visits in terms of color. The first visit in the late summer everything was blooming in the wonderful garden. It's hard going up the stairs and knowing how to bring some certain focus. I talked about the garden and then I thought it'll be good to go into the garden and I took lots of photos of the garden. I showed them to Ann. She loved seeing them, and she said, "Oh, you haven't taken one of the little tree right at the corner." So, I went down and I took one of the tree as well. It's very symptomatic of her wonderful eye for detail and completeness. She wanted to see the *whole* garden, and it meant so much to her. It meant much to me that she appreciated it, and that was focusing so well and that she always was doing art throughout her illness.

And the second time was a harder time—well they're both difficult times. The second time it was dark and wintery. The garden was dark and all the color had left. And she was looking darker. The only thing I could do then, really, was Gail sent shells from Sanibel. And I shared them with Ann at that time.

I think of those two visits very much, and I think always of her tremendous sense of wanting to have all of the details, all of the accuracy, so she could have a complete picture of things.

Gail Holst Warhaft

I just got back from Greece last night. Ann, I know, had spent quite a long time in Greece, so would have normally shared stories about Greece, since she would've asked me how Greece was. It was one of the many things I shared with her.

You know that I said a lot of what I had to say to her in the form of poems that I sent her. I used to be rather envious of Ann, she seemed to have a degree of control about her life and decisions and aesthetic that I never had. I always used to think of her as one of those people who, very early in life discovered a sense of what she thought was right, and what she wouldn't put up with. Aesthetically, she wouldn't put up with *anything* that wasn't to her taste. She'd rather sit in a bare room with one beautiful cushion in a corner, than have it full of furniture. I always rather envied this completely definite personality, and I think she maintained that right to the end. The last time I saw her she was *so* in control- and I was sort of verging on out of control because, of course, I was terribly upset. And it was *she* who was comforting me, not the other way around. She was saying, "Now, I'm at peace, I know what's happening, and don't be sad." You know, as if I was the person who needed some sort of comforting. I'm sure she shared that with you and a lot of her friends.

Nancy Pollak

Hi, yes, just hearing what Gail and Zellman are saying is so consistent with what I know of Ann. Also, what I saw when I visited her in August. When we were also talking about the garden. I had brought a plant and then I thought, "What if this plant doesn't measure up?" But Ann was saying something about the garden and she actually said, "The person is more important. It was interesting because, yes, she had this sort of aesthetic sense of how everything should be, but she also had that other thing that was so open and welcoming to people. And also what Gail was saying about Ann being the one to comfort. Again, she seemed to want to make me feel better, I was just astonished by that.

Gilly Taylor

I've got memories in chronological order. First of all, going to meet you and Ann. John [Peter's father] had noticed that something was happening, and we arranged to meet in Italy, in Rome. We had that Christmas dinner in Rome. I didn't know you were planning going north, and we went up to Florence and Ann knew *so much* about the culture and *everything!* She knew the places to go and it was so wonderful.
I found out all about her mother being here, and John, her father, not liking sea voyages. And I thought of him being in the Battle of Coral Sea, where Australia was saved from the Japanese Invasion, really.

And then the gardens, I mustn't talk too much, but I love the garden that she had with the swimming pool and the balcony garden that you both had. I was *pleased* to hear Zellman took those photographs because I was thinking Ann when she couldn't get down the stairs, "She *must get* photos of the garden."

And *Picturing Nature*, the book that I've shared with so many people whenever they come to my place. The way that she's inspired people. Always the knowledge—and her laughing eyes in that lovely picture you sent out with Tom and Pamela and Ann *really* laughing.

The other time was when, I think, at Cornell, and I was just reading all these scholarly books and things, and Ann said, "You've gotta read something else. " She gave me David Lodge. *Every* academic should read this. She knew just which one to give me. And helping to choose some suitcases and the different ways of packing… And most of all, the Glen Helen gorge where I saw all of you and your partners. That was the most precious week and coming all that way and meeting up. And I thought that, when Andrew was talking about the special bonding with Georgia. Georgia and Ann got away in a bar and drinking their white wine together and were talking about taming the

Taylors. That was very good because I think that both Ann and Georgia had a lot to do with taming the Taylors.

Sally Taylor

I'm Pete's sister, his older sister. Sorry, I'm getting emotional here. I only met Ann three times. The first time was in 1988, when Pete and Ann were in Berkeley. My partner and I were living in Northern California and we met in Stinson Beach. There's a beautiful photograph my other brother took of Ann, Pete, me and Andrew—actually, I think my partner took the photo of my family all together. I always loved looking at that photo, and particularly at Ann because she wore these distinct large glasses that just seemed to be part of her style. You know, it was just incredibly stylish, and she was just sitting there in her bikini—it was a cold day so she had a pullover on. You know, sitting on the sand looking very classy and that was just my first impression of her, you know, this classy looking woman but also highly intelligent, with an amazing sense of style.

Then I came to visit Ann and Peter in Boston in 1999, that's eleven years later, and stayed in their former house. I don't really remember much of that visit, except it was really enjoyable and amazing how easy it is to speak to Ann, even though we didn't know each other very well and we had led different kind of lives. There's something about the art of conversation that Ann just radiated naturally. And I've often pondered about that—what is the art of conversation—because in a way, it's a lost art. I was thinking about what it was in Ann that made it so easy to converse with her, and I think it was a combination of, not just her intelligence and wide breadth of interest in things and curiosity about things, so therefore, ability to talk about a diverse range of topics. But also just her—it's like politeness that I've often noticed in Americans who've come from sort of "well-bred Eastern U.S. backgrounds"—just a capacity to listen to others and absorb and assimilate what others are saying. So you really feel that the person is listening and absorbing what you're saying, and his response comes from not just parroting back, but assimilating that and then speaking their own feelings back. So there's an actual real conversation going on. I reflect on how rare that actually is, that you'd have that quality of interchange and relationship in the world. It's really special to have spent that time with her conversing, and to feel the unique aspects of her personality—and rare, really, that you'd have somebody of that artfulness in relation with the spoken word.

In 2008, Pete was going on an academic visit to Portugal. I'd been considering going to Europe, and our mother, Joyce (Gilly), was talking about coming. I don't think it would've happened except that Ann just said to all of us, "You MUST go! You must make the most of this time to be together." And those words that Pete introduced to us -get together with "celebrate, appreciate and build upon." I feel like Ann had such an eye for the moments in life that were important to celebrate, appreciate, and build upon. It was really her enthusiasm and encouragement that got all three of us to make that trip. And it was the most extraordinary trip because Mum was seventy-eight at the time, so it wasn't easy for her to travel on her own, but being with her two children, we were able to make that long flight to Europe. Pete hired a car in Portugal and researched the interesting places to go in Portugal and Spain, and we spent the most wonderful week in the car together travelling through incredible and historic places, like Cordoba and Grenada. I always feel incredibly grateful to Ann for insisting that we make the most of that opportunity.

And the last time together I'll just speak of briefly. It was my wish for my sixtieth birthday that all of the family came together, which is no mean feat, given that we live in different parts of the world. Near my sixty-first birthday—it took a bit of planning by my sister, Anne—everybody came together in Central Australia, which has the monolithic rock, Uluru, that most people are familiar with. And Ann came as well, with Pete. All of us went to this rather remote and run-down motel. We stayed there for about five days, and each day, Mum would wait at the motel and the rest of us—all of us brothers and sisters and partners would go off walking on the Larapinta Trail. It was completely, for me anyway, the most remarkable experience. We were in the desert on this trail through gently undulating rocky desert, with sparse trees. And you come across these amazing deep-blue water holes against the red rocks. Visually it was stunning. We'd be walking along together, forming different walking partners, everybody talking away. And the fact that Ann was there sharing that with us, I was so grateful that she made the effort to make the trip. She could've gone to Mexico and got on with her studies. It was such a great time and conversing with Ann was such a pleasure.

Thanks, Pete, for this opportunity to say a few words, and I'm sorry I can't be there in person.

Liz Taylor

I've been thinking back about the time that Peter and Ann had met and were getting married. I knew Peter and then met Ann through Peter, and was so thrilled to meet Ann because—your brother said this so well—that you had just met Ann and knew she was the right person for you, Peter. I remember feeling the same way at that time.

I want to tell a funny and true story that brings back a lot of memories of that time. When Peter and Ann got married, Len and I, my husband, tried really hard to think about what kind of gift we should give them to represent their union and celebrate their lives together, and capture something about them that really struck us. So we decided to give them a very unique bowl. And I remember bringing it by and giving it to them and Peter saying something like, sixteen, maybe twenty-three, maybe you'll remember the exact number of your many friends who also had given you bowls. I thought that was pretty funny, and I still think it's funny to this day. But what I've been contemplating for the past week is, why a *bowl*? So I just have a few thoughts about that.

I know that we were very struck by the lovely gatherings that you and Ann gave. The pot-lucks we were invited to and the conversation that wasn't just about trivialities. It was talking about where we were going, and who we were at the time, and what our lives meant to us. We were also acknowledging that this was a gathering with food, that food played an important role. I remember how Ann and you would take the time to create space for the food and have beautiful bowls, and utensils—that the aesthetics were important. So that, of course, made us think of giving both of you a unique bowl for food at your pot-lucks.

I also know I was responding to the very precise and thoughtful way that the two of you created a life together. It's something that has strongly influenced me and that I've tried to emulate within my married life. The very thoughtful merging of two lives. A relationship that's based on shared values, and shared visions, and shared aesthetics. But also one that acknowledges the tension and the difference between two people that celebrates what they create together, as well. And how, if we are fortunate enough, brings out the best in the other person.

On this thought about the bowls and about Ann, let me say that one of the things I treasured about Ann, among the many other things that people have mentioned here, is her ability to celebrate you, Peter. The fact that the two of you *together* could create a life and a way of being in the world that brought out and highlighted the things that were both special and best about each other.

And then I would like to comment that I doubt that Ann and you have any of those bowls because of the spartan life that Ann preferred to live. I just look back on it and I laugh—I don't think I chose the bowl that Ann particularly liked. And you know what? That is fine with me because that is one of the other things that I liked about Ann. I think Zellman and Gail commented on so clearly that she had a strong sense of aesthetics and the way things should be.

Peter

About bowls—I think it might be something about people getting older and slightly more conservative, but what people give us now is the salad spoons, an interesting pair of spoons, rather than the bowl itself. So they don't take the risk of getting the wrong bowl. When one of our teak bowls cracked after many, many years, I did find one online. It was perfect and I was so pleased—*I* knew it was perfect, I didn't even need Ann's approval, but it *was* a great replacement.

Gail

I wanted to get in on the bowl conversation—Ann and bowls. I have a number of bowls that remind me of Ann. She gave me several of them. We both had a love of painted pots and she had given me wonderful bowls.

I remember going for a wonderful walk with Ann. I was staying with you for just a day or two in Boston, and we went for this walk where we discovered that this house that she'd grown up in was for sale. And she said, "We just have to go in." It wasn't really an open house, though it did say "For Sale," so we just marched into the house. Ann was telling me exactly where she slept, where her mother slept, where her father slept—and she was so excited to be able to get into this house that had been her childhood house.

Then she took me to a nearby Indian shop where there were antique shop where there were beautiful bowls, beautiful pottery bowls. We went through them and we kept saying, "This is the one, *this* is the most beautiful one." We both sort of fell in love with this particular bowl and she said, "Just buy it, just have it." I would've hesitated because it was both heavy and fragile, but she said, "This is the bowl you have to have." So I remember carrying home this beautiful old Indian bowl, which I still treasure. Every time I look at it I think of Ann, and the last thing she gave me was a pair of Mexican bowls with this very simple green design. She said, "You know, I thought, 'It's just so wonderful and so like the sort of pots I buy when I'm in Greece." She said to me, "You know what we'd like? You and I'd like to see the hand that's painting, the hand that's moved inside that bowl." It brings her back so vividly, what we shared about the beautiful bowl we liked.

Zellman

I would just like to say a few words. Others have commented on the relationship between Peter and Ann, but your personalities are quite different. The unity and the visions you had were so similar. It was a wonderful thing for Gail and me to see that.

The other thing that I wanted to mention, which is hard for Peter, is how amazing he's been over these many, many, many long months. It's something that I've watched, and it's been an example of strength and love that has just been something amazing to see.

Peter

Thank you.

Gilly

I'm wearing a scarf at the moment, it's one of the lovely things she gave me. It will *always* be just right, just what I need to put on with so many things.

Tom

Ann always had the best taste among my siblings, that's why she loved Peter. One of the things that I love about Peter is his love for Ann…

I don't have *one* story. I did write some comments on the blog that Peter orchestrated. Ann has too many influences on me. One thing, when I think of Ann: I have worked in New York for many years. What I love about it is it's so diverse and particularly the Latino, Puerto Rican and Spanish cultures are very, very strong there. And walking down the streets of New York I hear languages, every time I hear Spanish I realize in the back of my mind I think of Ann. That was one of the first things I wrote on the blog and it was actually one of the most important ones because we didn't see enough of each other. That's it. Peter's love for Ann is a great thing.

Vann

Hello, everyone. I'm finding it difficult to think about these things and to express everything in words. But I definitely lost my mother way too soon. I had such a great mother, and the years I had with her were so filled with joy. She was the best mother that anyone could've had, so I got twenty-five really great years. I'm very, very thankful for the time I had and the mother I had. If I had to share a story, there was one time, it must've been high school—second year of high school, tenth grade—and I had some appointment that I had done outside of school. So I made up an excuse that I shouldn't do any work that night even though I got out, probably around 7, and I clearly could have done my work. So I got Ann to write me a note to say that I was excused from work. I showed up in class and gave the note to my teacher and said my mother has excused me from work tonight. And she goes—which is *not* like her at all—actually, she learned over the years that if I didn't want to do it, I wasn't going to. The teacher then proceeded to take the note and say 'thank you very much,' and hand out a pop-quiz to everyone in the class. And I threw such a fit that I thought the world was ending. My mom stormed right into that school, was more mad at me than anyone else, but gave everybody her mind at that school and it was one of the hardest car ride homes. But she yelled at the principal, she yelled at the teacher, she yelled at everyone all the way through. And then she looked at me and she goes, "What the hell are you thinking, bringing me in here just to save your butt!" So, that's who my mom was. She always had my back, always loved me. I couldn't have asked for a better mother. I was always wrong, usually—if you asked her—but she always loved me, and she always cared about me, and she always was with me for the hard times. So, for all those reasons, I feel very lucky to have had the mother that I had for the time that I had her.

And lots of love to everyone on the phone, and hopefully we'll see you all quite soon.

Peter

I just wanted to say, in terms of the connections in the world, that Zellman and Gail are from Melbourne. They left about ten years before me and they're about ten years older than me. But it was Nancy Pollak who connected us. Nancy who was in Ithaca, the Pollak family who'd been very close to the Blum family for a period in New Haven. So that was quite an alignment of the stars. They had just adopted Zoe, and she was crawling on the floor of Nancy's place during Sunday tea, and Vann was watching, he wasn't yet crawling, but he was very interested in this other little being. And it continued from there, and so, I'm not sure if Nancy invited them because we're all from Melbourne, but it's a connection that's continued to this day.

Sally

Pete, thanks for the blog. It's been wonderful, absolutely wonderful, for me to read given that I didn't know Ann very well, to read all these things that people have written about her. Things that otherwise I'd have no opportunity to know, and they've also just been really interesting. I'm sure Ann would really appreciate what you've done—it's much more enduring to have everything in the written word. It's wonderful, because it will always be there.

Peter

Well, Zellman said that Ann and I are different. The blog isn't actually Ann's aesthetic, but I feel she'd appreciate the way I would find structures that allow people's voice to come out, just as she would allow people's voice to come out by talking with them. It's a difference in style. I hope it does help her live on, in her ways.

Gilly

Thanks, Pete. Can I also say that the flowers that people brought me in memory of Ann with the blog have been so wonderful. I've spent so much time listening and thinking about the variety and the strength of Ann's friends. The beauty of the garden, and the garden summed up her aesthetic and her friends—everything about her. She had so many friends, I loved hearing it. Thank you very much.

FAMILY & FRIENDS, BY GOOGLE HANGOUT
12/13 DECEMBER 2015

Memories from those gathered for a party

Peter: Ann asked for a potluck party—No speeches. But everyone will get a chance to share something short—a story or even just a phrase—that will be recorded about how having Ann in your life has influenced you—about how we will carry that influence into our future given our good fortune that we are still alive.

We will do this every hour for ten minutes; I will start each time. [Full audio recording of stories, with emotions and sides and remarks: http://bit.ly/AnnPotluck.]

In 1984, Christmas and New Year, Ann and I went to Italy. She taught me that you can go somewhere, like to the Uffizi in Florence, and you can just stay there for an hour. You don't *have* to see everything. In fact after an hour, you don't see; you don't really look. So she taught me how to look, and one of the things she said is: "We're in Florence, we're going to cross the river, it's the Arno, and there's going to be a church, and in that church in the corner, there's going to be a painting by Pontormo, and it will look like this..." And she described the painting [The Deposition from the Cross]. She had seen it when she was... thirteen? So by then she was thirty-four, or something like that. She still remembered it after twenty years because she *looked*. One of the ways she influenced me was to teach me how to *look*.

Ashley Seal

One of my favorite things with Ann was Thanksgiving, when she was so excited to have us here, and to eat. But she said, "Well never mind, I'm having my dessert first, even though its not part of the rules." So, I will always want to eat dessert first because of Ann.

Pamela

I tried to pull her legs off in 1950, and she ended up with really beautiful long legs.

Tom

When I was about eleven Ann had me stick a paper clip into a light socket, assuring me that nothing bad would happen. Fortunately, nothing *really* bad happened. But, I think she felt bad about that.

Sam Rosenbaum

What I remember most about Ann is being outside with my mother and gardening. Both of them working their minds working together and forming that beautiful garden outside.

Richard Frumess

I think one of my greatest memories of Ann is the relationship she had with Pamela, and listening to them talk on the phone or when they got together. It was one of the most wonderful relationships I have ever seen and I will treasure that.

Peter

In 1990, I got a position at Cornell. For the first semester, I was commuting back and forth from Berkeley. We started to look for a house. Realtors would take you to places, and there was this really run-down place downtown in the flats area. I was just describing this by phone and eventually, Ann said, "that's the place we need to get." Alas, someone had bought it already; someone put cash down and bought it. But it came back on the market. The bank wouldn't let us buy it unless we put a lot of money in to repair, so it had to be a construction mortgage. Come to Halloween, the house is somehow fixed up, and people would come to the door in this neighborhood and say, "So *you're* the people who bought this house!" We'd let them look inside so they could see what she had done to rescue this house. And it's still a wonderful house—from 1870 early days of balloon framing. And it survived thanks to Ann's vision.

Josh Konigsburg

I'm a newcomer, *very* recently married to Mary Sue. I had the privilege of getting to know Peter and Annie just a little bit. An extraordinary privilege, blessing, joy. I was just talking to Peter a few minutes ago about what it means to me that Ann gave Mary and I, for our wedding, a very beautiful, artistic and beautiful pitcher for cream. She said it was very important for us to use. It has moved me very much to use this creamer every day for my half and half for my coffee. It's really important to me to do it, and important to keep doing it. I figured I'd cite that story.

Reyes Coll-Tellechia

I worked with Ann at UMass Boston for seventeen years. I never had a fight with her. We disagreed many times; we never had a fight. She and I talked every morning, along with Peggy. We commute on the T every afternoon. Ann taught me and showed me what gentle tenacity is—I do have the second part; Ann tried to very gently teach me the first part. I failed but she didn't mind. She accepted me without hesitation. That's what I learned from her. I think of Ann every day at work, every time I take the T, every time I fight without the gentle part. I will never forget Ann Blum.

Emily Joselson

I'm a friend from Cambridge days in the 70s. Lots and lots of wonderful memories. Ann is probably one of the smartest people I know in such an un-egotistical way. But the thing that I take with me, forward into life, which is *such* a gift, is facing death, and *talking* about that, and making decisions about your own end of life. Through knowing Annie, and watching the way she made decisions, and talk about them, it's helping *me* talk *with* people about that. So she's a hero in many ways, but *that* is the big one.

Brad Bellows

I met Ann on a hot summer day, probably around 1982. I was living on a place between Harvard Square and Porter Square, in Cambridge, on third floor of a triple-decker. Ann came by one day with one of our friends. She was working at the Peabody Museum at the time. She made an instant impression: big sparkling eyes, super smart, sweet, funny. Sometime thereafter, she was introduced to Peter, I think maybe in that same apartment circle. I think you were rooming with us for a summer,

Peter. There were so many things from that time that stick in my mind. I think she was teaching writing at Harvard, and she still hadn't graduated from college herself. Which is a credit to Harvard, honestly, for recognizing Ann's genius for so many things. But the incredible honor, and a lesson to see the beautiful and sort of, brave, and ethical and ultimately, incredible way in which Peter and Ann embarked on the adoption process that brought us their incredible son, Vann. We had the chance to get together with our kids, and it just was an inspiration to see how Ann and Peter grew into parenting in such a wonderful way. I wish I'd spent more time with Ann over the hectic years since then, but it's been an immense honor to have known her, to have had her in my life and to have had her example in all these ways. There aren't that many people who manage to be both principled and light, serious and brilliant and unpretentious, all wrapped in one—she really had that down. Thank you Ann and Peter.

Meri Sue Glasgall

I've been a friend of Ann's almost forty years, and we met through our *men* at the time, who working at the Harvard bookstore. We decided one night that we were going to go out *by ourselves* because we were always with a million people. We formed this bond at that early juncture. I came to know her as the most gracious, and I would say gentle, person I've ever known. She helped me through a lot of things, and I hope I can say the same for her. One Christmas, she invited me to New Haven to her family's Christmas. It was just was perfect. There was tea at 4 o'clock. The table was set perfectly. This is when I found out that Ann's mother told her that carrots were dessert. It made me want to be an Episcopalian because it was just so beautiful. But there's one thing more recently that she said to me; we were on the phone; it was about a year ago. I said something about, "Well yes, I'm going to have to be the grownup, here," and she said, "Meri, you have been a grown up for a very long time." So, that was my Ann, and I'll miss her terribly.

Michael Manning

I remember when I first met Vann, I was nervous being welcomed into the home. She was very generous, and I just have fond and funny memories of when Vann and I would hang out in our own little space in the house. She would make sure everything was there. It's just her generosity that was appreciated and I remember in terms of just welcoming me in. When I dropped off my art, I remember showing Vann and being unsure of it; she was very generous to reassure me that she appreciated it. On moving in day, into *this* house that I'm familiar with, that was a fun time. I just appreciated her presence and her smile and everything—always good memories with Ann. Much love.

Peter

A very simple thing that I got from Ann at an early stage is that, if you couldn't do something, if you missed something, you didn't give an excuse or give the whole explanation. You explain, I didn't get to do it, I'm going to do it tomorrow—or, whatever. It's very relevant in my teaching, and I'll say this to my students, "Don't give me an excuse, you can miss two classes out of thirteen without excuse; that's how your lives work out." (It's still very hard for them not to tell me that their grandmother died and everything.) It's a deeper principle than just that. I got that from Ann.

Margery Meadow

Ann was the best listener I've ever known. She could empathize, and she could really listen and give constructive feedback—not in a detached way, but in a thoughtful, deep connection. Non-ego, but, yet, herself there but not getting in the way of what you were looking for. I'll really miss that.

Alan Hewat

I'm part of the prehistoric generation here—I knew Ann back when she was "Annie" in Cambridge in the early 70s. She came down from Smith with her then boyfriend ("excuse me, Peter"). A bunch of us were working at the Harvard bookstore and she sort of folded in with our crowd, so we were all part of a gang. She was "Annie." She didn't become "Ann" until much later and I never knew her as Ann. Right from the beginning she had this magnetism that attracted everybody's attention. She became not a central part—she wasn't showy she didn't call attention to herself—but everybody *understood* that this was a excellent person. This was a person to cherish, and I've cherished Annie all my life. There have periods of up to five, maybe six years, where we didn't see each other or weren't in touch. And then we would turn up again, Annie would turn up in Vermont, or I would come down here, and we'd continue our conversation as if it had just ended ten minutes before. She had this total presence when she was with me that connected so thoroughly and so comfortably and we just blended so beautifully. It's very difficult for me to believe that I won't be able to sort of drop in on her in another six months, or eight months and pick up the conversation again. I miss her very much.

Jon Zorn

I'm part of that Cambridge crew myself. The thing I want to say first is, when people we speaking earlier this afternoon, several people as they were speaking I was nodding my head because of the adjectives they used about kindness, intensity, being able to look at you while you were speaking. You realize: This person is listening to me! And cares about what I'm saying. Annie was like that all the time. A beautiful spirit, who we met through the bookstore crowd. I realized that she worked at the Museum of Comparative Zoology, across the street in Harvard Square, and she realized that I was interested in Natural History, and was doing basic reading on the subject. She would welcome me to come visit her at her office, would open all the cases and show me all the butterflies, and all the bees, and things like that. We talked about evolutionary theory, and she presented me with a beautiful sepia picture of Charles Darwin in profile, in that big, floppy hat that he used to wear. I kept that in my apartment for *years* up on the bookshelf. It's been very interesting to talk to people today—thank you, Peter, for inviting everyone here to hear stories from different parts of Annie's life, except it's the same adjectives about a sparkle, and a spirit, and a generosity, and an intensity. I'll just end with one quick thing I've mentioned a couple of times…There was a time that I said to Alan, I said, "Alan, it could be really easy for a guy to fall in love with Annie Blum!" and he said, "Zorn, you idiot! Every man *in Cambridge* has fallen in love with Annie at one time or another." I said, "Oh, oh, right, yeah."

John Macleod

I just remember Ann as a wonderful person to be with, a dear friend. She did have a sparkle and an intellect, and a depth. I personally really miss her. We need her right now, as a person with such a deep and humane understanding of history and politics—we need that to construct and make our world. In so many ways she was like one of the tallest trees in the forest. That was Ann.

Karla Martineau

I had the pleasure of taking care of Ann in the last year of her life. As a hospice nurse, I am besotted. I mean, there are seminars about boundaries, and I was not able to keep my boundaries. She is a great listener; she always wanted to know about my life. I happened to be visiting her when my sister went into labor, and she said, "Oh my god, you've gotta leave!' I said, "I'm not done with you!" and she goes, "I don't *care*, you've gotta leave!!" And then I said "okay, okay." So the next visit she goes, "What did she have?!" So there was no keeping boundaries with Ann. She was the most selfless person I have ever known, and was worried about everybody else. She was a pleasure and it was my honor to take care of her.

Nate Blum

As some of you probably know, Ann's mother—my grandmother—passed away this summer. The Blum family Christmas was a "capitol T tradition" and it's the only thing I've ever known on Christmas Day, for twenty-five years. It's going to be *profound* in a few weeks. Now, without that warmth and humor, as people said, that receptiveness, it's going to be a hard December.

Grace McConaghy

I was Ann's caregiver for her last two months. I didn't have the privilege of knowing her as long as you people have, but she was able to share a lot of her thoughts and memories with me. I felt like I got to know quite a few people through her, the love for life, and for flowers, and for the people she cared about, her family, Peter, and Gilla was *amazing*. Just the compassion that she had, you know, I'd be bending down so close to her bed taking her socks off, and I'd say "Jeez Ann, I don't know, either my butt's getting bigger or Peter's doing something with this bed!" She'd say "well get down a little closer." I would get down on my knee, and she remembered me saying my knee was bad and she'd say, "Ooh, get off your bad knee," even though she was so fragile. And I would walk up the stairs and I'd hear her say, "Grace, is that you?" And I'd go right over and kneel next to the chair and say, "Hello, princess.' And she'd go, "Huh, *princess*." I would hold her hand, "So how are we doing today?' She'd tell me, "Well, I have bad news," or "I'm good today." And I would say to her, "Yesterday is gone; don't worry about tomorrow; today we're in the day. Today, we'll maintain. And that's the most we can do." I got to love her. I'm Karla's aunt, and that's how I got to take care of Ann. I'm just glad I was able to have Peter, and Ann, and Vann, and Gilla, and Pamela and Richard, and to get to know them. They'll always be in my heart.

Peter

We ended up working at the same university. The day I signed my contract at UMass, Ann got a one-year position—someone was going to be on medical leave. He did retire; she was a candidate for the position and got it. No nepotism. There we were in different buildings, different spheres—graduates versus undergraduates. We could share some of the same characters that we wanted to complain about, some of the stuff and nonsense about the university. I got more tangled in it than she did; it would keep me up at night. She said, "Look, keep your eye on the prize." Which means you've got to define what the prize is, what are those things you *really* want to have put into place, and *work* steadily to put into place. Don't bother to imagine you can change the rest of the things. So, that was one of the things that she's left with me. And I'm not saying—you don't have to say—that we actually learnt these lessons well.

Rachel Rubin

I'm a colleague from UMass Boston. I was thinking about what I wanted to say, and then I thought the best way to acknowledge and honor Ann's collective vision—because I thought the solidarity I felt with her on campus was really important—I'd like to do a call and response. I'm going to read a line, and then you all will say back, "We will remember her."

In the rising of the sun, and in its going down,
    We remember her.
In the blowing of wind and in the chill of Winter,
    We remember her.
In the rebirth of Spring, at the blueness of skies, and in the warmth of Summer,
    We remember her.
In the rustling of leaves, and in the beauty of Autumn,
    We remember her.
When we are lost and sick at heart,
    We remember her.
When we have joys we crave to share,

> We remember her.
> When we have decisions that are difficult to make,
> > We remember her.
> When we have achievements that are based on hers,
> > We remember her.
> So long as we live, she too shall live, for she is part of us as
> > We remember her."

Chris Bobel

I'm a colleague of Ann and Peter. Ann was kind of my work-wife in a lot of ways. We both commuted to and from Arlington, so we often spent time on the T and the bus, which was a plus because I often connected with people on the T, but then not also on the bus. So we had usually an hour and a half to kvetch. She was so sane and reasonable, when I was always so erratic and unreasonable and out of control. Ann was always had such a grounding influence on me *and* a sense of humor. Because we started around the same time and we were on the tenure track together, and we were both just freaked out about earning tenure. I remember she bought me a little button that sat over one of the keys on my computer, and it was a red button that said, "PANIC," so that I could press it at the appropriate time. So I've come up through UMass Boston with Ann and I really don't know how to do it without her. We talked a lot in the last couple of months and usually the theme was how pissed we were that we couldn't be crusty old grey haired feminists on campus together making a mess of things without apology. So I will have to do that without her.

Sandra Haley

I met Ann her first year at UMass Boston as an undergraduate student. I was lucky enough to wander into one of her classes. She became my advisor; she talked me into applying for grad school; she talked me into applying for a PhD program; she mentored me all throughout. So, when Rachel was talking about when we have achievements based on hers, I really heard that. The best I can hope for is to somehow reflect well on her influence. I'm just so grateful to have known her.

Diane Paul

I have a story that is sort of light-hearted, but also illustrative of Annie, who I met, I think in the mid 70s. It was a long time ago. And then in 1983, I saw the film, "Zelig," and shortly after that, we had lunch and I mentioned that I had seen it. And she said, "Oh! I have a story about that." She said, "Woody Allen called my dad…" I said, "Your dad?" "Yeah! He was in Zelig!' I said, "Really??" So you all probably know, but there are five historical witnesses in Zelig: Susan Sontag, Bruno Betelheim, Irving Howe, Saul Bellow, and John Morton Blum. I had known Annie by then, maybe eight years and I had no idea that her father was John Morton Blum. So anyway, the story that she told was that her father got a phone call from somebody saying he was Woody Allen—an assistant of his had been a student at Yale. Her father never considered for a second that it might really be Woody Allen. Apparently, her brother, Tom, did great impersonations, so he said, if I remember the story correctly, "Oh, come on, Tom!' and hung up! Woody Allen then called back, and he was very persistent and called back a third time. Then he said something that got him to believe that he really was Woody Allen and so he ended up in the film. But what was illustrative for me is that I could've known Ann at that point, for eight years, be in a field where of course you would know who John Morton Blum was, and find out that way. I thought that was quintessential Annie.

Kate Hartford

I knew Ann originally because of Diane, who had persuaded her to go to UMass to finish up her undergraduate degree. At this point, of course, she'd been working at the MCZ for some years, she had published even when she had been working at Princeton for some years, that *phenomenally beautiful* book on scientific illustration. And so, she arrives at UMass her first year, and she comes to me for help because they were telling her she had to take freshman English. This was actually one of the most fun things I ever got to do, bureaucratically—composing a letter to the Advising Center explaining to them that somebody who had published a book through Princeton University Press really doesn't need to take freshman English. She succeeded.

Peter

Ann has something called the "Laundry Arts." That's to say, doing laundry is something which has some skill, there's a way to learn how do it efficiently. If you don't appreciate the laundry arts, if you don't appreciate that it actually takes some attention, then what you're really doing is, saying "it'll work, even if it's sloppy," meaning, "if you want it done better, you do it," meaning, you're really actually leaning towards having someone else do it. If you're a male, that usually means you're expecting someone else to do it. So it's actually a very subtle form of sexism to *not* appreciate the laundry arts. But Ann didn't say, you're being a sexist, a typical sexist guy, even though you don't think you're being a sexist, because you're not doing the laundry. She would say, "You know there's something called the Laundry Arts." And I think it applies to lots of other fields besides the laundry.

Rajini Srikanth

I'm a faculty member at UMass Boston, and so that's how I know both Peter and Ann. (We always wondered how the two of them got together, but that's another story.) But I will say I first got to know Ann when she came to teach for the Honors Program, now the Honors College, which is something that I head up. You know, her course on Mexico was absolutely beloved because she expected the students to be rigorous, complex thinkers—that was Ann. And I think she expected no less from her faculty colleagues. Very recently, I was trying to put together a course proposal, and Ann look at me and would say, "You're not getting it." I said, "What do you mean, I'm not getting it? I think I'm addressing everything you want me to do." She would look at me kindly and say, "Let me send you some things that will help you understand." And we did this back and forth, I want to say, several weeks, and it finally dawned on me that Ann was telling very kindly that I wasn't paying attention. So I sort of really got down in there, and opened my ears and opened my eyes, and listened to her. I think we finally got it right. I want to say that it was worth all of the effort that she extracted from me, because I think what we finally have now is an absolutely fabulous course, an intermediate seminar, that others use as a model. I think in some ways maybe is similar to the Laundry Arts that Peter was talking about—insisting on getting it right and not tolerating sloppiness. So thank you Ann, we will keep that with us always in The Honors College.

Elizabeth Bussiere

I'm a staff member in the Political Science Department at UMass Boston. I first got to know Ann when I was a Department Chair, from 2009/10 ish-2013. And Ann and Janice Kepler in Economics, and Roberta Wollons in History and I were a group of four department chairs who met every month for lunch. The idea initially was to share ideas and strategies for dealing with new administrative mandates and bureaucratic absurdities and things like that. Often times it became a gripe session, which was very therapeutic, I think, for all of us. But what stood out for me, which—and it sounds like it overlaps with what both Peter and Rajini were saying—Ann had this very unique a mix of the qualities of broad vision and meticulous attention to detail, and also a feistiness combined with a patience and tolerance. So I often felt very inadequate as a chair in relation to her because her department had archived all sorts of documents and they could easily access them, like their department constitution. Our department constitution was in some folder, typed, not even in a computer but typed on a typewriter.

Ann had this ability to make everyone feel valued and affirmed. Ironically, given I was somewhat intimidated by her talents and her skills, when I finally stopped being chair, and I was going to put time into writing, she was the person I went to. I said, "I would like to have dinner with you. And I would like to get your advice on writing. I have writing blocks; I have a lot of insecurity around writing." We just had this great dinner. I knew she was a passionate scholar, so it's one reason I wanted to talk to her. Like, how do you keep that light lit when you have all these other responsibilities? I was struck by her incredible patience and empathy, despite her being "up here" in terms of talents and skills. So, she made being department chair bearable, and I will always be grateful for that and will always remember her very warmly.

Nancy Hafner

I'm Ann's sister-in-law. You know, we always got together on holidays, sometimes a bit more than that, but that was mainly it. So I think of Annie within the family structure. I think of all sorts of pieces that of the family that came through her. One, which people have all talked about are STANDARDS. There were standards to be held, but Ann always seemed to temper the standards with a laugh, with humor, where it really became fun and a game, rather than something to worry about. What I mostly feel is that you really can't take anything for granted. You have to seize the moment with the people you love and do it often. And she will be missed.

Anissa Lane

Hi everyone. We often had a conversation that went something like this: It's funny how people come into each other's lives for whatever reason in whatever season. My experience is a little different from everyone else's—I actually met Ann via Vann. I want to give a little back-story—I won't be long. Vann and my son became fast friends when Vann first came to Beaver County Day School and he came in ninth grade—in high school. And Steven and his friends had been there since middle school. Steven tells me—and Vann tells this story too—"I was walking by the science room, I've seen this kid sitting in there." And he was like, "What are you doing sittin' in here?" And he was like, well, he was new, he didn't really know anyone. So he was like: "Come on out here with me." Ever since then, Vann has been a part of my family, and he has made me a part of his. What I love most about Ann was her willingness to share him. You know, my house was "convenient"—let's just say that. I live near Beaver Country Day, so *all* the kids came to my house. They'd walk there during lunch. It's where they'd come when they'd cme home from school. Her ability to share love was just *amazing, absolutely amazing*. Vann has been a part of my family, and it's so funny, people come up to me and say, "Oh *you're* Anissa, *you're* his other mom!" One of the things I said to her years ago, "You guys know you have me *for life*. So when Vann gets married, I'll be sittin' on the pew with you all! Just understand that." And she was like, "we wouldn't have it any other way."

A quick story, I—young single mom—wasn't able to go to school. I found that when my son went off to school, our *kids* went off to college, I was like, "Ann, I think I want to go to school." "Do it! DO IT!" And she guided me all the way through. I would call her often and say, "I can't do it, oh my gosh!" I was working full time and going to school full time. "You can do this Anissa, you're almost there, you can do it." I'm proud to say that I graduated from school last year, and I went straight into a program. I was like, "I want to teach"; she was like, "Go into graduate school—Do it!" I was like: "Okaayy." So anyway, I'm proud to say that I'm on my last week of grad school. And I'm like, I'm upset, just- I have all this going on, and a lot to do, and papers to write, and things to do. I keep hearing in my head, "You can do this...you can do this..."

What I'll remember most about Ann is her love. She accepted me for where I was. We'll continue to share Vann. I'll never replace her. But I let her know that I will be there for him; I will *always* be there for him (as for Peter). I just wanted to share that with you all because she's an integral part of my family, and I plan on staying there. They can't get rid of me, I already told them. So, thank you.

Abby Blum

I am Ann's niece. She is one of the few people I have known my entire life. I am going to share three things that I learned from her. One: I don't know how many of you know her parents—my grand parents—they are pretty formal people. For our generation, Ann taught us, from a young age, the importance and value of going our own direction; find our own path. Second: She never shied away from having the important conversations in life at the dinner table, no matter how old you were. Talking about things like social justice, economic justice. That helped me develop the values I have now as an adult. Lastly, Ann had great style—whether it was her garden or how she dressed—really how she went through life, with wonderful style and grace.

Ruthie Gilmore

Ann and I were best friends for fifty years. We met when we were 15 years old at the Day Prospect Hill School for Girls. From about 1984 forwards, we described us as identical twins separated at birth. We had a reason for this, well ,many reasons. One: our mothers would confuse us when looking at pictures of us and not know which was which. We spent some time apart out of contact, for no good reason, after she was best person at my wedding we were not in close contact. We got back together in late 1984. We discovered when I unpacked my bag that we were reading the same book, Not in Our Genes. And we were wearing identical socks, which were really quite noticeable—they were bright orange argylls. On the basis of these two bits of evidence, we decided that we were identical twins separated at birth.

Many people have spoken of Ann's generosity and love. I wish I could talk to you of this all night, but she said no speeches so I'm not going to give one. But there is one last thing I want to say, when we finished PhDs in 1998, thirty years after we graduated high school. By vastly different paths we ended up at the same place at the same time. She sat down to help me go on the job market. She wouldn't do something for you; she would help you do it really well yourself. She, the queen of teaching expository prose at Harvard, pulled a job application letter out of me like unto I never would have composed myself. In all ways I am a better person; I am a better scholar. And I am heart-broken twin today.

Peter

One of the things I have seen with Ann: She would get up very early in the morning, make her coffee, and go back to sit in bed. We have always been in places with good morning light. She would watch the dawn or early morning light. Be quiet. It wasn't the time she wanted me to be come and do anything in that room or make noise. She would reflect. Or just be quiet. She would tell me: "You don't have to think." In the last months, I would be the one who would bring her up—she wasn't drinking coffee then; she was drinking green tea. She kept doing that till almost the last day.

Stephen Robinson

I went to high school with Vann, but we were closer than that. Vann is like a brother to me. Him being a brother means Peter is another dad and Ann is another mother for me. Ann always wanted the best for me. Even if I did something bad or wrong and my mother was digging in to me, Ann would say: "You can just do your best; just do your best. We want the best for you." She was always there for me to talk to if I needed advice, schoolwise. And I needed a lot of that; I did appreciate that.

Her smile is what I remember most.

Jacqueline Berthet

I have known Ann and Peter since the early 80s. I read a quote this week that made me think. Simone referred to pain and suffering as a currency we pass on. Just occasionally someone doesn't. I think of Ann as someone who doesn't pass on pain and suffering. That is what I have learned.

Anne Taylor

I am Peter's sister. I haven't had the opportunity to spend a lot of time over the years Peter has been with Ann. But we were very privileged to have a family holiday a few years ago in the center of Australia where all the siblings and partners and my mother got together. I was wondering how this holiday would go—think back to a holiday when you had all your brothers and sisters. We would go on desert treks each day. I particularly remember one resting point where Ann homed in on me to have a conversation with me. It left a strong impression—I have heard it here many times. Attentive listening, a desire to get to know you and make you feel very important. That holiday has very special significance for me.

Pamela

I am Ann's sister. I just want to tell you all how much your love of Ann has meant to me. How she has talked about you and the importance you have held in her lives. I particularly want to thank Ruthie Gilmore who has been Ann's great soul mate since ninth grade. Even though I have met many of you just for the first time today, I felt your presence as she talked about you. I can't tell you how deep and rich the experience has been.

Kevin Barnett

I am co-parent along with Alison of David, our son, and Vann, David's half-brother. We have had such a rich life raising our boys together from the opposite coasts. I had such a sense of uplift from Ann, from the beginning when we often struggled. She would bring a philosophical view of the world, a sense of positivity, a village in how we raised our families together of community. I will never forget that richness in the way we have come together. We could not be more happy to be here. We also thank Vicki, the boys' birth mother.

Joe Levine

I got to know Ann in the middle 70s when I showed up at Harvard absolutely certain that I didn't belong there. Her smiling face as the interface between me and the intimidating amount of knowledge stored in the MCZ library was always very helpful. I remember the joy that she exhibited about to us the knowledge she had about how to find knowledge.

Deborah Dumaine

I spent my twenties with Annie. We grew up together. We traveled in Greece a little bit together. I remember visiting Annie at the Museum of Comparative Zoology and thinking what a magical place she worked. We tried to figure out what we were going to be when we grew up. She was such a soulful person; she was so profound; she had such great thoughts; such a wonderful compass about what she was doing and where she was going. I admired that as I was a compass-free person at the time.

Victoria Munroe

I knew Annie first in Athens. She was living there and I was in school there for a year. We shared many years together after that. I was living with her in Cambridge as she was writing her beautiful first book. She taught me a lot about how to look at drawings from any particular field. She, of course, was looking at scientific illustration and trying to understand the evolution of technology and how that affected natural history. I hope you all know her book well—it is incredible. I am an art dealer, so I learned a lot from Annie about how to look at everything. I was always impressed by how articulate Ann would be when she wanted to express herself. It's a crystal memory: having conversations with Annie. She was so clear. I have never admired anyone searching for the best words to express whatever it was she wanted to express.

Steve Cadwell

I knew Ann from age 18 when we first were away at college together. Annie was always the home base for me. She was here as I would come back and forth through various parts of my own life. She, as others have said, was a great listener. The last big time I had with her was reading poems with her that I had written. She was such a great audience. [Steve read the poem, *Missing Ann*; see page 14-15.]

Paula Chandoha

Ann and I met in 1973 at the Museum of Comparative Zoology. We were work colleagues. I was the scientific photographer and she brought work from archives that needed copying. We kept getting to know each other more and more; talking about images and scientific illustration. We lived around the corner from each other. We would have our dinners together. I was a photographer who wasn't confident then. She always looked at my work and she was honest when she critiqued. We had a wonderful exchange and I'd say to her, "We grew up together." We had long absences in the friendship, but I knew she was always there. When she started writing the book, I remember walking into her apartment and seeing her by the window. It was wonderful for me to see and experience. She was always there as a friend. The suddenness of when she got sick. I really miss her. I turn around thinking I could talk about that with Ann. One thing I did remember recently: There was a thirtieth birthday party at her apartment on Mass Ave. There was these wonderful photos on Polaroid SX70 film. There are only 4, but they are wonderful to look at and think about.

James Simpson

I am a very old school friend of Peter. In 2012 I was living in what seemed to be to be a very fragile house 300 yards down the road. You might remember that in November there was an almighty hurricane. As I was lying in the upper floor of this house in bed, the whole place felt as if it were about to take off. I remembered the advice of my son, who had been in the military: "You have to have a battle buddy, someone who will look out for you." I immediately rang Ann—Peter was away. We agreed that we would be battle buddies. It turned out we didn't need to call on each other. I knew that I felt a whole lot safer with Ann as my battle buddy. In addition to that, I will say that Peter and Ann have been fantastic, extraordinary, inspiring model—battle buddies for each other over this last year.

Vann

I met Ann in 1990 when she decided that she wanted to be a parent. I generally have all the same things everyone else has to say about her: Incredibly compassionate, loving, thoughtful, knew just the right way everything needed to be, opinionated. The experience that I had over the last year and half watching her die reinforced everything that people have been saying. When you are dying, when you know it's over, you have the right to be as angry at the world as you'd like to be. But my mum was nicer to me when she was dying. She has an incredible way, she had an incredible way of making a real connection with everybody that was involved in her life, from the person giving her coffee in the morning to the Chancellor of her University to the people she worked with to her friends especially. I think that's something she has given to me: the ability to make deep friendships and relationships. The two people who cared for her when she was dying, I feel like they became part of our family. She knew everything that happened in their lives. You find out a lot about somebody when they know they are going to die. And about who my dad was; taking care of someone like that is not easy. I love you all for being here. I know my mum cared for each of you in her own way. I appreciate you being here and sharing your love for her with us.

Peter

One of Ann's influences on me is a sense that you are not doing what you are doing for fame, for accolades or external recognition. It is not what you are doing it for. If it's not important to you personally to be doing your research and writing, to be connecting with people, then loosen up—it has to be important. The other side of "no fame" is that she was overly humble; she wouldn't put herself up for prizes. Yet she got awards for her book. A very interesting influence to have is to imagine that in a world where there is so many things in bright lights that that is not the important stuff.

Brad Bellows

I got a beautiful letter today from Iain and Gill Boal from England [see page 101-2]. Iain and I were lucky to see Ann two weeks before the end. Iain has spoken of the influence Ann had on him in setting up the May Day rooms, an archive of documents of dissent. He is planning to try to set up a scholarship in Ann's name. Ann meant a lot to all of us in a group that was called The Pumping Station; Iain would have loved to have been here personally to tell you that.

Ben Schwendener

I didn't know Ann as well as I know Peter. The many times she answered the phone or met me at the door, it was always so embracing, warm, and wanting to get to business. She was an incredibly dedicated person.

Shari Repasz Schwendener

There is obviously an incredible amount of love in this room for this woman.

Tommie

I'm Ann's little brother. Peter and Ann started a brilliant blog [the basis of this book] when Ann went into palliative care. The question was "I think of Ann when…" I think of Ann all the time, in my life, when I hear Spanish on the streets, when I hear the news from Greece, when I read the news from Mexico, when I see a nice market of fruits and vegetables, in the moment of being ripe. When you think about the reaping in the fall, when you think about the sowing in the spring, I think of Ann.

David Terkla

I am at UMass Boston. I first came to know Ann indirectly when I was chairing the College Personnel Committee and her tenure case came up. I was thinking I'd really like to meet this person. What a wonderful body of scholarship and teaching. It turns out I joined the administration not too long after that and interacted with her in her role as Chair. I loved her organization and commitment to the Department and also her fairness and her calm way, but firm way, of asking for things. I then had the privilege of serving with Ann on a committee at the University level to look at salary anomalies. Ann and I served on the committee together for two years. I was an administration representative; she was one of the faculty's. We tended to see eye to eye. Her sense of justice would always come out in these cases. Both of us ardently advocated for much more money than we were given.

Alison Negrin

My husband and I raised Vann's brother, David. I met Ann even before David was born. I thought it was odd at first to stay so connected. But now I am so thankful—to have Ann, Peter, and Vann in our lives, and now to meet the rest of the family—our family. I love you all so much.

Peter

The garden is definitely into the winter phase now, but there's still color—yellows and greens and reds in some places—even the color of the dead plants. The garden would go through its phases in the summer. It was definitely Ann's creation, which dates back to summer jobs in New Haven in the Parks Department or working in a greenhouse in New Mexico when she dropped out of college. This summer I started to do the garden work. I would go out early after getting her cup of tea and walking Gilla. I learned to be a gardener in the sense of, before you do anything you really like to do, you weed. You have to put weeding first because weeds will take over. I did that and I also made the flagstone path—that was my project. In the fall I came to appreciate the way the different dyings happened, the cutting back you need to do. I mentioned this to Ann. She said: "You know that has to be planned." It's not just something that happens because gardens are nice. You have to work to make sure this plant goes yellow before this one, and so on. Underneath a beautiful garden—which someone told me is a legend in the neighborhood—there's a lot of planning, a lot of work. We started a notebook so she could pass across information to me, but we only got one page in. So it's over to me now to learn.

Estelle Disch

I was at UMass Boston for 30 years. Ann and I got to overlap. If I were to define a great colleague, she would be at the top of the list—just a wonderful person to chat with. Ann ended up teaching the book written by my late partner about the grandmothers of the Plaza de Mayo. These were the mothers of women who were disappeared and their babies were given out in phony adoptions. Ann invited her each year to talk to her students. Rita adored those sessions. It was a very important part of Rita's life. It makes me smile.

Vann

Ann got Pamela, her sister, to get a planner for 2016. She couldn't get up to walk, but she had a planner for 2016. She asked Ashley what we were doing for Christmas because we were going to have Christmas here. She was looking ahead, chugging along, fighting. I feel very lucky to have so many wonderful friends, so much family around, so many people who care about my mum and care about my dad and care about me. I'm excited to move forward in 2016 with all of your friendships and all of your love. To develop our own stories, to make new traditions. It'll be too bad she's not there. There's a lot of great things she'd want us to do. It's all going to happen. To 2016!

Pamela

She said: "Don't wallow in misery. Go live."

Kevin

I so appreciate everyone's comments. A number of your sentiments and reflections stick out: her sense of clarity, of love, of spareness. These are things that resonate with my memories of Ann. Thank you for the reminder because this is really about looking forward as well, how to carry forward that spirit. I have lost a number of friends in recent years, but somehow this passing has affected me more. We were so close in age; it is a reminder of the fragility of life. Do things that are important and to approach life with that sense of clarity. I am taking this time, this event as an important marker in looking for ways to carry forward the spirit she exhibited so well.

Peter

One of the things Ann did once she knew there'd be no more treatment: We want to do things that we had been putting off that we wanted to imagine being there in the future. So we had the bookcases in the next room built, the screens on the back porch and the handrails on the stairs to make it easier for her mother to visit. Ann was doing two things: Looking forward to a future that she wanted to imagine people being able to appreciate and enjoy. It was a gift to the future that she wouldn't be part of or wouldn't be sure of being part of. What she was also doing—I didn't understand this until I thought about it over the last few days—was telling us: how about you also have that attitude to your own future. That leads me back to one of her little principles: Do yourself in the future a favor. The most mundane example is when you leave home in the morning, don't leave dirty dishes in the sink. The future you coming back would come home to dirty dishes—that's not nice to the future you. A mundane example of a larger principle, a wonderful principle.

Carol Cohn

I have been resisting speaking; I don't know how you speak after thirty years of being friends. I have been thinking about a few things. Ann and I knew each other before we had kids. There was a plan we had: we were going to write a novel together, Fertility: A Comedy of Manners. Ann and Peter started raising Vann 11 months before I started raising my daughter. Ann was always a guide to me, with a set of standards I could never live up to. The pleasure we had with the little ones together is something I'll never forget. One thing that really strikes me about Ann is that she loved to laugh, seriously loved to laugh. At the dinners that Paula, Cheryl, Ann and I had these last ten years, there have been a lot of crap in our lives, a lot of hard things. You can count on those dinners to have bright moments of tremendous laughter. It was Ann. It was Ann who really moved that laughter forward. She somehow managed to take very seriously what needed to be and figure out what was funny about it. Belly laughs that were a tremendous gift that I will miss a lot.

Peter

It is Friday night. (Ann died on Saturday morning after Thanksgiving). Ann is back in her bed—she wanted to go back there from the hospital bed where she's been in for a few days. She's saying, "Now I can focus on strengthening." (It had been too hard to maneuver from the hospital bed.) She would need some help with swallowing, liquids and she would ask for help. I was sitting beside her and then she looks at me, "I need to cover the suitcases." I wanted to reassure her. Thinking about covering the suitcases like putting them in nice fabric patterns, I said "It's OK, I have already done that." She looks back at me and says, "No you haven't." By the time the night's over, she has asked for help at different times, but never quite finished a sentence. So, when in the morning she stopped breathing, I looked back and saw that's the last coherent thing she said: "I need to cover the suitcases." You can interpret that in all kinds of ways. "Cover" could be: "I need to *hide* the suitcases, I'm not yet ready to go on a trip, I'm not yet ready to leave you"—that's what you do with suitcases. But it could also be— and this is what I am taking into my life—"I need to cover the suitcases so you don't think about traveling, about moving on if something is not quite right. So you can be here now with the wonderful house we have set up, with wonderful memories, wonderful family support. Just build on that." That's the story I wanted to finish with.

Pamela

Thank you. It's been a very powerful day.

Peter

It will carry us in the future. Thank you everyone.

Richard

It is has been wonderful to meet and connect with people we didn't know. And carry on relationships and friendships. That's the best memory of Ann we can have.

FAMILY & FRIENDS, AT A DAY-LONG POTLUCK PARTY
13 DECEMBER 2015

Memories of Ann from Anne

My family (the Australian Taylor family) and I only had a few opportunities to spend time with Ann over differing periods of our lives. Living in different countries the opportunities were few. My brother Pete had been overseas for many years following his academic leanings and we were intrigued to find he had met a special girl in America who he was to spend the next 30+ years with.

How quickly time flies and in retrospect the time we get to spend with family and loved ones takes on a special significance.

Ann came with Peter to Australia in 1987 before my third child was born. I think Australia was a shock to her or so I thought at the time. Looking back and having first travelled to The States in 2011 I realize Australia probably was a shock to Ann. Ann and Pete came to stay with me one night while on this visit and I remember the meal and some laughs shared but with two young children under 5 they would have been the dominant attention grabbers.

The following years as our lives unfolded my contact with Ann was occasional chats over the phone when she answered or during some Christmas long distance conversations. Skype and other commonly accepted modes of communication we now take for granted were not available to us then. We relied on letters and the occasional photo. Ann always answered the phone with such warmth and made you feel she was so glad to have had the chance to speak with you.

We received the news of Vann's arrival in the family with much joy and enjoyed seeing the pictures of him over the years as he grew. Impressions of Ann enjoying family time were gained from these photos and letters. Peter did manage to visit with Vann over the years but unfortunately Ann did not come with him due to other commitments but we enjoyed hearing from Pete stories of their lives together.

In 2011 my partner, Randolph and I managed to visit the States for the first time and came to stay with them in Boston for two weeks. In this time I was able to witness many aspects of Ann, her love of coffee, warm smile, infectious laugh and beautiful sense of style. Ann had to leave suddenly to attend to her parents needs so we did not get to spend the full time of our stay with her but enjoyed helping Pete build some of his first garden beds and knew Ann took delight in her garden and the future plans for its beauty.

I was delighted to know that Ann was to accompany Pete on our planned family holiday meeting in the centre of Australia. This was a special occasion instigated to celebrate my sisters 60th birthday and amazingly all Taylor siblings and their partners could be present together with our mother. Each day siblings and partners would choose a walk to embark on across the desert landscape. I vividly remember one rest spot where Ann deliberately sought out my company, sitting beside me with a keen interest to engage in conversation with me. What we talked about has long since faded but she left me with a strong sense of being a person who wanted to engage and get to know her husbands sister and understand the essence of Anne , what made me tick. I felt deeply acknowledged and recognized in this moment and it has always stuck in my memory as special and now even more so.

We decided after this holiday that there would need to be many more to follow as each Taylor sibling reached their milestone 60th year. I looked forward to the opportunity to spend more time with family and partners in the coming moving to retirement years. It was hard to hear of Ann's cancer and the subsequent months and being so distant. We will not get the opportunity we had then but I am so glad we had this time together and the essence of Ann lives on in memory and spirit.

ANNE TAYLOR
13 DECEMBER 2015

Excerpts from condolence notes

* Ann was truly a remarkable woman, was loved in our clinic.

* I could easily see her intellect and compassion. I know from Carol what kind of incredible friendship she showered upon those who mattered to her.

* I will remember her for her warm smile, energy and optimism. Buoyant spirit trumped her diagnosis and I'm sure she was an inspiration to others as she was to me. Although my meetings with Ann were few, she made a profound impression upon me, one of intelligence, deep curiosity, opinions, generosity and kindness. I remember vividly the dinner I enjoyed at your home one snowy night when we discussed her research in Mexico, the impact of Catholicism on female behavior and myriad other things. This was our first meeting, but her warmth and zestful conversation was so delightful that I felt as though we had been friends for years. Then when I fell ill and was in pain, Ann wrote a note expressing concern and offering practical help. I was deeply moved by her loving kindness.

* The Ann I knew and remember most vividly was wild and fierce—despite or against the gentility of her upbringing—a very young woman whose soul loved the mountains and the open sky of the Southwest.

* In many ways, you and Ann were so pivotal as guides into adoption—and the making of a family for us. For this we were and are still so very grateful. You were both always so generous and supportive—and Vann, a model baby!

* I will always remember the first time I met her. Ann and Sarah walked over to see a tree that had fallen in my yard after the microburst. Ann radiated warmth and compassion with a beautiful smile. What a pleasure it was to walk by your house and see Ann as she worked in your magnificent garden. Though I only knew Ann for short time, I will always remember her smile, her warmth and the pleasure she shared with others by making our neighborhood more beautiful.

* She was a meticulous scholar and department chair, generous in serving both students and her colleagues, and a lovely person. She will be terribly missed on campus....

* I am no longer amazed by, but I still wonder at and am grateful for, the ways in which people we have never met can impact our lives. While I never had the pleasure of meeting Ann, I will remember her whenever I am in the garden from the stories I have heard from Peter.

I will remember the lesson that by sharing even small pieces of the many reasons we love each other, we allow even broader dissemination of our loved ones' contributions to our lives and the world—often in unexpected and enduring ways.

Deep friendships, love and rememberances

Dear Peter, and Vann, I was so moved by Sunday's celebration of Ann's life.

So many warm-hearted and caring people united with the powerful positive energy that Ann brought to us all. A feast on many levels of life and with enough food to feed the block! Thank you for creating such a memorable event. Much love to you both.

BEN
15 DECEMBER 2015

Study Spanish with these beliefs that come from Ann

Carrying Ann forward, I will study Spanish for a few minutes regularly, say, a few early mornings a week, with these beliefs that come from Ann,

- truth comes from the struggle to understand, a person never completely masters a subject
- a new person emerges from the study of a new language, no matter how fragmentary and incomplete
- my Spanish person will be a better person in greatest part because it will reflect my sister Ann

Much love,

THOMAS
21 DECEMBER 2015

My mother would have given anything—anything—to have been able to believe and expect Ann would be alive and with us here at this gathering

Welcome, everyone. I'm Thomas, the son, here with my sister Pamela and our families, including the grandchildren Abigail, Nathan, and Vann. I'd like to call us together for a moment to give some context to this event.

Right up to the last, my mother at times could surprise me. When my sister Pamela discovered my mother's will and instructions in the freezer (a surprise), we found handwritten instructions "<u>No</u> funeral or memorial is my preference."

The emphatic, underlined "No," not a surprise. Nor the "no funeral" directive. "No memorial" surprised me and gave me some pause. If no memorial, then what...

"Prefer a private gathering...," she wrote. This is that gathering.

My sister Pamela and I, and our families, are very, very pleased to be here at the festivities for my mother with you all: The Evergreen Woods community and staff, long-time New Haven friends, some now far flung, and my cousins and second cousins, the family of my mother's sister.

In a few moments, I promise you a toast to Pamela Zink Blum, Babou as we called her. But these are very difficult times.

As many of you know, when my mother died last August my sister lay very weak and terminally ill up in her home in Arlington. She was enormously frustrated that she could not come down to be with my sister and me, and help us put my mother's affairs in order.

But after 176 Sherman was cleared out, Pamela, Ann, and I planned this gathering together. We originally wanted to have a more timely party in October. However, we decided to postpone the date to focus more on visiting, being with, and talking with Ann—frankly, the logistics of organizing an event for before Thanksgiving just got in the way of that.

So we set the date for today after the new year with the hope, but not the expectation, that Ann might be able to vicariously participate in these festivities.

Sadly, our expectations proved all too accurate. My sister Ann died over Thanksgiving weekend.

My mother would have given anything—anything—to have been able to believe and expect Ann would be alive and with us here at this gathering. She could not, because she knew Ann would not—a source of great anguish and grief to her.

Ann's death and these thoughts bring the idea of an event and celebration to a complete, full stop. And I do not want to say we should, or we must, or "so-and-so would have wanted us to." That's stuff and nonsense.

But here's what I propose, with my family, in the spirit of what we think my mother meant when she wrote her preferences for a private gathering.

We have a gathering. Let's celebrate because we're here and we can.

I promised you a toast, and you'll have it in a moment. After the toast—

• In our private gathering, rather than public speeches or eulogies, let's socialize and foster conviviality among the gathered—which my mother loved to do and did so very well.

• In our celebration, let's engage and talk with each other together and make small toasts to her and all she cared about: friends, culture, ideals. Let's say to each other what we've been thinking about her, what we came to say, what we may need to say.

• And finally, let's take these conversations, engagement, and toasts out into our worlds and continue them while we can for the entire time we're here.

Now here's the toast I promised. I give this toast in spirit with my brother-in-law Peter Taylor who wanted to be but could not be here this afternoon, let's raise our glasses together:

Here's to love and commitment, learning and knowledge, and to weaving together the social fabric of our lives, to my mother, Babou, Pamela Zink Blum.

TOM
9 JANUARY 2016

Late 2015 end-of-year letter

2015 for me was a year of caregiving for Ann as chemotherapy failed (mid-February) and we shifted to palliative care. But labeling this as *care* doesn't point to the tremendous hard work that has to be done by the *patient*—

medicines, movement, meaning, letting projects be undone, visitors, relationship building with caregivers (whether paid, family, or friends), bodily functions, passing time, plans, monitoring, experimenting, arranging, boundary definition, what to say when, resisting..

One way to appreciate this experience is indicated by my blog post, "Living under constraints" [see p. 230] which I wrote when trying to make sense, after Ann died at Thanksgiving, of why the death and dying and cancer books and websites hadn't been much help.

One way to appreciate this experience from the caregiver's side is indicated by my blog post, "Multiple roles as a health caregiver" [see p. 181] I wrote this in the early days of palliative care when trying to make sense of why the advice of bringing in others to help seemed not very helpful. Composing the list helped me to be mindful about giving space to the different roles. (To protect myself from well-meaning readers worrying that Ann's death was imminent, I didn't make the post visible till much later when a relative was starting to be the caregiver for a partner in the very early stage of diagnosis and treatment for a serious illness—see also "What I see here" [p. 210])

Another way to appreciate what this year has been is to acknowledge all the people who showed, before and after Ann's death, how important it has been to have Ann in their lives. The Ann(ie) Blum in Our Lives blog/archive and daylong pot-luck party in December was my way to help give voice to this [see transcribed stories, p. 233]. The tense is awkward—"has been" versus "have Ann"—because (and in this I am not alone) I am moving towards integrating bits of Ann into my future self [see UMass Memorial, p. 305].

People continue to show their caring, many asking about how Vann and I are doing. We would both say that we miss Ann a lot and are sad that our futures will not be shared with her. And we are both grateful for your concern. I would also say that I am *unsettled* and that this seems appropriate and ok. (I have been writing about the various, evolving dimensions of being unsettled. I can share some of these if you ask, to be seen as "threads that you draw into your own making sense of possibilities for change, [so] that you unsettle some things and do not wait until the death of someone important to make space for that.")

While I do have to show up to work teaching & etc. etc., I also hope to spend more time in what I call the basement archives, bringing to light—and out of their dusty boxes—letters and documents from Ann's 65 years. These are likely to keep me being unsettled for some time yet or even for more time than that.

In the basement there are also suitcases, which suggests a literal meaning of Ann's last sentences about needing to "cover the suitcases" [see p. 226]. But I continue to hear those words metaphorically.

Love and thanks,

PETER
2 FEBRUARY 2016

Beyond falling in love again

One of the winds that gusts into my emotional space since Ann's death is the feeling of falling in love with her again.

In a way that's very understandable—the comments of family and friends, spoken and written, the pictures, the memories of falling in love the first time—there's a lot there of Ann to find oneself in love with.

I don't know if this is been the case for you, dear reader: falling in love also involves the fantasy that the other person fills your heart—the holes and gaps of past hurts and anxieties get forgotten for some time. (That is, love [at first] is blind as in blinded by the light.)

That's not to say I don't like—or one might say *love*—the feeling of falling in love with Ann now. For falling in love with Ann when we first came together was something that opened the door for building a Relationship that, among other things, could allow for hurts and anxieties to be given their due and healing attention.

So, whenever I feel the jab or the ache of missing Ann, I can let that in and can also see that it's a feeling heightened by the love-falling. So, I should not bathe too long in feeling sad about the absence of the person I am falling in love with. Instead, I should start looking for the door that is being opened and needs to be walked through—to build a Relationship with my changing life.

I am probably missing and misreading some things. This, last night's attempt to put something into words, is subject to revision and complication as other thoughts/ feelings/ things arise.

PETER
29 JANUARY 2016

Gilla, part of Ann's life for 10 years

Ten years and a bit ago, Gilla was let into the room where we were waiting at the Morristown Seeing Eye Dog Center to meet this dropout from their training program. Tail swinging, she bounded up as if we were meant to be her friends for life.

Indeed, assuming any new acquaintance would be a friend was the lesson teacher Gilla taught anyone ready to learn it. Of course, she didn't know, but, in her Gilla dog way, was prepared to go along with, where she'd be taken by the Taylor-Blum family. The photos at http://bit.ly/gilladog show her making friends—and being a dog—as far as Idaho and Portugal, and in every pond and culvert of the Middlesex fells here nearby.

On Friday she splashed around in her favorite stream in the lower Fells, both on the way out and heading home. The walk was on the short side, as had become usual, but gave no sign that, later that day, she'd need to be carried up the stairs. A visit to the vet the next morning led to a weekend in the Blue Pearl animal hospital, where the picture emerged of heart troubles combined with (or because of) lymphoma. We expected to start chemo yesterday, but the morning news was of fluid buildup as her heart had trouble pumping strongly. She was very pleased to see the "family" as we arrived at the hospital—Jen (her dogwalker and close close friend since she arrived in Arlington), Vann and girlfriend Ashley, and me. She was able to lift her head to take us in, snuggle in our laps, relax as we stroked her head. But everyone was surprised by how quickly her congested heart failed; she was gone before sunset. But still beautiful. Now missed by many.

My thanks and love to everyone who let her into their lives.

PETER
23 FEBRUARY 2016

Gilla and Ann, Guimarães, Portugal, November 2012

Memorial Event
Remembrances

RMCLAS, Santa Fe, New Mexico
1 April 2016

(Full audio recording of talks, with tone, emotion, and audience response, at http://bit.ly/rmclas16)

Bill French

We're here to mark the passing of a very close friend and colleague of many of us, and a good friend of the Oaxaca Seminar, of RMCLAS [Rocky Mountain Council for Latin American Studies], and of all of you in the room.

Before we start, I'd like to acknowledge Elena and Amanda, who are on the RMCLAS organizing committee, who encouraged a panel in honor of Ann. I'd also like to acknowledge the presence of Peter Taylor in the audience—Ann's partner and my friend for many years.

Now, I'd like to turn the floor over to Lois Rudnick before she has to leave. Lois was Ann's undergraduate professor at UMass Boston.

Lois Rudnick: "Ecstatic because Ann was one of those people that made teaching at UMass Boston absolutely wonderful"

Thirty-one years ago, Ann Blum walked into my office. I was director and chair of American Studies for about four hundred years before I retired in 2009 and moved to Santa Fe to escape the New England Winters. But I'm still a recovering academic because I can't stop teaching. I had never met a student like Ann. I started teaching at UMass Boston in 1974 part-time, then in '77 got tenure and then became director of the department. It was 1985 when she walked into my office and started telling me about her *multiple careers*—before she decided to go back and complete her BA. And I don't know whether she thought I'd be concerned or upset, but I was utterly ecstatic because Ann was one of those people that made teaching at UMass Boston absolutely wonderful. Extraordinary young men and women who had all kinds of alternate lives, and travelled and experienced the world, and then in their thirties decided, "Maybe I do want to finish my degree, or get a degree." I fell in love with her in five minutes, and was thrilled to be her mentor and chair. I believe—I don't know this for a fact, I have to check this out—that she may have been the first person to do an independent study in American Studies. (It took a while for us to become a major.) She was an *absolute joy*. When she joined the faculty and tenure track in 2000, I'd never had an undergraduate student at UMass who became a faculty member at UMass Boston. That just wasn't the trajectory of most of our first generation of working-class students, and I knew that she would be a phenomenal leader in her department, which she was. I felt so fortunate to have her there as a peer after having had her as a student. And I'm just thrilled to be able to have these two minutes worth of memories of Ann before you do this wonderful presentation.

Bill

Before we go too much further we were going to share some Sauvignon Blanc in honor of Ann. But we decided, as a RMCLAS gathering, we would perhaps go with two different kinds of tequila as a way of toasting, as we go along. If that's of interest please come and help yourselves. There are little red shot glasses in the back. *[joyful chatter]*

Bill: "We were there together [in] a great space of collegiality"

I have to admit, I don't know what kind of tone to set in this kind of a session. I'd like it to be celebratory in the sense of acknowledging a tremendous colleague, a tremendous scholar, a friend—someone whom I taught with for more than fifteen years in the Oaxaca program. That's the tone I'm going to try to maintain. Actually, I was taken by complete surprise when I was thinking about this session and about my relationship with Ann because I thought that we had taught in Oaxaca maybe, six or eight times or had been there for a few years. I'm not very good at history and have no sense of time. I went back to 2006 and I'd found a letter I'd written for some promotion, or something to do with Ann's career—and I talked about the eight years that we'd spent in the Oaxaca program up to 200*6* and we had another eight after that. So we had a long, long and very, very productive and very, very enjoyable relationship in the Oaxaca Seminar.

There are a number of memories I take with me about that seminar. One is how absolutely dedicated Ann was to mentorship and to modeling the kind of relations that we had as scholars at the front of the room, and as scholars with graduate students. I remember that we would meet to get that front and center in all that we did in the Oaxaca Seminar—to try to stress those kinds of relationships and that kind of modeling. I also remember the tremendous time that Ann would take, willing to meet with all the graduate students over coffee or lunch, and I'm looking at people nodding—I see lots of people from the Oaxaca program in here. So it's nice to see that nodding Ageeth, Robbie and Eddie and Rob and Shayna and Amanda and other people in the room, people up at the front.

The other thing that struck me as I was thinking about the period of team teaching in the Oaxaca Seminar is the tremendous range of Ann's scholarship. I realize now, looking at everything that we did, is that every year when we came back together in June to teach that there would be a new article, or new chapter, or some new piece of original research. So what really, really strikes me is the tremendous generosity and sharing of this constant research with her colleagues and with the students in Oaxaca and elsewhere in publishing it. We had a chance to do a presentation of Ann's book, *Domestic Economies,* in the Oaxaca Seminar, and she was so generous as a scholar, it was so amazing to read and re-read the introduction, and to look at the bibliography in this book because it's like a "who's who" at RMCLAS. It attests to her range of interests. Not only family history, but certainly centered in family history. I think that she was a labor historian as well, who took class as a category very seriously. She engaged with John Lear's work, and with many other people's work in here. She was a family historian who engaged with Donna Guy's work, Ann Twinam's work, Susan Socolow's work, in this book. She was a gender historian, again, engaging with Donna's work and many, many people at RMCLAS. She was interested in social reproduction, she was interested in so many different things that ranged across so many different fields. She was also a scholar of the Porfiriato and a scholar of the Mexican Revolution. Reading her bibliography and who's she's engaging with and speaking to in her work, really is a tremendous testimony to the kind of community that we're building through both the RMCLAS and programs like the Oaxaca Seminar. I think she's a very generous scholar in recognizing all those kinds of engagements and all those contributions to her own work. I think in promoting the next generation of scholarship around the history of childhood, and I think we'll hear more about that.

I didn't want to go on very long, but I have to say that one of the most memorable things for me about The Oaxaca Program, other than going with Ann to Paquita la del Barrio concert, which was touring, where sons had to carry their screaming mothers and grandmothers out of the venue in a fireman's carry. And we tried to make sense of it as gender historians, about what was actually going on. That was a very memorable experience, but what most comes to mind is that almost every morning in the time that we spent in Oaxaca—I kinda call it "Oaxaca Time" because we would go back every year for a month, almost, and we would pick up some of the things that we like to do every year. We would walk up the hill above the Guelaguetza auditorium. All students and faculty who were around were invited to join us, and we would spend an hour, an hour and a half, walking and talking. I don't think Ann and I missed many mornings in the time that we were there together. It was a great classroom, it was a great space of collegiality, it was a space of friendship, and we would learn things about the emergence of the "Chicatanas," the flying ants that would come out that people would collect to make salsas, and things like that. We knew all the names of the dogs that lived on the hill. And actually, I planted trees up there as well, so I have a living connection, as well as a memory-one to the hill, and walking the hill.

Ann's scholarship is going to have a continuing and on-going impact that we see at the front of the room today, and in the audience as well today. I'd just like to toast the memory of a fine colleague and a very, very good friend.

Katherine Bliss: "Seeds of generosity, compassion, humor, and open engagement that she has planted in each of our hearts"

I met Ann in the summer of 1992, when I was in Mexico City to do some exploratory dissertation research. I was spending a lot of time at the Archivo General de la Nación, working in the section that housed document collections related to public health, public welfare, and other social services in the late 19th and early 20th centuries.

Much of the time I was by myself, but one day I noticed another researcher had arrived, a slender woman with pointy glasses, hair clipped up in a sideways ponytail with a long barrette, and a striped shirt.

Curious, I wandered up to the main desk to check out the request slips she had submitted—who was this Berkeley graduate student, I wondered? Was she looking at the same documents I was? Did this mean I was going to have to search for a new dissertation topic? You can imagine the many thoughts swirling through my head.

Imagine my pleasure when Ann later came over to the table where I was sitting to introduce herself. Over a brief discussion then, and coffee at the AGN cafe later that week, we discovered that we were indeed looking at overlapping, yet different issues—Ann was researching the lives of children without parents, societal perspectives on orphanage, and the public and private institutions that arose to support adoptions and other services for babies and young children without families, whereas I was looking at public health and the experience of adolescents and young women who became involved in sexual commerce in Mexico City. Ann's enthusiasm for her subject was contagious, and she was anything but competitive. As we compared notes on how we had become interested in the topics and shared information about some of the other archives we had found useful, it very quickly became clear to me that Ann was a gem of a colleague, and I hoped we would also become friends.

Over the next two plus decades, I was indeed fortunate to count Ann as a close colleague and good friend. She and Peter generously put me up for a night in Ithaca as I drove from Chicago to my first job in Amherst in 1996, and Ann cooked an amazing chicken molé dinner, even as she, Peter and Vann, their 5 year-old son, were preparing to move to Pennsylvania within the next few weeks.

We shared rooms at numerous conferences over the years—LASA in Miami, Las Vegas, Guadalajara, Washington, DC, and the European Social Sciences Conference in Berlin—resolving always that the rooms should be safe spaces in which to both debate new and different approaches to old themes or decompress after a difficult panel or strange encounter. I should add that these conversations were frequently mediated by cups of strong coffee that Ann brewed herself using a small cone filter and hot pot she brought from home.

And we shared some interesting adventures on the margins of the Oaxaca Summer Institute, too—one time dragging Bill French with us to see Paquita, la del Barrio, at a concert venue on the outskirts of town; another time getting thrown out of a restaurant near Yautitlán with Bill Beezley and John Hart after a conversation with the local mayor and chief of police turned sour once the topic turned to the legacy of the Mexican Revolution in the southern part of the country; and yet another being flashed by a man standing on a busy street corner wearing nothing but a sombrero and a very colorful blanket, which he expertly adjusted to expose himself to us as we passed by.

I have throughout my house decorative reminders of Ann's generous spirit—a small talavera plate she found at the Coyoacán market, baskets from Oaxaca, a copal incense burner, and collection of historic photographs from Mexico City. One of my daughter's favorite books is one Ann gave her when we met for a walk through Radcliffe Yard back in November of 2013—it's "Press Here" by Hervé Tullé, the one where you press colored dots to activate different situations in the text—back then, at 18 months, Isabel found it a bit challenging, but now she's a pro at working the dots, and I think of Ann each time we read it.

Others will be speaking about Ann's role as a mentor, but let me share one thought before I go on to describe what I have found to be inspirational about her work as a scholar: sometime in the fall of 1995 I was asked to share some of my dissertation research at the University of Chicago Legal History Workshop. This was not the usual workshop I attended, and I think the members were not accustomed to presentations about non-U.S. topics. In any event, my proposal that by examining prostitution and sexual commerce I was looking at private life was met with derision, particularly by two law students who, in retrospect, were probably using their barbed comments to me as a way of scoring points against each other. Perhaps now I understand why they objected to my argument, but it was an unpleasant situation, all the same. Back home, nursing my wounds, I wrote about the experience in an email to Ann; I don't have the correspondence any longer, but I remember that in her reply she wisely observed something to the effect that "life is not a competition" and that scoring points or winning arguments at the graduate workshop level was not what it's really all about. She instead emphasized the importance of having other interests, friends, and commitments to keep one "grounded and centered," in her words, in the midst of chaos and fray.

In many ways I think it was Ann's sense of grounded-ness and the fact that she took delight in so many things outside of work that made her such a compassionate and insightful scholar.

First, I should note that Ann was an extraordinarily disciplined researcher. From the early 1990s, when we first met, I knew Ann to have a laser-like focus on using her time well to get her work done. Perhaps she brought some of this focus to her research from her work as an archivist at the Harvard Museum of Comparative Zoology, during which time she completed her undergraduate degree and also wrote an award-winning book, *Picturing Nature*. But I think it was also the fact that Ann's trips to Mexico were usually relatively short that enabled her to focus so intently: Vann was a young child at the time, and if they didn't all travel together to Mexico, Ann and Peter would take turns traveling, doing research, and managing child care over the summer months.

But I mean, Ann's focus was impressive—she would show up at the archives as soon as they opened, around 8 am, take a quick break to down a box of Jumex mango juice for sustenance at 11 am or noon, and soldier on until the archives closed around 3 or 4 pm. Sometimes we would search out a new venue for comida in the Centro Histórico, but then, when I might be heading home afterwards, Ann would continue on to another archive or periodical collection that was open late, and only after that go back to her room to analyze the day's work and prepare herself for the next one.

Over the period between 1994 and 2001, Ann and I co-organized several conference panels—from AHA to LASA to the New England Conference on Latin American Studies (NECLAS)—on topics ranging from social welfare programs in Mexico and Argentina to scientific networks in post-revolutionary Latin America. Her approach, whether as panelist, moderator, or chair, was consistently collaborative and curious—even when she disagreed with a panelist's methodology or conclusions, she offered her comments in a diplomatic and open-minded manner.

I also had the opportunity to appreciate how Ann's approach to her own research changed over time. Following our early archive conversations about "dead babies and forgotten girls," I had the opportunity to read her dissertation when I was a member of a NECLAS prize committee, and we awarded it the best dissertation prize in 1998 or 1999. A few years later I read her manuscript for the University of Nebraska press and was impressed at how she had transformed a prize-winning dissertation into a book that went beyond an institutional and social history of welfare programs for children into a nuanced examination of "family practices and class formation in Modern Mexico."

From 2002 until 2006 I working with Ann on an article about changing ideas regarding adolescence in 1920s and '30s Mexico City for the volume Bill and I edited on Gender and Sexuality in Post-Independence Latin America. We initially discussed the project over lunches in Harvard Square or at an amazing little Mexican restaurant around the corner from where Ann and Peter and Vann lived in Arlington. One time we were so involved in a conversation about orphans and sexual abuse that a woman eventually came over to us and asked, "Do you KNOW how you sound to the rest of us?" We were apparently oblivious to the intensity of our discussion and insensitive to the effect hearing about the tragic lives of homeless children might have on others less interested in the topic.

I mention that episode, in part, because it was a bit out of character. What really struck me over the period that Ann and I collaborated on the article was the careful and sensitive way Ann read the documents, most of which were case files from the Consejo Tutelar para Menores Infractores, patiently peeling away the judgmental language of the social workers to find poignant stories of love and hope, which she described with sincere compassion and her typical, beautiful prose in the text.

Let me end with a few observations about Ann as a role model, particularly during the course of her illness. Throughout our communication over the last year of her life—primarily email—I saw that Ann brought the same compassion, grace, and humor to her experience of being a cancer patient that she brought to her scholarly work. On the one hand, knowing that I had been devastated by the loss of my mother to lung and liver cancer just a few years before, Ann confessed that she had been worried about upsetting me when sharing news about her own diagnosis. Even when describing a recent round of treatments or a setback she had faced, she always inquired about my family and wanted to know how my father's latest surgery or procedure might have gone.

And yet, Ann found ways to see the positive or humorous in her encounters with the medical system. One time she wrote about the joy of discovering that one of her caregivers at Mt. Auburn Hospital had been a nursing student—and a minor in Latin American Studies at U-Mass Boston, the very program in which Ann taught and the department which she had chaired. In another email she wrote about the effects of chemotherapy, including hair loss: And here I quote: "And I got tired of hair everywhere, and had the barber around the corner shave my head yesterday. When I put on my glasses and saw the results I couldn't believe how much it makes me look like my father! Uncanny. Of course, he didn't wear a scarf or hoop earrings."

Even after infections and other complications prevented Ann from continuing chemotherapy and made it difficult for her to be very physically active, she took pleasure in describing the beauty of the natural world and changing seasons outside her window; thinking about the wonderful garden she had cultivated in her yard below; and considering the vegetable seeds she might order from a worker-owned supplier in Maine that had been her go-to source for many years.

Having shared many bottles of beer, and a few shots of mescal, with Ann over the years, I now look forward to joining you later in this session in toasting her memory, her scholarly contributions, her friendship, and her mentorship, and most of all, the seeds of generosity, compassion, humor, and open engagement that she has planted in each of our hearts.

Elena Jackson Albarrán: "She changed the field of Mexican History for me."

I don't mind being redundant on some of these points because I think they bear repeating. I don't think anyone minds dwelling on her scholarly interventions, her generosity—that's the word that comes to the forefront of everyone's mind when talking about Ann—or her mentorship.

First I wanted to talk about her scholarship, and what her scholarship meant for me, and for those of us who are working on history of family and history of childhood and welfare. Then I want to talk about her mentorship, and what I put her through a little. So, I'm sorry, Ann.

Ann made an indelible imprint in the scholarship of family history, the history of childhood and welfare, and gender history in modern Mexico. She changed the way that we think about the relationship of the state to the family, following in the footsteps of people like Mary Kay Vaughan and Donna Guy. One of the things she did really well was to define and characterize the state, to render it palpable in the form of institutions, agencies, ideologies, program resources, and individuals that Mexicans interacted with every day. From my perspective, her contributions broke open the history of childhood as a viable field of study in Modern Mexico and beyond.

She started in her dissertation, and in her influential article in *The Journal of Family History*, by looking at how motherhood was unevenly constructed across classes, in large part, by state policies and prevailing moral ideologies about illegitimacy, by looking at patterns of child circulation and welfare policy. She dismissed the fictive script of the monolithic welfare state, deftly demonstrating that state-sponsored orphans actually circulated among and between networks of mothers, domestic workers, and state officials. And she brought those individuals to life in ways that help us to envision the way that the state was working. In her chapter in *Sex and Revolution* she looked at petitions to the orphanage to reveal the ways that potential adoptive parents and potential adoptees themselves articulated their understanding of the state's message about the revolutionary family.

These published scholarly interventions, along with conference presentations as she revised her dissertation manuscript into a book, reveal the development of an increasingly child-centered analysis, and she began to look at discourses about and experiences of children as fertile ground for understanding the evolving state and popular understandings of the family. Ever-attentive to the material, symbolic, and semiotic power of work as a social force, she was able to describe families in terms of their respective labor—compensated or not, gendered, and unevenly distributed of its individual members. In her work of the Tribunal de Menores, she described the developing tensions and overlap between the categories of protected and working childhoods, and the ways that these distinctions were implicated in a vast network of childhood practices.

The sensitivity to the intimacies of labor politics is reflected in her service to the profession at the university level, demonstrating a rare continuity between scholarship and professional activities that many of us would like to emulate. In her own words, in comments that she sent to me from a 2011 AHA CLAH Panel on Latin-American nationalist policies intended to socialize, educate or benefit children, she asked, "Did the policies or programs that flowed from these rationales benefit children? Undoubtedly, albeit, unevenly. Were the advocates of child health, welfare, and nutrition sincere or cynical? Most probably, they were sincere and well meaning. Thus, concepts in childhood, conflicted and contradictory as they were, in many instances produced healthier children and more fulfilled lives. Still, we must never lose sight of the fact that these concepts also reified and widened the social and economic distance between those who benefitted and those who were left out of the national family portrait." These thoughts that she wrote capture an essence of her intellectual vision. She saw in modern Mexican history the flawed individuals that toiled, and litigated, and legislated as part of a national family. As messy and misunderstood, and well intentioned, and poorly communicated as any family.

In her last RMCLAS presentation when we met in Santa Fe in 2013, she presented an evocative paper called, 'The Color of Home" [see page 159ff]. I don't know how many people were at that presentation about fatherhood and work, nuancing our understanding of the shape of the family. When I caught up with her after her presentation, she told me that she was loving this new project because she was finally getting "out from under the state." She was not to deal with the state anymore and free to explore the more affective, emotional and sensory aspects of family life and gender relations that her previous work had not allowed for. Understanding what it feels like to be trapped under the weight of a long dissertation-to-book project, I was so very much looking forward to watching her model the second project transition with as much grace and erudition as she did the first. I'm sad that we won't have the opportunity to see that.

I want to change topics and talk a little bit about her mentorship. Bill Beezley has this assignment in his seminar where the students have to read a recently completed dissertation, and contact that person to interview them. In 1999, I was a Master's student, and I was working on a topic of the history of gendered state welfare in the 1960s. It was a bad thesis. I subjected Adrian Bantjes to this thesis as well, so I'm feeling really guilty in the RMCLAS family right now about some of my earlier scholarship. Ann had just completed her dissertation, "Children Without Parents; Law, Charity and Social Practice, Mexico City 1867-1940" in 1998, at UC Berkeley, so she was the person that Beasley said I needed to interview. And I was terrified, I was a Master's student, and I was uncertain of my choice to pursue history as a profession, and I was apprehensive at the daunting task of writing a dissertation. I read hers. And I remember calling her on my land-line, lying on the floor of my first apartment in Tucson, my elbows propped on her daunting four-hundred page manuscript, wrapping the phone cord around my wrist and interviewing her nervously, first from my scripted questions and then increasingly informally, as she began to warm me to the ins and outs, and ups and downs of historical practice. We met in person shortly thereafter in Oaxaca, where I was a student in the Summer Institute of 2000. We walked down Alcalá, and she took me to the restaurant, Maria Bonita. She introduced me to the delicious bread soup. And entertained my elementary questions with characteristic grace and nurturing encouragement.

I returned to Tuscon and enrolled in a PhD program in history. Her research drew my attention to the child-centered decades of the 1920s and 1930s as a space for exploring the history of childhood through tracking down and analyzing child produced documents—an unthinkable task made thinkable through her demonstration that the state really was paying unprecedented attention to the nation's children for lots of transparent, and also insidious reasons, in the decades following the Revolution. I embarked. I'd like to say that those seminal conversations on the phone and in person with Ann set me on the path to success. But unfortunately for her, the increasing proximity of our research interests forced her to bear witness to many of my most awkward and egregious conference faux-pas and over the course of my fumbling graduate development. We sat on more panels than I'm sure she would've cared to remember: at the AHA CLAH, at the Society for History of Childhood and Youth, numerous RMCLAS panels, and at the Mexicanistas Conference. On one occasion, on one of our earlier conference presentations, I showed up to our panel armed with a twenty-page paper that was probably printed at about a space and a half and that was going to be my conference presentation. This was one of my earlier conferences, and she was chairing the panel. She graciously let me pass the fifteen-minute mark before passing me the five-minute note. I started to sweat, and had about eleven pages to go. I didn't have any experience with extemporizing. I had no confidence in my ability to summarize or omit any part of the argument that I deemed essential to everyone's understanding of everything I had to say. So I powered on. Then the two-minute note, the one-minute note... how many of you have gotten more than three notes? Then Ann passed me a note that said, "YOU'RE DONE." I was pretty sure she was talking about my career and not just the conference paper. And I was pretty sure that I had just burned a very significant bridge. She was also the first person on a conference panel to ask me to consider how I would go about gendering childhood. I had no idea what she meant, so I dramatically fumbled with a completely off-base answer. After the panel she gently, but sagely, suggested some ways that I could deepen my analysis along the lines of gender historical inquiry, and tactfully provided me with examples without being condescending.

We continued to appear on panels together, and she continued to provide clear, generous, enormously intellectual and productive feedback on mine, and all collaborators' presentations. She met with me in Cambridge for coffee when I was in town and helped me think through the organization of my book. She directed me toward archival collections at the AGN, and the Archivo de Salubridad. She always communicated with me and encouraged me through my process in a way that helped me through some of those awkward moments, and feel like its possible to be such a good and generous non-competitive scholar and mentor. She changed the field of Mexican History for me, and I feel like I will always be scuttling along in her wake.

Maria Muñoz: "This knack for asking key questions—the really gutsy important questions you probably didn't want to ask of yourself."

My colleagues have talked quite a bit about Ann's intellectual contribution and the work that she did. I'm going to focus more on the mentoring part. I don't think I could say anything better than my colleagues have said about her academic contribution. In all honestly, it's been really difficult to put into words anything to do with Ann. It's been four months since Peter, Vann, and siblings, friends and colleagues, and our intellectual community…since *WE* suffered this great loss.

I posted on Facebook what I could convey in the days after she passed [www.facebook.com/ann.blum.7], but since then, frankly, I've not been able to—nor *wanted* to give voice to the loss of her. So now here I am trying to find the words that can come close to even conveying the impact of her on so many lives, on mine in particular. Out of everyone here today on this panel, I probably knew her the least amount of time. Still, her influence on a personal and professional level is immeasurable.

I met Ann in 2003 as part of the Oaxaca Summer Institute. I was in the middle of my M.A. program and was making the transition from French Algeria to Latin America. One of the assignments during Ann and Bill French's week on gender was to think critically on how we might imagine gender, and/or questions of gender fitting into the work that we were doing, whether it was M.A. or PhD research. I remember that we had to go around and give reports on how we might do that. There were about fourteen of us in that group—so about seven MA students and seven PhD students. There's a couple of you guys in here that were part of that group, Ageeth, Robbie, Steve. I was person number six or seven as we went around the table. Most people gave thoughtful answers when it was my turn I said something like, "I really gave this a lot of thought"—most likely I had not—"but currently in my research I don't think gender analysis is at all useful or important." Right? I don't really know what Ann's or Bill's thoughts were at that precise moment. I don't think I ever *asked* or *wanted* to know. But I sat there, kind of like the little kid in Shel Silverstein's poem *Smart,* where he trades the dollar for two quarters, two quarters for three dimes, three dimes for four nickels, four nickels for five pennies, and then goes back to Dad and is really proud. "Then he closes his eyes and shook his head, too proud of me to speak." So, I actually sat there really quite proud of myself, thinking I had given a pretty clever answer. That somehow I had circumvented that situation.

A few months later at my first RMCLAS—it was actually here in Santa Fe, in 2004—I was trying to decide where to go to grad school and had narrowed it down to Oxford and the U of Arizona. Ann was so gracious and kind—she was still talking to me after the Oaxaca situation—and we discussed my options. Ann never really told anyone what to do. She had this quality, this thoughtfulness, this knack for asking key questions—the really gutsy important questions you probably didn't want to ask of yourself. She allowed you to draw your own conclusions and make and own your own decisions in that process. I ended up going to U of A. In my first years I actually made a *lot* of time bugging her, sending her emails, and in my times of desperation, calling her. She shared her graduate experience with me as a way to make me think of mine in more useful ways. She was really kind, but really firm, reassuring, but challenged me. And she pushed me to be intellectually uncomfortable in order to grow as a scholar and a person. I stayed in the PhD program because of Ann. She gave so much of her time and herself just to get me through that first year.

A couple of years later, when I was dissertating, she asked me to mentor a couple of young scholars. It was clear to me that it was my turn to do for others what she had done for me, and certainly *countless* others besides me. In many ways I'm a work in progress, working on becoming a better scholar, a better colleague, a better mentor—as she modeled for me.

I also had to eat my words when my research eventually revealed that, yes, I would need to consider forms of gender analysis to understand how indigenous women framed their demands in the language of motherhood, familial obligations, and femininities, and masculinities in regards to the post-1940s indigenous movements. She was too classy to say anything to me, but I think she really relished the moment when the "g-bomb" came out of my mouth.

When her book *Domestic Economies* was published, the Oaxaca Summer Institute held a book presentation for her in 2011. She asked me to provide comments on her book. I was both feeling honored, but also quite sheepish at that moment, reminded of our first seminar together years before. I also think that it was her way of welcoming me on board as I joined the seminar as co-director. It was also her way of taking me seriously as a colleague in the seminar and in the academy as a newly minted assistant professor.

What I intend in sharing these stories is to convey her empath as a mentor in the field. As a woman, and the work that she did in terms of research on gender, masculinities, fatherhood, children, the ill. She also taught me as a scholar I didn't have to tear someone else down for my own work to matter and be valued. She showed me how important it is to encourage and mentor young scholars. She modeled how to be a historian, how to be a colleague, how to be a mentor, how to be strong, kind, and generous, and enjoy life. She modeled for me how to be a consummate professional. I was fortunate enough to say these things to her last May when I visited with her. For those of you who may not have had the opportunity to do so, I want you to know that I made sure that she knew that I was not the only young scholar whom she meant this much to. And I made sure that she knew that part of her legacy in our field, in our craft, in life, would be carried on by many of us.

There are many things I will remember. I will remember the ritual search for a *frutero*—the perfect endless, elusive drive for this *frutero*. Our market visits for avocado leaves for our *frijoles negros* in Oaxaca, our coffees, our *limonades*, our "foodie" conversations, sharing cooking tips and recipes as well as wine ideas. And I will always remember that infectious smile and joyful laughter. Above all, I will remember that keen mind, the kindness, the compassion, the strength, the love of our dear mentor and friend. I chose to think of how privileged I am to have had her in my life, and that Peter and Vann shared her with all of us.

Bill

I'd like to open the floor in the time we have left.

Walter Brem: "Always had a smile; she was always positive"

First I want to thank the panel and Amanda for organizing this. I've known Ann for *thirty years* and I didn't really know anything about her until today. When I arrived at the Bancroft Library in 1985, she was a student and I could tell she was older because we were both older. She was in the *manuscript* division. This was not a happy place, but she always had a smile, she was always positive, and when I had questions she always answered them. She knew a shit-load more than I did about what was down there. But she was one of those among a very few others that, when I asked questions, I would get answers. But then later I got to know her through these various RMCLASes, that's how I got to know her. But she never never pushed her own history or research agenda. I had to ask her; I had to draw stuff out. Bill and I had a conversation earlier and I said, "She was always so secretive," and he says, "That's not the person *I* know." I just had to draw her out. I am so pleased to learn how much she did—not just Oaxaca, but in the "biz." So this has been a wonderful panel because now I really know who Ann is.

Susan Deeds: "She had this incredible grace I'll never forget"

I probably met Ann in 1998 or 1999. She came to Mexico City when I was on sabbatical and so I introduced her to Elsa Movido, who worked on children also—she was another colleague that we lost a few years ago and was a really close friend of mine. Over the years when Ann would come to Mexico- this was before Oaxaca, she had a friend in Coyoacán where she stayed and we would get together. We would talk about our graduate school experiences—we had some similar kinds of experiences finishing our PhDs. But mainly we talked about family. I never met Peter or Vann, but I really felt like I knew Vann. Vann was younger than my son, Colin, who was almost like an only child because he was born so much later. We would have these incredible conversations. What I remember the most about Ann is that we would invert the mentorship—I mean, I'm supposed to be the mentor, I'm going to be seventy-three this year and I've probably mentored quite a few people, and maybe some of them are even here. But I felt like it was Ann who mentored me. That she had this compassion and warmth and understanding. We've all talked about her generosity, which was great, but I would also say that she just had this incredible grace that I'll never forget.

Bill Beezley: "She had the ability to make everybody in the room better."

First, I think Ann and John really represent what Berkeley *should* be, what UC *should* be, and their impact on the profession. Berkeley's gone in different directions now, but for me, Bolton, all of those greats from years past at Berkeley, Ann's in that line. Tremendous scholars (and so is John). So, it's great to know that she was there.

Second, I went to Tufts one time to do a lecture. Because Ann knew I was in town, she invited me to go sightseeing in Boston, and she took me to Walden Pond. Ann knew of all these wonderful things going on there. She talked about Walden Pond, she talked about Thoreau, she talked about biology, about Thoreau's involvement with plants and flowers and all that stuff. So, for me it was a short course, well, maybe a long course on botany and biology. And I wanted to be a biologist or a botanist when I first went to college. So it was wonderful, you could *see* how much she respected that. I always think about Ann and Thoreau—not enough to read Thoreau.

The other thing I wanted to say is that the whole initial idea of Oaxaca was that in the U.S., England, Canada, Mexico, and other places, there are people of great quality who don't teach at PhD-producing schools. But, they deserve to interact with graduate students, and graduate students really need to interact with them. So that was the idea, that Ann wasn't at Chicago, or Texas, or Berkeley, but students had a chance to go and spend time with her by going to Oaxaca. She made things happen there that were simply unbelievable and they will always continue.

For me, the two words that I would use to describe Ann's experience, or, my experience with Ann and what I think she meant, is first of all, Ann was a person, rare, rare, who had the ability to make everybody in the room better. *Better.* And she did it because— Susan stole my word—she lived with grace.

Amanda López: "Ann was so smart, but she made being smart look *easy.*"

I want to speak for all of us who where influenced by Ann and maybe she didn't know it, that she influenced us so much. When I did Oaxaca in 2002—and a lot of Oaxaca 2002 people are here—I was doing a part-time Master's program in San Antonio. I wasn't even serious about graduate school, and somehow you get to Oaxaca through people—so I got there, I'm not going to explain that. Ann was there, and I honestly, probably, when I talked to her, was like, "Oh my god, this is the maybe the smartest person I've ever spoken to in my whole life," and I was *very* intimidated. I was intimidated by a lot of things. But anyway, "Whoa, this is not gonna work out!" Ann was so smart, but she made being smart look *easy*. So democratic about it, that I was like, "Wait, I *can* do this." Like, *I* can do this. Oh, I can't be Ann, she's one of a kind. So this is what I'm talking about how she influenced, but maybe she didn't know.

So, right after I got back from Oaxaca in 2002 and I applied to the U of A program, I wrote Ann a letter to thank her for everything that she had done for me, and how she had inspired me to actually go on to do the dissertation research. But, I was a little shy and I decided never to send it to her because, I don't know, I just was like this is showing too much emotion. When I moved to my tenure track job in Chicago, in all the cleaning out I found the letter that I never sent to her, I probably should've sent it then, at that point, but I never did. At *this* point I'm finally trying to tell Ann, "thank you," because I wouldn't be here without her.

Robert Weis: "It all kind of comes together—the flesh and the blood, the paper and the ink."

I was just thinking about Ann. I was thinking about Adrian Bantjes and how when one is coming up—and I came up with Maria and Rob, Ageeth and Amanda… —one comes to people not *as people*, but as books, as articles. Then it's a tough process to think, besides paper and ink, they're are also blood and bones and flesh. And then when one *meets* people, "Oh, that's you!" Ann, though, is really important, as a lot of people have said, in helping us make that transition. That could also be you! You're a part of this group and you could do that. I could see her diving a fork into some food and saying "So what are you working on?" That's really helping me get to a higher place. Then I'm thinking about those people, they come and go and then become books again. But when I read Ann's book, it's not a book, it's *Ann*. It's Ann talking to me. It all comes together—the flesh and the blood, the paper and the ink.

Thinking about Ann, it points out to me we're a tribe that's pretty vital; there's a lot of people along the way that say, "Hey, man, you're doin' all right." Ann was one of those very important people. I'm also happy that there are so many people like Ann that are still with us, that are still like, "I'll email you, send you his email, help you with this…" I'm happy to be part of this group.

Liz Hutchinson: "Adult Children of Academics"

I met Ann my first week of graduate school, so I share a lot of the stories here. She had almost no hair, she had those brilliant eyes, and the pointy glasses. We bonded *fleeing* Tulio Halperín's seminar in order to photocopy together a three-hundred page book—it took days. I think it was in those first conversations that, I, a lost graduate student—not sure yet of Latin American studies, or history or political activism, or where I fit—found Ann, and that was really comfortable. We bonded over xeroxing and quickly formed a small society, the ACA—Adult Children of Academics—because we found we shared a peculiar insecurity in so far as we felt like were supposed to know where we were and what we were doing all the time. But you still had that relationship with the parents that sometimes was nagging. I think it nagged me a lot more than it nagged Ann at that point. The compassion, and the grace, and the generosity of spirit that people have pointed to was a nurturing and a safe space.

And from then on, I think I lost out on the roommate roulette at many conferences, because you've gotten her first. When I had that chance to room with Ann and share that coffee that she would make in the hotel room, it was always with gratitude. I felt that space preserved a lot of the humanity and the community that was vital to even staying in this profession. I always appreciated that because it would've been very easy to fall out of the program and back into a kind of obsessive competitive professionalism that I felt at odds with. So that's the part of Ann that really modeled for me a career, during graduate school and throughout our work together, dropping "g-bombs" where ever we could.

Toni Loftin: "I really thank her and I'm really going to miss her."

I met Ann at Oaxaca, in '13- three years ago. And I found her to be generous, and interested in what I was thinking of doing in my dissertation. And so, when she wanted to meet the students I was really pleased because I was so intimidated by all you guys. Bill, Bill and Monica and Maria, and Gabriela—they were all these people who knew so much more than I did. I was going to get a chance to spend a month with you. When we sat down and talked, she asked me what I was thinking about doing. I said I was thinking about looking at American influence on retail in Mexico, and so I told her a bit about the research I'd been doing, and how I found archives at SMU. She said, "Well you know, you should consider gender, and looking at how Mexican women interpreted American ways of commerce." And that was something that I had not considered at all. I said, "okay" and I kind of put it in the back of my head.

Oaxaca '13 ended. I went back to school, passed my exams, got my proposal in. Gender made it into my dissertation proposal. Women in the home and domesticity and consumption, and the way that women went about interpreting that, is going to be a major part of my work. So I really thank her and I'm really going to miss her.

John Lear: "She would mentor by pretending that you were mentoring *her.*"

I think about Ann a lot. And I think about her in a lot of different places, at Berkeley, in Coyoacán where we often coincided with a dear shared friend, and I think about her in Santa Fe because we would often meet here. The last time we did what we'd often do: we just walked. She described this town that she had lived in between the different times in college: "This is the house where three of us lived," and "this happened," and "I would wait on tables…" She took me to a part of Santa Fe I'd never seen before—I don't know if she conjured it or if it really exists—this street with all these little restaurants. All this just reminded of one thing that's extraordinary about her: Ann had this very circuitous way to academia and it gave her a perspective that I just loved.

When I met her, I was finishing up at Berkeley and didn't know why I was there. I thought I was faking it and could walk away from it at any moment. And she came with all this humility, and generosity, and yet, she was one of the most intensely intellectual people I'd ever met. I remember having dinner with Peter and her and thinking, "Oh my god, these are real intellectuals!" One of the most amazing things— and other people have mentioned this as well—she would mentor by pretending that you were mentoring *her*. So, I was ahead of her, wasn't sure where I was going, and she always believed in what I was doing—read my dissertation, read my book chapters.

One last memory that I'll just throw in very quickly is the Querétaro meeting of Mexican historians and we did our walking routine and walked a lot. She and I were both dealing with people close to us had died. I believe it was a close friend of hers who had lost a child, and I had lost a friend who was a little bit older than me. It was The Day of the Dead. Part of our walk was working through this, and we went to this exhibition of these very personal altars. We both turned that—with the help of these Mexicans and this Mexican tradition—into a joyous afternoon. As Katherine mentioned, she did some of that as she was dying, and reached out to us. I remember a phone call where I said, "How are you doing?" then I thought, "DAMN!" I had told myself I would never say that. She sort of nurtured me out of that moment.

I'll miss her, but she is here, in Santa Fe.

Peter: "We're not ready to leave this—there's still more stuff we need to work on."

Ann and I were married nearly thirty years. You should all relax because, if you think you took a long time to learn lessons from Ann, I was with her for thirty years and there's so many lessons I didn't learn very well. The things I want to say are not going to be linear.

When I found out about this event and I was going to be in California, it was so wonderful that I could make my trip back to Boston come through here. Not just to hear what you're saying, but, I mean, you all lost her too. People send condolences to the spouse and the son, and so on, but I recognize it's very important for you to have a voice. It's wonderful to be here and I thank you for what you're saying.

If any of you haven't visited yet, there's a blog—really a repository—annblum.wordpress.com [now this book]. Full of wonderful things; some of those things date back before I met her. She dropped out of college twice in the late 60's and early 70's. Lois told us about how she came back, and that's about the time that we connected. So she was going back in the academic world, but there's a whole life before then. You'll get some glimpses if you go to that blog and maybe listen to some audio recordings connected. What I'll say is non-linear. I'll get back to the time before later.

We always worked in the same study, back to back—there were times when that's all the room we had. Over her desk, from the conference where they had collected all the diaries that she's been working on the last number of years, there is a poster. It has five generations of women in her family. It still sits on that wall, so even though I don't have *her* back to me, doing *her* stuff, I still have that. You can imagine that [see p. 149].

One thing that she taught me, one thing I *did* learn, what she articulated for me is she'd say, "We're not finished with this topic yet." She thought longer to gestate issues and to get things written. She wasn't terribly good at writing during the academic year. She put all her time and heart into teaching, advising students, being on committees, and so on. While I'd just take every crack of time, I'd be working—I could think about problems while I was walking to the bus. Ann gestated. She really needed the clear time in the summers, and so her writing took longer. So fads would come; I'm not going to name them; you've probably seen them. And she was able to see and say that "there's still more stuff we have to work on." That's a nice image to have in the change versus continuity schema of doing history. And it helps me a lot in my own work to think, "The reason I'm still working on this is because people didn't finish working on it. They let it go being unresolved." That's a helpful thing to think about.

We share an office and the phone rings. With the advent of the cordless phone, you could take it to another room. Yet at the times I overheard her, things might be really rough with campus politics or something else and people calling would ask how she is. She would automatically be able to tell them about the good things that were happening. I was stunned by that. I would often tell the truth while Ann would never show the bad stuff going on behind. What you are saying about generosity extends to her somehow seeing that "that is not important for me to share." The generosity comes from having, as they would say in psychology, very good boundaries.

To go back to there being a life in Cambridge before, when she was working in archives. We had a wonderful potluck party for her in December; people got to tell a lot of different stories. One friend, Sharon Kingsland, flew up from Baltimore just for a couple of hours. As she left, she gave me a packet of letters Ann had written to her over eleven years [reproduced in this book]. It is a most incredible thing. Sharon and Ann were research assistants for a Canadian professor who was doing a history of the Museum of Comparative Zoology. They'd work together in the summers. They were both beginning to write their first articles or give their first talks. Was it any good? Should I go to this party? I really should get up tomorrow; it's my one day to work— she was starting to work on the book that became *Picturing Nature*. All those struggles.

That led me down to the basement to find Sharon's letters to Ann. There they were, in neat archive folders. And there are all her research boxes. So there lies a puzzle for me, which maybe you can help me with. How to let go of it? Or is there anything you can do with work that had been percolating? There is wonderful stuff in there. What she was studying about families is also about life course. The letters she was working on reminding us of the letters she had been writing for all those years. Is there a way to recover that and have it honored—the letters, the vulnerability, the life course.

Bill

I will draw this session to a close. Thank you to the panel, the audience, Peter, everyone, and know that the conversations will continue. Thank you.

UMass Boston
21 April 2016

(Full audio recording of talks, with tone, emotion, and audience response, at http://bit.ly/ASBEvent)

Maria Cisterna-Gold (Chair, Latin American and Iberian Studies [LAIS] Department): "Always remind[ing] us of the ironies and incongruities of our daily lives"

Good Afternoon, hello. First, I want to thank all of you for coming today to share with us Ann's life and work. It's been a very difficult couple of years for us. For most of it, Ann was very present, responding to emails before anyone else. She had great ideas for all our concerns, and projects, and always had an answer for all our questions and challenges.

It was not easy to plan this event, this memorial, without her. She was the event planner of our department, impeccably organized and diligent. For this event, she would have created an agenda from day one that would have been circulated several times and very little deviation from it would have been allowed. However, she always managed to finish every task with a huge smile, making all of us feel as if it was our joint effort that made it all possible, when the truth is that success would have been clumsier without her.

Ann's work transcended categories and (indeed) disciplines. Her research examined childhood and adoption, connections among the urban poor and their children, family practices, and class formation, social reform and national formations. She has published multiple articles, essay collections and monographs, all while teaching a full load—that is "three/three" for you young ones out here—and being chair for four years. Her second book, *Domestic Economies: Family, Work and Welfare in Mexico City,*

1884-1943, received an honorable mention for the Mexican History book prize at the 2010 American Historical Association Conference on Latin American History. Also, later on, using a rich collection of men's lives writing, her latest work explored the intimate histories of authors—daily work, social roles, childhood, and affective lives within a world bound by family and community. However, she was always seeking to elucidate masculine and paternal renderings of domestic space and family life—a take not as popular when thinking of domestic tasks and responsibilities.

When Ann passed in November, we became even more aware of what she has meant to all of us. Today, we choose to think of Ann's passing, not as a loss, but as a presence. "An intellectual and critical radiance," as Walter Benjamin would say, from which to think about community, family, social responsibility, partnership and governance, because to her, that is what mattered. Remembrance of a life that will serve as a point of reference for the challenging times, for the difficult questions, and for when compassion and gratitude seem scarce. And most importantly, a sense of humor—a brilliant sense of humor like hers, that always reminded us of the ironies and incongruities of our daily lives.

Today we will hear from different friends and colleagues who are eager to share what Ann has meant to all of them, and how she touched every one of us by the scope of her research, as a colleague, as a mentor, and a teacher. I will be calling them by name, one by one. The first to speak will be Chancellor Motley.

Keith Motley (Chancellor): "Some of us are really from here...."

Thank you so much for the opportunity to be a part of this memorial service for someone who meant so much to us, to me personally. Someone who I smile every time I think about her. She was one of the people in my life who checked me. When she checked me, she taught me and nurtured me. But every time I asked her to do something for the University, she said yes.

"Strength and dignity are her clothing, and she laughs at the time to come. She opens her mouth with wisdom, and the teaching of kindness is on her tongue." Dr. Ann Blum, proud member of this University, UMass Boston Class of 1986, always let me know there was something she has that I will never have. Which was: the degree from here. "Some of us are really from here…."

Winston Langley (Provost): "Ability to link what appears to be footnotes in other areas of history."

…I'd like to make three or four points about Ann as I remember her, more in a scholarly sense. She had as an intellectual burden the re-centering of our understanding of the family, its place in social life, and the ways in which the realm of scholarship may be broadened and its approach properly tooled to understand this institution. And how our approach to historical inquiry may be properly enriched by an understanding of the role of the family.

Her work contributed in many ways to a broader understanding of children, childhood, domestic servants—an area where she spent time to do research and all of meticulous effort to secure the requisite evidence for respectful historical inquiry—public policy, social policy, child labor, public health, history of medicine. They all had a bearing on what she sought to do. In that sense, she played a major role, not unlike Charlotte Perkins's *Women and Economics* in the 1890s in showing that what we call micro-history is intimately tied to macro-history. And how she illustrated this—how a proper understanding of the family, of children, of orphans, of private charity may express itself in the goals and values of a revolution, and may find themselves expressed constitutionally and in governance and later in interaction with public policy. The ability to link what appears to be footnotes in other areas of history, to enrich our understanding of the importance of social history and how it informs any other sense of history. It is a remarkable goal and achievement…

I think the best professor is the student, one who is always seeking to come to knowledge. I think of Ann and Peter and the Department, which has played such an important role in our push for inter- and of transdisciplinary studies in recognition of the fact that life is multiple intersections and we grow within those intersections. I know we'll miss her very much, but I know the University has been enriched by the contributions she has made.

Estelle Disch (Sociology): "Ann presente!"

A couple of things about Ann—one is that she was willing to teach a General Ed Seminar as a tenured person. Those of us who worked in that Program know that was like pulling teeth. Ann loved this place and loved our students, and was always ready to work. Secondly, I knew Ann indirectly because my late partner wrote a book about the grandmothers of the Plaza de Mayo. Ann assigned the book in her courses, and every semester she would ask Rita to come and speak to the class. I don't know what Rita said to Ann about this, but Rita would come home so happy. Rita was dealing with her own cancer crisis at the time and she would just glow at the chance to meet UMass students and to talk with Ann's class. Every time that course got taught, there Rita was. So you're about to see a 2013 video [https://vimeo.com/64758505; see text earlier in the book] in which Ann is cheering on Rita because of the archive of her interviews of the grandmothers of Plaza de Mayo, which UMass has housed and made available. Ann spoke at the inauguration of that. If Rita were here, she would be singing Ann's praises and cheering her on. Ann presente!

Daniel Ortiz (Dean, Healey Library): "She graduated from here, she wants to give back"

I met Ann many years ago, when she was hired and I heard from one of the librarians that there was this scholar who had started working at UMass Boston, who came from a lineage of scholars. He was surprised that someone of her pedigree would come to UMass Boston. And I said, "I think you're missing the point. She graduated from here, she wants to give back." So, I went and met with Ann, and it was actually a formidable moment to meet someone who actually got the campus, got the students, and could go anywhere they wanted, and wanted to come back here. I really treasured that and enjoyed it. I didn't know that over the years I would be working with her more closely than I had before. We actually worked about three years, with the help of other faculty, in the then Hispanics Study Department to build a Hispanic Speaker Series. It was a collaborative between the Library and the Department, which brought wonderful speakers to the campus, and that did unique things. In those days we didn't have the technology to videotape everything that we wanted to. I wish that we would be doing that now that we have brand new apparatus in the library to do those kind of things.

Working with Ann, having her hand, supporting every single idea that we had, looking for speakers, fomenting the exchange of faculty, students, and a different kind of mentoring was something that I treasure very much. Then Ann became a member of the Library Committee, and she fought very arduously for a number of different things and represented the library very well at Faculty Council and a number of different forums. And she always did that with passion, as Winston said, she was not timid, she would speak her mind in a very nice tone. So, she was a good teacher for me in that sense…the Puerto Rican in me still comes out from time to time….or maybe it's my family, I'm not too sure about that.

Anyway, one day, I had moved to Arlington, and I'm minding my own business, and suddenly I see this woman. I'm like, "Oh. Oh, is that Ann?" It was Ann. She was walking her dog. I was surprised; she was surprised to see me. And so we had our sidewalk chats every so often. Every time she was walking her dog and I happened to be outside, or sometimes I would walk by her house, and admire her garden where she had been working for a long time, and it was really beautiful. It always reminded me that she was a true Renaissance woman in many ways. Her scholarship demonstrated that, her many interests, her desire to do things, for the good of doing the right thing, is the Ann that I met and enjoyed being colleagues, and friends with. I am going to miss her very dearly, and I miss our sidewalk talks.

Neal Bruss (English): "Ann carried on her back the mission of this university"

There's just no question that Ann picked up and carried on her back the mission of this university. And particularly the mission toward its students, as decisively as *anyone* in our history, and as decisively as anyone in this room, and there's several in this room who have done this. In the past five years of working very closely with her, I was amazed by this, by her simply picking up the mission and carrying it, in her classroom, in the transformation of her department, in NEASC and several other projects that we worked on together and in the Faculty Council.

Five months later after her passing, what I recall most is Ann's laughter. I have to tell you that before her illness, and early in her illness before its severity got through to me, I deliberately looked for ways to make Ann laugh. And I did it selfishly. I did this selfishly for my own benefit. I loved to hear her laugh; it rejuvenated me. Ann's laughter was the natural wonder of this campus. All that brilliance, that great iron of her character, her own sense of humor—all of it illuminating any room she was in.

One story, for NEASC the two of us were trying to get a *certain* type of data, to make a *certain* type of argument. And I told her that she understood what I was doing better than I did, and she should just go do whatever I was trying to do, and ignore me. That made her laugh, and I actually didn't intend to do so then. It was just so completely obvious that in these big projects—the biggest projects, she understood everything, and particularly, what was needed. She understood *me* completely, and I appreciated that very much.

I would say that *this* is what Ann means to me, the laughter, and this understanding, and the carrying of our mission. I cannot do justice to this dimension. She certainly was a person, but she is the whole kind of a person that we are with her. She is *US*. All this Spring, the first Mondays of the month, when I've gone to the Faculty Council, I *almost* see her on the front left corner of the table, that corner of the counsel table she held down with Jane Adams. I really have to tell you that, five months later, I navigate through my own responsibilities from day-to-day, with Ann's powers of discernment, *and* character, *and* understanding, *and all her iron* and her laugh, with me, *every day*. I valued her enormously. I still rely on her. My gratitude for having known her could not be greater.

Rachel Rubin (American Studies): "I will say to myself, 'Hey, Ann, it's good to see you again'"

Ann Blum was never boring. I say that feeling like I have known her a long time, because I knew her before I knew her—which I will explain in a moment. This acquaintanceship was a series of delightful surprises.

I am a faculty member in American Studies. Ann Blum was an American Studies major here at UMass Boston before we had an American Studies major here at UMass Boston. Therefore, I heard a lot about Ann from our previous chair (who, if you knew her, talked *a lot*). Ann's sophisticated innovation as an undergraduate shaped our major when we did establish it, and did develop it, just after I was hired. There are ways, you could say, that Ann shaped my job and institutional home, prepared it long before I even knew I was going to be an American Studies professor. So when I finally met her in person, for the first time, I was like, "Oh, hey, Ann, good to see you again."

I am probably not supposed to say this, but when I was on the CPC, I was blown away by Ann's 4th year review. Because she wasn't just an American Studies innovator who turn into a Latin Americanist! She had a whole other career as a zoologist! Gorgeous illustrations of animals washed over me—which, again, made me feel like I knew her, because my parents both really cared about nature—my mother, because she had grown up in the country, and my father, because he'd grown up in the city. Ann's 4th year review---people, we are talking about personnel work here—her 4th-year review made me glow and think of the beautiful natural world and sing, "Oh, hey, Ann, good to see you again."

This is not unique to me, but during my time here at UMass Boston, I have dealt with some really, really heavy personal situations. Ann could tell when something had landed on me, took me aside, and got me talking. She gave advice, she gave support, she let me swear like the Baltimorean I am. Ultimately, I would practically fling myself at her, sobbing, "Oh, hey, Ann, it's good to see you."

Of course, personal grief and joy notwithstanding, there are plenty of workaday responsibilities here. Over the years, I served with Ann on several committees—the FSU executive committee, the Faculty Council, the CHCS steering committee, and for a while a regular, informal chairs' gathering. Committee work can feel like you are in a magic realist story by Nicolai Gogol or Italo Calvino. It can be more boring than anything, but you really can't let your mind wander for a second. On more than one of these occasions, I'd be banging my head against an internal wall, and it would be starting to ache, and then Ann would ask the question that made it all clear. It was like strategic Advil that I would gulp down while saying in relief, "Whew! Ann! Good to see you again!"

And then Ann became ill, which filled me with first with rage, then with sorrow. And in the midst of her illness, she remembered everything to ask about. She gave me advice about my kids and my students and my scholarship and neighbors. I felt so lucky to have those visits, which sometimes I could see were costing her. Filled with gratitude, I would kiss her cheek and whisper, "Ann, it is so good to see you again."

On one of those last visits, she sent me home with a "daughter growing up poem" as my daughter was in her first semester of college. After we lost Ann, I hurried to my computer to read the poem again, and found, of course, that it has more than one meaning. I am going to read it now, for us and for Ann.

The Writer   Richard Wilbur, 1921

In her room at the prow of the house
Where light breaks, and the windows are tossed with linden,
My daughter is writing a story.
I pause in the stairwell, hearing
From her shut door a commotion of typewriter-keys

Like a chain hauled over a gunwale.
Young as she is, the stuff
Of her life is a great cargo, and some of it heavy:
I wish her a lucky passage.
But now it is she who pauses,
As if to reject my thought and its easy figure.
A stillness greatens, in which
The whole house seems to be thinking,
And then she is at it again with a bunched clamor
Of strokes, and again is silent.
I remember the dazed starling
Which was trapped in that very room, two years ago;
How we stole in, lifted a sash
And retreated, not to affright it;
And how for a helpless hour, through the crack of the door,
We watched the sleek, wild, dark
And iridescent creature
Batter against the brilliance, drop like a glove
To the hard floor, or the desk-top,
And wait then, humped and bloody,
For the wits to try it again; and how our spirits
Rose when, suddenly sure,
It lifted off from a chair-back,

Beating a smooth course for the right window
And clearing the sill of the world.
It is always a matter, my darling,
Of life or death, as I had forgotten. I wish
What I wished you before, but harder.

Ann, we are feeling your loss sharply here, but I am sure---I am sure---that around the corner will be many, many moments when I have a realization or hear a joke or drink pomegranate tea, and will feel lucky and will say to myself, "Hey, Ann, it's good to see you again."

Clara Estow: "Some very human qualities, of which I want to mention a couple, just to touch up the portrait a bit."

To be quite frank, I come here today and find UMass Boston greatly diminished. No, not because I retired, but because Ann is no longer here. I knew her as a student, as a colleague—I take some credit here for hiring her—and as an extraordinary citizen of the University.

I could recall for you all her many, many virtues—blah, blah, blah—but the other speakers today have covered that ground already, and better than I could. She was virtuous to a fault. As Reyes once said, how frustrating to some of us that you could try to fight with Ann, but she would NEVER take the bait. She got her way in other ways. The phrase iron fist in velvet glove comes to mind. But that is not quite fair. If one has ideals and principles and sticks to them, it's impressive how much one can accomplish.

But we are not here to canonize Ann; or, at least, I'm not. She had her flaws. OK, not flaws exactly, but quirks, no not quirks, eccentricities, no; simply some very human qualities, of which I want to mention a couple, just to touch up the portrait a bit.

You have heard and/or read about her outstanding contributions to the Oaxaca, Mexico summer school program, where she went from graduate student participant to co-director. Was it because of her abiding interest in modern Mexican history? Perhaps. Or, was she driven to leave her family during the summer because of her passionate love of Oaxacan food? And the month-long opportunity to savor the seven different local moles? I challenge anyone to say that her gustatory efforts do not qualify as legitimate doctoral-level research opportunities.

When not in Mexico, Ann was occasionally known to enjoy a good piece of steak—medium rare—and a glass or two of scotch. No research associated with that, however, at least not that I know of. Pity, don't you think? Or, is there a course proposal in the offing? Skeptical? I can tell you that my daughter teaches a college-level course on the psychology of food!

Lastly, as all who knew Ann noticed, she was always impeccably dressed and groomed, in that elegantly minimalist signature style of hers. Yes, of course; all of us did. Did you happen to notice the shoes she was wearing? Always the latest fashion and in the best taste. For Ann, loved shoes. I mean really loved shoes. Imelda, move over.

So, I hope I've done my feeble best to tarnish the reputation of our beloved Ann. Food lover, red meat eater, scotch drinker, shoe wearer. All too wonderfully human.

Thanks Ann for all you were: brilliant social historian of Mexico, devoted mother and wife, and a great colleague and friend. You have greatly enriched my life.

Efraín Barradas (University of Florida): "I wasn't talking to the student I had in class, I was talking to a new teacher that I had"

I should begin by telling you that I feel like the prodigal son. I taught at this University from August 1974 to December 1999. My return is not because my father calls me, but because my sister, Ann, calls me. If the Chancellor said Ann could tell him that she studied here, I could brag and say, "Hey, I taught Ann here." I was a teacher. During that period, I had *brilliant* students. Maria Cisterna was also my student; her husband, Ian Gold was also my student. Ramon Figueroa, Luis Cosme, Cindy Schuster, there's a long, long list of brilliant students. But among them, Ann is numero uno.

When I taught Ann, I think I planted in her the idea that she should not really do American Studies, but Latin American Studies. When she left UMass, she came to me and said, "I'm sorry. I am so sorry, I am not going to study Latin American Literature;

I'm going to study Latin American *History*." And I said to Ann, "*Great!*" That's what I wanted her to do.

I was invited by the Department to give a talk to the students a few hours ago. I gave that talk, and all through that talk, I was only thinking of Ann, because I structured that talk because I learned from her. The roles were reversed. Ann was no longer my student, Ann was my teacher. I met Ann at academic conferences, especially in LASA, Latin American Studies Association. I remember we were waiting for a plane in Montreal, and my partner, Enrique Moreno, Ann and I sat down and organized a panel for the next LASA on "Autobiography and Narrative of the Self in Latin America." I realized when I was talking to her that I wasn't talking to the student I had in class, I was talking to a *new* teacher that I had. So, I am very, very honored that I could be here with you today, looking at some wonderful colleagues of mine that I haven't seen in sixteen years. But I'm really not the same person now. I realized this afternoon, when I gave a talk, which was not about Latin American Literature, it was really about culture and history. In many ways I owe that to Ann. Gracias.

Chris Bobel (Women & Gender Studies): "A Love Letter to My Friend Ann"

A few weeks ago, one of our WGS graduates, and a student of Ann's, wrote me a newsy email. In it, she asked if I had seen Ann lately. My heart sank. She did not know Ann was ill. She did not know Ann was gone.

When I mustered the courage and some modicum of tact, I wrote and told her the horrible news. Her sadness palpable, she replied:

I would have loved to tell Ann how much she meant to me and what a difference she made in my life.

How many of us here today feel the same?

I had the privilege of seeing Ann off and on throughout her illness, up to a few days before she died. During some of these visits, we lamented the damned injustice of stupid evil cancer's plan to steal her from this world. A few times, we laughed, ruefully, about the trouble we were planning to cause in our shared old age—two cranky old feminists roaming the catwalks, stirring dissent. But I regret that I did not say more. I failed to convey to her how much she meant in my life and so many others.

And so I offer this—my tragically tardy love letter to Ann.

Dear Ann:

We joined UMB within a year of each other. I can't place how we met, but I vividly recall the feeling of it—profound gratitude. You were smart—so smart, and humble, so humble. And honest and kind, and endlessly clever. Because we were both caught in the tortured tangle that is combining motherhood with the professoriate [and you probably used that word], I felt an immediate bond. I remember telling Thomas about you, feeling much like a 4th grader on the 1st day of school, "I made a new friend." I planned to keep you.

After a long day on campus, we would find each other on the sidewalk waiting for the shuttle—remember when it parked outside Quinn? We'd chat, our voices rising and falling over the din of the bus-then train-then bus all the way to Arlington.

Through the years, we processed and problem solved, commiserated and kvetched, We discussed the evolution of our roles as mothers, daughters, sisters, and partners alongside and often clashing with our careers as moved from neophyte assistant professors to relieved associate professors to exhausted department chairs.

Through it all, you had this way of both hearing and seeing ME.

You were quiet, characteristically unflappable, and often serious. But not always. I loved the way you would throw back your head and laugh. Remember the Spring before your tenure file was due and you joked about cursing the bright green shoots as they emerged from the ground *"Get back in there! It can't be Spring. I need more time to write."*

You were a peerless mentor, gracious and wise skilled at guiding with a steady hand that never pushed. You made everything you touched, better.

Remember when I attempted to write a historical analysis of a little known social movement --I shudder at the memory now---I had no proper training to do such a thing and you knew it. But rather than telling me to stay in my lane, you agreed to read the draft. And somehow, you deftly transformed that sow's ear into, if not a silk purse, certainly a sturdy enough everyday bag. Today, that journal article gets cited more than almost any other I've published to date.

You were incredibly generous. With your time, your experience, your astute way of sizing up a situation and seeing a way forward.

You put others first, even at the most impossible moments.

Remember one of our last conversations, when I sat with you in your sun washed bedroom. You were desperately miserable, through and through, too weak to sustain much chatter, and yet, you looked straight at me, smiled and quietly uttered, "You look so beautiful."

My dear, dear friend Ann I keep looking for you on the train, or walking on the pavement between Wheatley and McCormack.

When I see a tiny woman wearing a brightly colored scarf, short hair, glasses.

I want it to be you.

Love,
Chris

Sandra Haley (Brown University PhD student): "Pushing me to take not always the easiest path, but the right one"

Fifteen years ago, I enrolled at UMass Boston as an undergrad student. Fortunately and *completely* by chance, in my first semester, I walked into one of Ann Blum's classes, and it changed my life. My route to education was, shall we say, circuitous, at best. But right from the start, Professor Blum was having none of it. Not for a second did she imagine that my ideas, or the ideas of anyone in the room, for that matter, weren't important and didn't deserve time, and consideration, and work—lots of work. Her consistently high expectations made all of us better students, better thinkers, and at least in my case, better human beings.

I'm one student out of thousands, and all of us benefitted immensely from her commitment, and talents. I know this for sure, because I've seen the hundreds of cards and letters and post cards of thanks from former students, all of which she kept and treasured.

After a few years, I left UMass Boston with an individual Bachelor's degree, a loose prototype of what today would be the Latin American and Iberian Studies Degree, the degree that Ann Blum worked so hard to create. She was my teacher, my advisor, my mentor, all throughout. She encouraged me to consider, and helped me navigate applying to Master's programs, something I would never have even imagined doing, without her kind prodding. Most recently, Professor Blum was the outside member of my dissertation committee in the History Department at Brown—a project still in process.

All the best opportunities in my life, I owe directly to her influence. Here's an example: a few years ago, I was researching in Oaxaca, Mexico, and was able to meet with Professor Blum on several occasions, while she was also in Mexico working herself. The last time we met in Oaxaca was during a terrible time for me personally. I was struggling not only with my dissertation, but with life in general. Apparently she noticed. Previously when we met at conferences, or on research trips to the archive, we'd gone for an afternoon lime-aide in the Zocalo. This time, Ann gently, but firmly insisted that we meet for a sunrise walk up to the top of El Fortin, overlooking Oaxaca City. A good hours' climb, up an endless set of staircases, and then a steep gravel road, and not just once—*every morning* there we were at six a.m., marching upward as the sun rose on us. No amount of quiet begrudging on my part over the whole thing could diminish her sunny disposition one bit. For weeks she insisted we'd need to talk about work on those early morning walks, sometimes she'd include Bill French, another colleague who was in town. When she left town a week later, I'd continue climbing the hill at dawn, alone. And more importantly, I was writing again. Now, *that* is a commitment to mentorship—pushing me to take not always the easiest path, but the right one.

I want to say how utterly grateful I am for everything she did for me. Thank you, Professor Blum, just, *thank you*.

She was a wonderful teacher and mentor, and with all of her students, *incredibly* generous with her time and energy. Her belief in me continues to change my life over and over and over again, and *always* for the better. I simply cannot think of anyone who I admire or respect more deeply. Having Ann Blum as a model of ethical academia, helping me find my way in the world. Most of the best parts of my life were made possible by her advice, and I'd like to say, friendship. More than anything, I'm just glad that we shared the pathways.

Peggy Fitzgerald (LAIS Departmental administrator): "Her determination came with fairness, a true respect for students, administrators and colleagues"

Ann was not only a wonderful scholar, she was also a great administrator. When Ann became chair of the department for the first time, as with all new chairs, they don't know what to expect. But Ann embraced the challenge—from changing the name of our department, redefining our major and minor, guiding the department through an AQUAD review, to dealing with everyone's personal issues, and everything else in between. She was just as dedicated to being chair of the department, as she was in her teaching and research.

Working with Ann revealed her character immensely. She had a strong commitment to the Department, to students, and to the university causes. She had high expectations of herself and others, but was always there to lend a helping hand. I remember every morning, when she came in with her bigger than life smile, she would say, "So, Peggy, what can I do for you today?" Ann also had no problem with addressing issues. She would tackle them with the same tenacity as she did everything else across her path. Nothing was too big, nor too small for her to handle. She approached each problem and each set of circumstances with the same determination and vigor that she brought to the department every day. Anyone who had the pleasure of working with Ann knew of her commitment to excellent. Although petite in stature, she was a giant when it came to getting things accomplished. Her determination came with fairness, a true respect for students, administrators and colleagues.

The department has lost a great colleague and friend. We will be forever grateful for her contributions and the legacy she has left to the department.

Reyes Coll-Tellechia (LAIS): "By not teaching Latin America, we're imposing unfair limits in the education of our students"

On behalf of everyone in the department, I want to thank each one of you, whether you spoke or are going to speak, for coming here and for helping us remember Ann's life and celebrate it. There's very little that I can say now, every body has spoken very eloquently, so I will say a couple of things.

Ann was one of the very, very few individuals who was a student at UMass, an adjunct faculty at UMass, and also a professor *and* an administrator. She didn't work in facilities, to my knowledge, but she might have had connections—secret connections that I didn't know, although I worked with her for fifteen years.

As several speakers have mentioned, we configured an entire academic *unit* which is a very difficult thing to do. She built a unit that is very special at the university, but will probably soon be very normal. But she did that fifteen years before anybody new. Among her accomplishments as an administrator are, the new Major in Latin American and Iberian Studies, the Minor in Latin American Studies, the Minor in Spanish and the Minor in Portuguese. None of these existed before Ann became Chair of the department. She was not done—not at all. She had already embarked on two new ventures. The Department is determined to bring those two ventures to fruition. One is a PhD in Atlantic Studies, for which she already designed a template. The other one, a Masters in Latin American Studies. In the last few conversations I had with her, I received strict orders to keep the information secret until the team—whatever the team was, I don't know—had all the information available to share.

The serious part here is that for years, as a person who knew this university well, and had seen the university and experienced it from different perspectives, Ann *deplored*– that's the word she used, the scarcity of courses dealing with Latin America in this university, the scarcity of research dealing with Latin America at this university. She saw this as profound intellectual shortcomings, and as a handicap that would not allow us to ever say we were international or transnational, or even diverse. Moreover, she often expressed the belief that not researching Latin America in biology, in political science, in economics, in gender studies, in geography, by not teaching Latin America, we were imposing unfair limits in the education of our students. So I would like to end with that memo from Ann as planned: "Chair, to each one of you, Research Latin America. Find spaces for Latin America in your syllabi. Find spaces for Latin America in your courses, in your research, in your departments. Have the Department of Latin American and Iberian Studies *extend*, or *come in* and embrace us. Signed, *Ann S. Blum*." Thank you.

Peter Taylor: "Perhaps all of us here might then integrate bits of Ann into who we are at UMass Boston"

Ann and I lived together for 30 years. We got together just before she came to UMass—the first time, when she decided to drop back in to higher education and get a B.A. The 2nd time she came to UMass, we were quite happy to get our faculty positions independently of each other.

And then to do our jobs independently of each other. Yes, we did talk shop at home sometimes, but not as much as you might think—or, perhaps, worry. It helped to have a child to redirect our attention—when Vann [over there] was 9 or 10—that was very early in our time at UMass—he interrupted his parents' dinner-table talk one night by exclaiming "The Dean. The Dean. The Dean" then stormed out of the room. We weren't actually complaining about a Dean that time, but the message was well taken—remembered at home from then on.

Something else about living with Ann for thirty years—in listening to what people recall about her—both today and collected on the website annblum.wordpress.com—there are lessons from Ann that I am still learning—I'm not sure if that kind of incomplete is allowed under the new policy, but…. Anyway, early in the New Year, as befits that season, I started to make a list of principles and practices of Ann's. My thinking was that, to the extent that I took them up and then keep them going, that would integrate bits of Ann into my future self.

I'd like to share some of them now—perhaps all of us here might then integrate bits of Ann into who we are at UMass Boston—and beyond.
1. Start the day with time for reflection, appreciating the arrival of morning light.

2. Always express thanks in real time and write thank you notes. [OK, let me pause here to thank Maria, Peggy, Reyes and the LAIS department for organizing this memorial, for bringing us together today. On a more personal note, I want to thank the speakers on behalf of Ann's family—and especially Vann and me—for painting pictures of the living Ann, the Ann in your lives.]

3a. Do yourself in the future a favor. b. That means not assuming that there is someone else to clean up for you or look after you.

4. (Corollary of #3a) Floss your teeth. Take your pills. Apply your lotions. Do your exercises.

5. Do not give excuses. Do not take up people's time and attention having to listen to your excuses (=corollary of #3b). Simply say what you plan to do going forward.

6. When a friend or family member needs to talk, put aside what you're doing and give them your attention.

7. Get rid of unused clothes and possessions. That is, *don't hold onto projects that with the passing of time you haven't got to.*

8. Prepare each meal to be a bounded event. Don't snack on ingredients while preparing, go back for a second or third installment, or pick at what's on the table because it's there.

9. Do not see the significance of what you do in relation to whether it is deemed significant in institutional/establishment spheres. Seeking fame gives others too much power over who you are becoming.

[Now Ann would *never* do what I am doing—commanding the stage to lay out "10 commandments."]

10. Model what you want others to take up, hoping they will choose to take it up themselves. (That's in contrast to their doing it, probably very imperfectly, because you're told them to.)

11. One hour is the maximum you can take in visually, e.g., at an art gallery. (Don't feel guilty if you are in, say, the Uffizi, not looking at every one of its famous works.)

12. Look for your daily minimum visual input.

13. When working in an institution, define your "prize" (a few things to get changed), then keep your eye on this prize and do not fret about not being able to change everything else.

14. At home and with family, devote resources to those things you want to visualize being there in the future—even when you are not.

Let me end by again expressing my thanks for everyone being here today.

Sharon Kingsland: "One of the greatest histories of natural history"

I know it's getting late, I'd like to share one thing, briefly. I met Ann in the mid 1970s and, therefore, I was her friend while she was writing her first book, called, *Picturing Nature*, which has been alluded to, it's a wonderful book on the history of natural history. In those days, in the history of science, all the attention was on the elites, the Darwins, the Newtons, and so forth. Almost nobody thought to look at the people who were doing the basic work, in this case, the illustrators, who were illustrating the great works of Natural History of the Nineteenth Century. So Ann was pioneering in focusing on these people. Some of them were amazing artists, whom nobody had ever heard of, such as August Sonrel, who was Louis Agassiz's artist. Luckily, Princeton University Press did not stint in producing Ann's book in the mid 80s, and produced an absolutely gorgeous book with large images of the illustrations.

To fast forward in 2009, I was at Cal Tech for the Bicentennial of the birth of Charles Darwin, for a conference. For part of the conference, we went to the Huntington for a special little reception. Huntington, you probably know, is one of the most famous institutions in the world for its botanical gardens, its fantastic art collection, and its library. They had put out an exhibit of natural history books, including Darwin's *Origin of Species*, and tremendously rare books of natural history that they had—very expensive. I'm walking through this exhibit, marveling at everything, I go around a corner and there's Ann's book! Part of the exhibit as they very appropriately realized, one of the best, one of the greatest histories of natural history that we have today. For those of you who don't know that side of her.

Rosemary Raymundo: "Takes her time to speak to everybody and get to know people and genuinely care."

I was fortunate enough to have Ann as a professor. I guess my favorite memory of her was once going to the Department. I had had a class with her, but I didn't really think that I had made any impact—I didn't think I *shined* in the class. I had a few conversations with her, but nothing really serious. I didn't feel like I had made a big connection just yet with her. It was really interesting because I was talking to Peggy, and I asked her a question, and Ann came by. She recognized me, she remembered me. Which I thought was great. I was like, "Oh, awesome!" because as a college student, they tell you to make connections with your professors. You want to get to know them and it's a great thing to do. I just didn't know I was there yet. Then she asked me, "Oh, how's it going? How are your classes?" I was actually taking an online class for the first time and it was really difficult for me. It wasn't my cup of tea; I really like being in class. Over the computer, it's just hard to really get to discuss things. I was explaining that to her and she just looked at me and said, "You know, it's hard but you can do it. You just gotta keep at it." That was something very powerful to me; she took her time to sit there and ask me how my classes were. Then she took her time to say, "Nothing's going to be easy, and it's not gonna be great if it's easy." So, I just thought that was such an amazing moment I had with her. I think after that, I fell in love with her; she was such an amazing woman. When I had another opportunity to take a class with her, I definitely jumped at it. This amazing moment that I shared with her echoes everything that everyone has said about her. She just really always takes her time to speak to everybody and get to know people, and genuinely cared. And I really appreciated that in her. Thank you.

Vann Taylor (son): "If you're going to incorporate one thing, really care about your students"

My mom was a good mom, and a good teacher. But she was an academic—I'm distinctly *not* an academic, because my parents were, so it's important to be the opposite. But she was the most amazing mom anyone could ever have. The best thing about her: she genuinely cared about everyone in this room and outside of this room just as much as she cared about me. I think having teachers like that is really important because people get fed up with the system, people get fed up with certain students, or their lives, and they forget to care about the people that need to be cared about.

I just have a quick story. I went to Bentley University and—this is probably not appropriate—I was in the library and there was a cute girl. I was like, "I'm gonna go talk to her"—it's a library and you're not supposed to talk. So, we start talking and I asked her about herself, and she actually went to UMass Boston. And she actually took my mom's class—which meant that I had no chance. The best part about it was that my mom was her mentor, and she chose Bentley University because my mom knew about it because of me. She meant the world to that girl, who I don't know anymore. The point is, if you're going to incorporate one thing, really care about your students because it makes a lasting impact. I have had teachers like that, and I had my mom. She still cares about me, and cares about all you, too.

Maria

Well, thank you everyone for coming. This was very important to us to be able to bring people together. She loved everyone, even if when she didn't. One of the ways that we are committed to continuing to remember Ann, and continue her path, we have established a scholarship in Ann's name [see verso page of book for details]. We are very invested in our students, just as much as she was. We think this is one of the ways that she would like to continue contributing to the university and to teaching.

Thank you very much.

Contributors

To the identity below of each contributor, append *and friend*

Abby Blum	niece, daughter of Tom
Alan Hewat	one of the 1970s Harvard Bookstore guys, aka aspiring writers
Alexandra Puerto	historian of women and gender in Latin America
Alison Negrin	mother of David, Vann's brother
Amanda López	historian of Mexico
Andrew Taylor	brother-in-law, younger brother of Peter
Anissa Lane	mother of Stephen Robinson, extra "mother" to Vann
Ann Blum	a.k.a. Annie Blum, 1950-2015
Anne Taylor	sister-in-law, younger sister of Peter
Ashley Seal	friend of Vann and hairstylist for Ann in 2015
Avi Chomsky	historian of Latin America, fellow PhD history student at UC Berkeley
Becky Jones	MCZ staff, at whose apartment Ann and Peter met
Becky May	met in Berkeley (through husbands) c. 1989
Ben Schwendener	musician and composer (gravityarts.org), sometime teacher in Peter's program at UMass
Bill Beezley	historian of Mexico, founder of Oaxaca summer institute
Bill French	historian of Mexico, co-instructor Oaxaca summer institute
Brad Bellows	architect, co-convenor of the Pumping Station discussion group in Cambridge/Somerville area, 1982-86
Candace Kunz	insightful advisor during adoption process, 1989-90
Carol Cohn	braided paths: met during her year of research on defense intellectuals in Cambridge, another 1990 parent, eventually a UMass colleague
Chris Bobel	UMass Boston colleague, Women's & Gender Studies Arlington resident, and fellow rider on the T
Claire Milne	met in 8th grade in Cambridge, England
Clara Estow	Ann's Department Chair for several years at UMass Boston

Craig Gilmore	Ruthie's husband
Daniel Ortiz Zapata	Director of UMass Boston Libraries, Arlington neighbor
David Barnett	Vann's brother
David Lakari	archivist at MCZ before Ann
David Terkla	UMass Boston faculty member then administrator, economist
Deborah Dumaine	girlfriends to brothers in 1970s
Dennis Piechota	archeological conservator
Diane Paul	met through brother of Meri Sue, guided Ann to complete studies at UMass Boston
Efraín Barradas	Ann's Spanish-language literature teacher at UMass
Elena Jackson Albarrán	historian of Mexico
Elizabeth Bussiere	fellow departmental chairs at UMass Boston, political science
Elizabeth Holmes	Ithaca neighbor, poet
Emily Joselson	originally, like Ann, one of the girlfriends of 1970s Harvard Bookstore guys
Emma León	wife of Raúl, social scientist at U.N.A.M. in Cuernavaca
Enid Ratnam-Keese	friend of Gilly Taylor
Estelle Disch	UMass Boston faculty member, sociologist, fellow rider on T
Gabriela Soto Laveaga	historian of Mexico and public health
Gail Holst-Warhaft	poet, musician, Hellenophile of Australian origin, Ithaca resident, adopting parent of Vann's friends Zoe and Simon
Georgia Blain	Andrew Taylor's partner
Gilla	lab retriever, family dog from 2006-2016
Gilly Taylor	mother-in-law
Grace McConaghy	caregiver in Fall 2015, aunt of Karla
Hamid Khouyi	hairdresser to Ann, then Vann, then Peter
Herzonia Yañez	host during visits to Mexico City
Hilary Charlesworth	graduate student in law at Harvard in 1980s, with Melbourne friends in common with Peter
Iain Boal	co-convenor and host of the Pumping Station discussion group in Cambridge/Somerville area, 1982-86, then Retort in Berkeley, 1986-present and MayDay Rooms, London
Irina Castro	junior researcher, U. Coimbra, 2012 host to Peter in Portugal
Jacqueline Berthet	graphic designer, partner of Brad
James Simpson	high school friend of Peter, then Somerville/ Arlington/ Cambridge neighbor during last decade

Jasmine	aka Steve Cadwell
Jen Burns	dog walker to Gilla
Joe Levine	graduate student in MCZ in mid-1970s, then partner of Steve
John Lear	historian of Mexico, fellow PhD history student at UC Berkeley
John Macleod	husband of Margery
Jon Zorn	one of the 1970s Harvard Bookstore guys, aka aspiring writers, in 1970s
Jorge Gaskins	met first year in College, later agro- and aqua-ecological social entrepreneur in Puerto Rico
Josh Konigsberg	newly married to Meri Sue
Judy Zeitlin	UMass Boston colleague, anthropology
Karla Martineau	Ann's hospice nurse from Care Dimensions
Kate Hartford	teacher to Ann at UMass Boston, later colleague, Political Science
Katie Platt	member of Pumping Station discussion group in 1980s
Katherine Bliss	historian of Mexico, later global health researcher
Keith Motley	Chancellor, UMass Boston
Kelley Castro	historian of Mexico
Kevin Barnett	father of David, Vann's brother
Laura Briggs	historian of reproductive politics
Liz Hutchinson	fellow PhD history student at UC Berkeley
Liz Taylor	biology student with Peter [not a relative]
Lois Rudnick	advisor to Ann at UMass Boston, later colleague
Lou Pollak	a legal scholar, then judge; from Ann's parents' generation
Mara Siegel	worked in the MCZ library in 1970s
Margery Meadow	housemate of Peter in early 80s; neighbor on our return to Boston area
Maria Cisterna-Gold	Departmental colleague at UMass
María Muñoz	historian of Mexico
Mariel Cohn	daughter of Carol
Marta Roriz	Junior researcher/ PhD candidate, U. of Coimbra, Portugal
Maxine Schmidt (Macci)	MCZ library worker, at whose birthday party Peter met Ann
Meri Sue Glasgall	originally, like Ann, one of the girlfriends of 1970s Harvard Bookstore guys
Michael Manning	high school classmate of Vann

Nancy Pollak	childhood neighbor in New Haven, later in Ithaca
Nancy Hafner	sister-in-law, wife of Tom
Nate Blum	nephew, son of Tom
Neal Bruss	UMass Boston colleague, English
Pamela Blum	older sister
Pamela Henson	Historian, Institutional History Division, Smithsonian Institution Archives
Patricia Ferreira	PhD Student, U. Coimbra, Portugal
Paula Chandoha	MCZ staff then freelancers together
Peggy Fitzgerald	administrator of Ann's department at UMass Boston
Peter Taylor	husband, together since 1984
Rachel Rubin	UMass Boston colleague, American Studies
Rajini Srikanth	UMass Boston colleague, English
Raúl García-Barrios	met in Berkeley through Peter in 1987; many trips and visits in Mexico together
Reaux	Paula's dog
Reyes Coll-Tellechia	senior Departmental colleague at UMass
Richard Frumess	brother-in-law, husband of Pamela
Robert Weis	historian of Mexico
Rosemary Raymundo	past student at UMass Boston
Ruthie Wilson Gilmore	friend since high school, "twin" since meeting up in 1984 both reading the same book criticizing studies of identical twins raised apart
Sally Taylor	sister-in-law, older sister of Peter
Sam Rosenbaum	son of downstairs neighbor
Sandra Haley	undergraduate student of Ann's, later historian of Mexico
Sarah Wright	downstairs neighbor and member of the "garden committee"
Shaari Neretin	psychotherapist
Shauna Helton	wife of Reyes
Shari Rapasz Schwendener	dancer, wife of Ben
Sharon Kingsland	met as research assistants on a history of the Museum of Comparative Zoology
Sheila Tully	Latin American studies scholar and activist, student with Ann in Berkeley
Stephen Robinson	high school classmate of Vann
Steve Cadwell	met first year in College

Steve Silliman	UMass Boston colleague, anthropology
Sue Harris O'Connor	speaker and writer on experience of trans-racial adoption
Susan Deeds	historian of Mexico
Susan Mraz	Departmental colleague at UMass
Susan Oyama	philosopher of biology, colleague of Peter in New York
Toni Loftin	historian of Mexico
Tom Blum (Tommie, Thomas)	brother
Twin	aka Ruthie Gilmore
Vann Taylor	son
Vicki Stephens	Vann's birth mother
Victoria Munroe	one-time girlfriends of brothers, later housemate and art gallery owner
Walter Brem	Latin America archivist, UC Berkeley
Winston Langley	Provost, UMass Boston
Zellman Warhaft	socially responsible engineer (of Australian origin), Ithaca resident, adopting parent of Vann's friends Zoe and Simon

"Love does not shield us from the turmoil of our inner and outer worlds; love itself responds and changes."

"I will certainly cherish the many things Ann taught and shared with me—from insights regarding the politics of labor and reproduction to how to brew a stellar cup of coffee in a less than stellar Oaxacan hotel room."

"I am reminded of many hotel rooms in the early morning.... reading, writing (usually me) and editing conference papers and enjoying being bad girls in academe!"

"I don't remember much of what we talked about, just the pleasure of easy conversation about children, family, Mexico. It always seemed when we met that we were able to pick up the conversation where we left off a year or two earlier."

"Visiting you last weekend pulled me right into the present; you radiate the focus of the moment. Yes, radiate. I bask in the warmth of you, Annie, even as you dwindle in flesh and fiber; it's in your eyes, which refuse to dwindle. Be comfortable, seek peace. I love you."

"You have said that you are becoming much weaker. This, of course, is distressing to all of us who love you. But—not sure how to put this, so I am going to invent a word—your *Ann-ness* is not weaker."

"I am thinking of you and what your living and dying are teaching me. And trying my best to be present with you—with as much of your rich and meaningful life as I know it—seeing you as endlessly beyond these impossibly hard months, weeks, days, hours while holding them, too.'"

"Cackling in my heart with you."

"But then, she looks directly into my eyes: 'I need to cover the suitcases.' To calm her, I reply: 'It's OK, I've done that.' She pushed firmly back: 'No you haven't.'"

'I would have loved to tell Ann how much she meant to me and what a difference she made in my life."

"When my mother died in 1982, Ann wrote to me 'It's wrenching to even imagine the loss. But I am slowly learning something that you probably already know, and that is – that we don't have to stop loving the person who has died.'"

www.ingramcontent.com/pod-product-compliance
Lightning Source LLC
Chambersburg PA
CBHW080523020526
44112CB00046B/2772